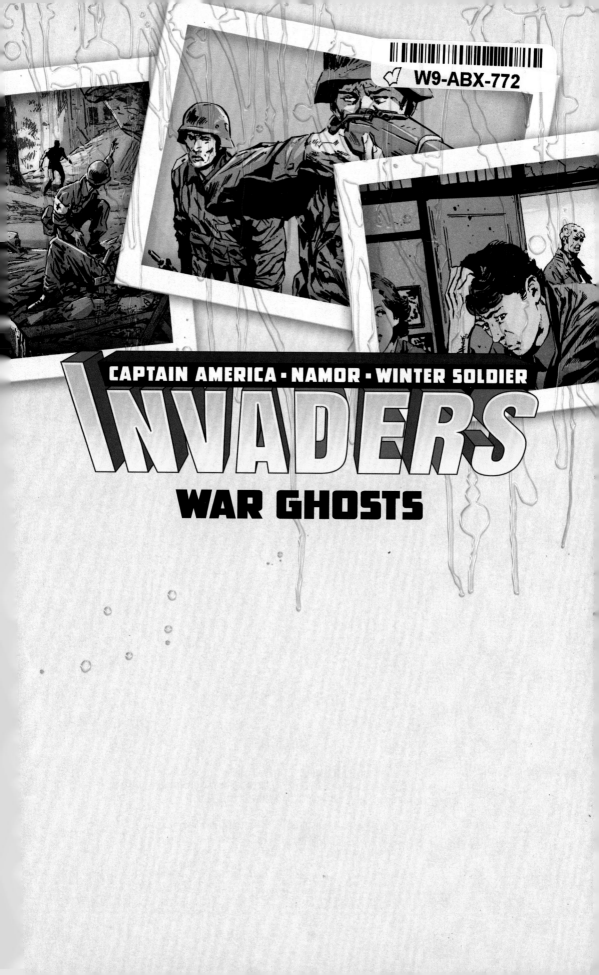

CAPTAIN AMERICA · NAMOR · WINTER SOLDIER

INVADERS

WAR GHOSTS

★ ★ ★

COLLECTION EDITOR KATERI WOODY   CAITLIN O'CONNELL ASSISTANT EDITOR
EDITOR, SPECIAL PROJECTS: MARK D. BEAZLEY   JENNIFER GRÜNWALD SENIOR EDITOR, SPECIAL PROJECTS
VP PRODUCTION & SPECIAL PROJECTS JEFF YOUNGQUIST   JAY BOWEN BOOK DESIGNER

SVP PRINT, SALES & MARKETING DAVID GABRIEL   SVEN LARSEN DIRECTOR, LICENSED PUBLISHING
EDITOR IN CHIEF C.B. CEBULSKI   JOE QUESADA CHIEF CREATIVE OFFICER
PRESIDENT DAN BUCKLEY   ALAN FINE EXECUTIVE PRODUCER

INVADERS VOL. 1: WAR GHOSTS. Contains material originally published in magazine form as INVADERS #1-6. First printing 2019. ISBN 978-1-302-91749-4. Published by MARVEL WORLDWIDE, INC., a subsidiary of MARVEL ENTERTAINMENT, LLC. OFFICE OF PUBLICATION: 135 West 50th Street, New York, NY 10020. © 2019 MARVEL No similarity between any of the names, characters, persons, and/or institutions in this magazine with those of any living or dead person or institution is intended, and any such similarity which may exist is purely coincidental. **Printed in the U.S.A.** DAN BUCKLEY, President, Marvel Entertainment; JOHN NEE, Publisher; JOE QUESADA, Chief Creative Officer; TOM BREVOORT, SVP of Publishing; DAVID BOGART, Associate Publisher & SVP of Talent Affairs; DAVID GABRIEL, SVP of Sales & Marketing, Publishing; JEFF YOUNGQUIST, VP of Production & Special Projects; DAN CARR, Executive Director of Publishing Technology; ALEX MORALES, Director of Publishing Operations; DAN EDINGTON, Managing Editor; SUSAN CRESPI, Production Manager; STAN LEE, Chairman Emeritus. For information regarding advertising in Marvel Comics or on Marvel.com, please contact Vit DeBellis, Custom Solutions & Integrated Advertising Manager, at vdebellis@marvel.com. For Marvel subscription inquiries, please call 888-511-5480. **Manufactured between 6/7/2019 and 7/9/2019 by SOLISCO PRINTERS, SCOTT, QC, CANADA.**
10 9 8 7 6 5 4 3 2 1

CAPTAIN AMERICA AND BUCKY BARNES! NAMOR, THE SUB-MARINER! THE ORIGINAL HUMAN TORCH, JIM HAMMOND! During the darkest hours of World War II , these four banded together as THE INVADERS — to battle the Axis Powers to the death in the name of freedom!

The war was a long time ago, but the Invaders are still haunted by the ghosts of their pasts — perhaps none more than the morally ambiguous King Namor of Atlantis, who seems to be igniting a new global war between the surface world and the seas his people call home.

The question everyone wants the answer to now is...why?

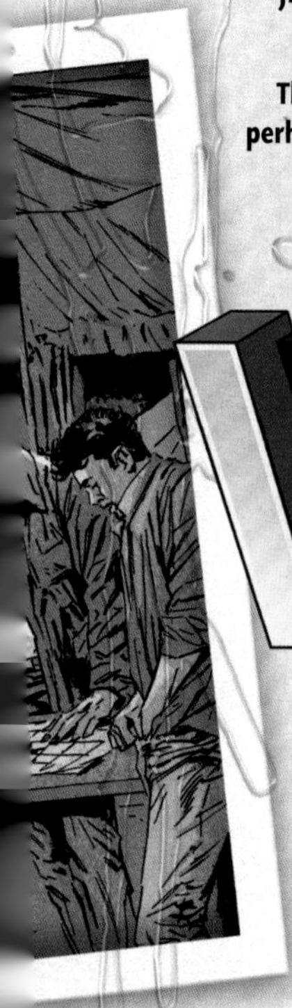

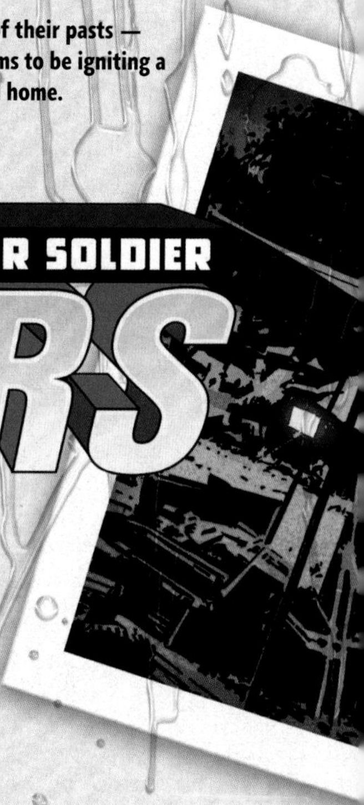

CAPTAIN AMERICA - NAMOR - WINTER SOLDIER

INVADERS

WAR GHOSTS

CHIP ZDARSKY
WRITER

CARLOS MAGNO & BUTCH GUICE
ARTISTS

ALEX GUIMARÃES
COLOR ARTIST

BUTCH GUICE & ROMULO FAJADO JR.
COVER ART

VC's TRAVIS LANHAM
LETTERER

SHANNON ANDREWS
ASSISTANT EDITOR

ALANNA SMITH
ASSOCIATE EDITOR

TOM BREVOORT
EDITOR

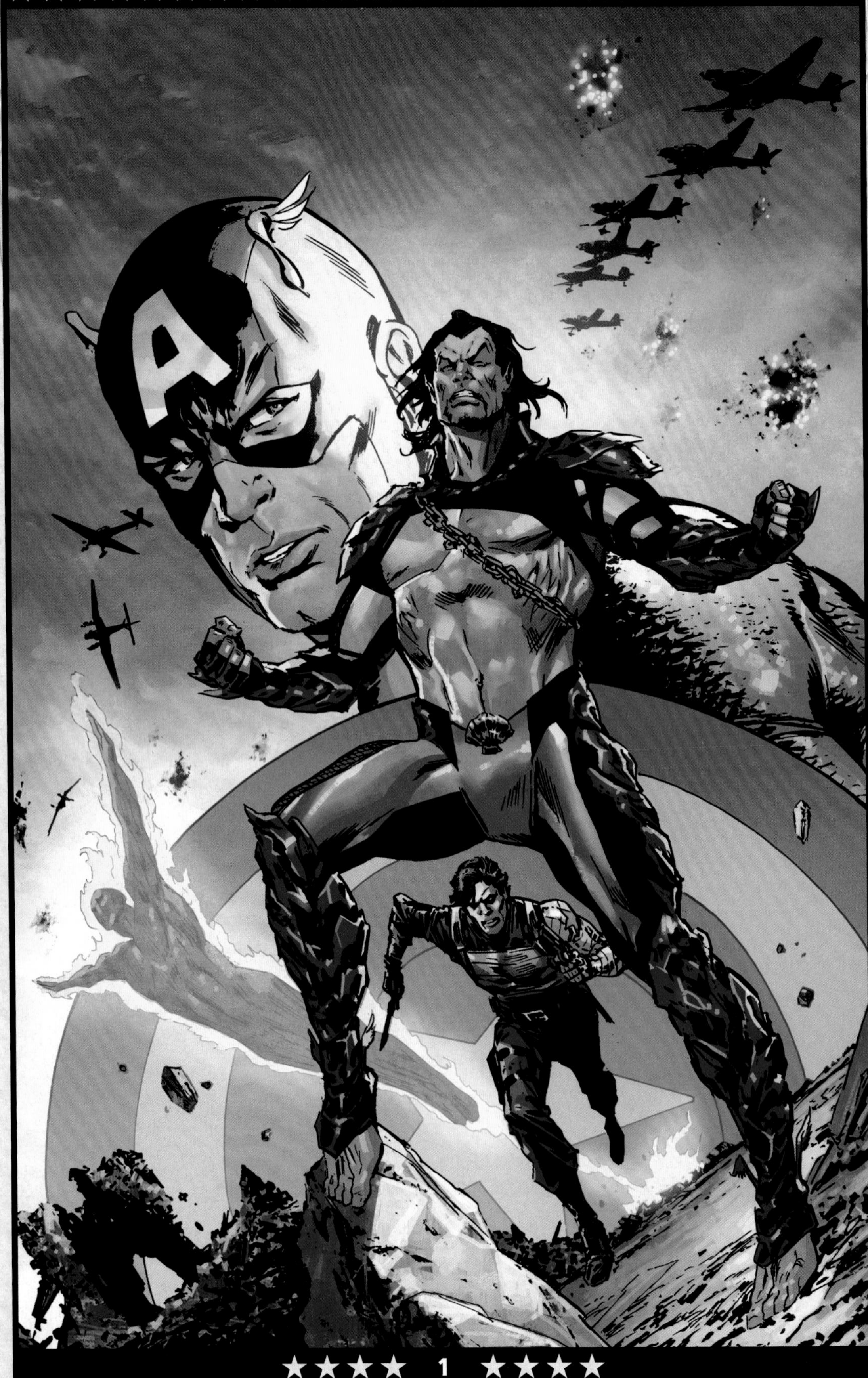

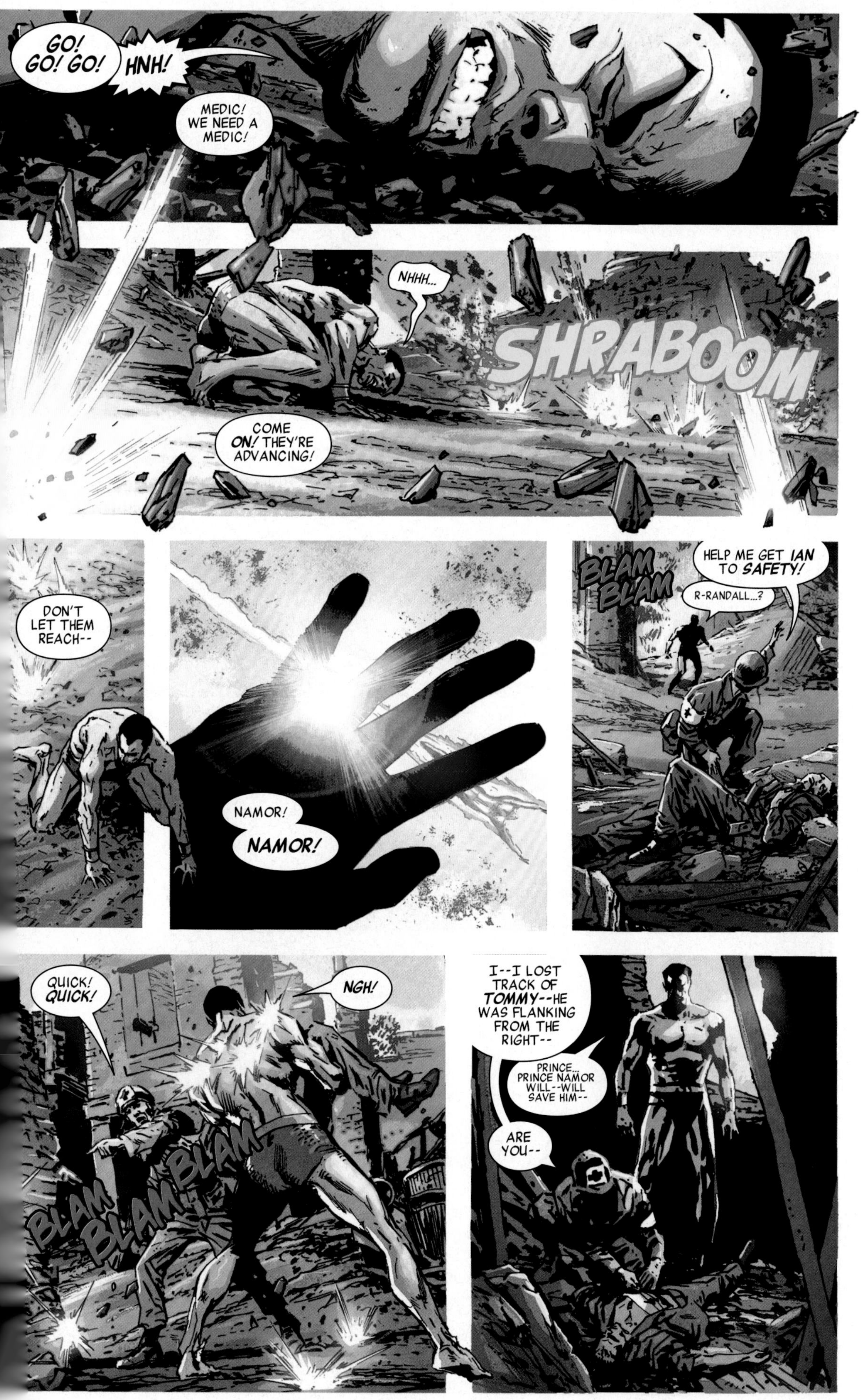
GO! GO! GO!
HNH!
MEDIC! WE NEED A MEDIC!
NHHH...
SHRABOOM
COME ON! THEY'RE ADVANCING!
DON'T LET THEM REACH--
NAMOR!
NAMOR!
BLAM BLAM
HELP ME GET IAN TO SAFETY!
R-RANDALL...?
QUICK! QUICK!
NGH!
BLAM BLAM BLAM BLAM
I--I LOST TRACK OF TOMMY--HE WAS FLANKING FROM THE RIGHT--
PRINCE... PRINCE NAMOR WILL--WILL SAVE HIM--
ARE YOU--

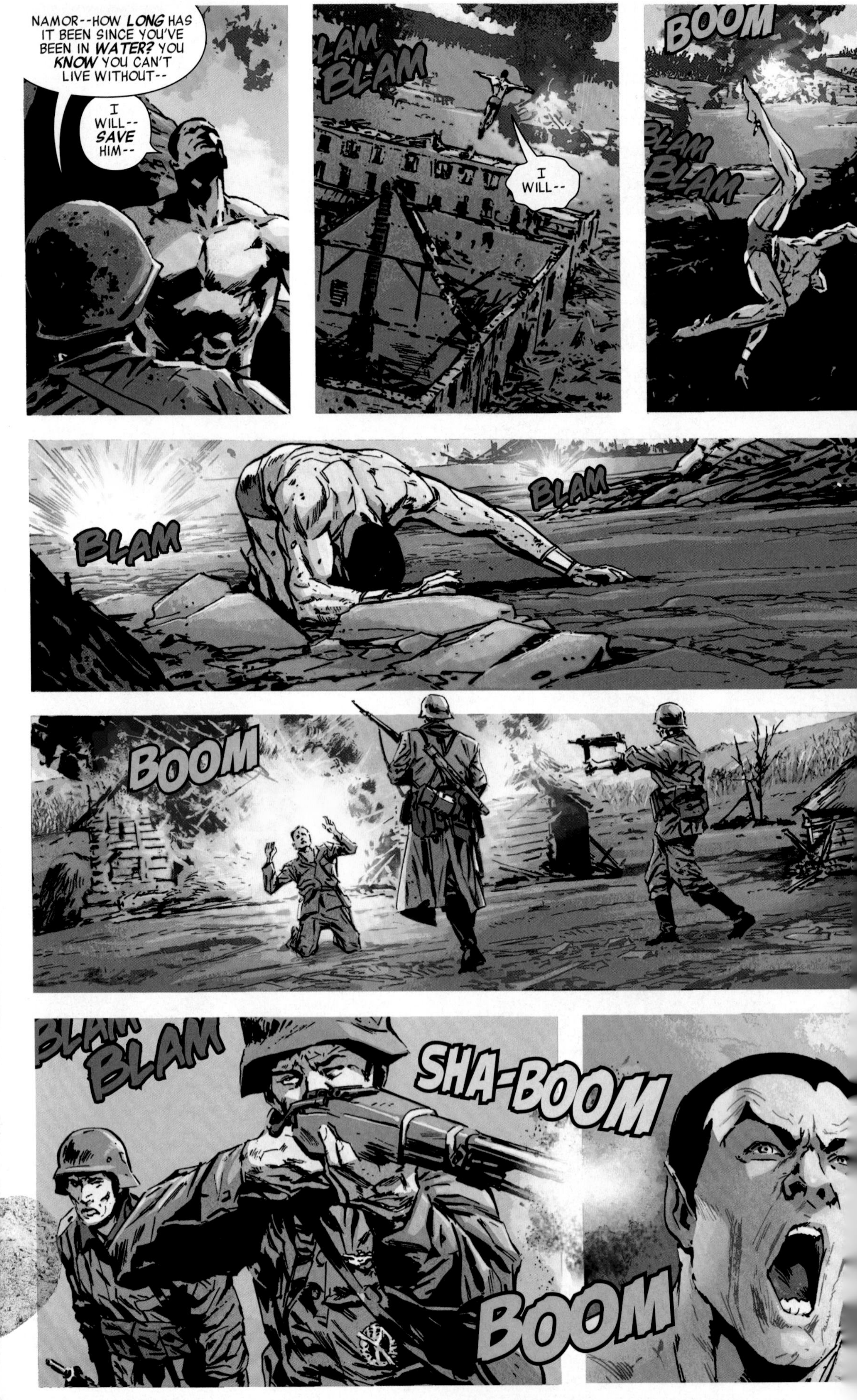
NAMOR--HOW LONG HAS IT BEEN SINCE YOU'VE BEEN IN WATER? YOU KNOW YOU CAN'T LIVE WITHOUT--
I WILL-- SAVE HIM--
BLAM BLAM
I WILL--
BOOM
BLAM BLAM
BLAM
BLAM
BOOM
BLAM BLAM
SHA-BOOM
BOOM

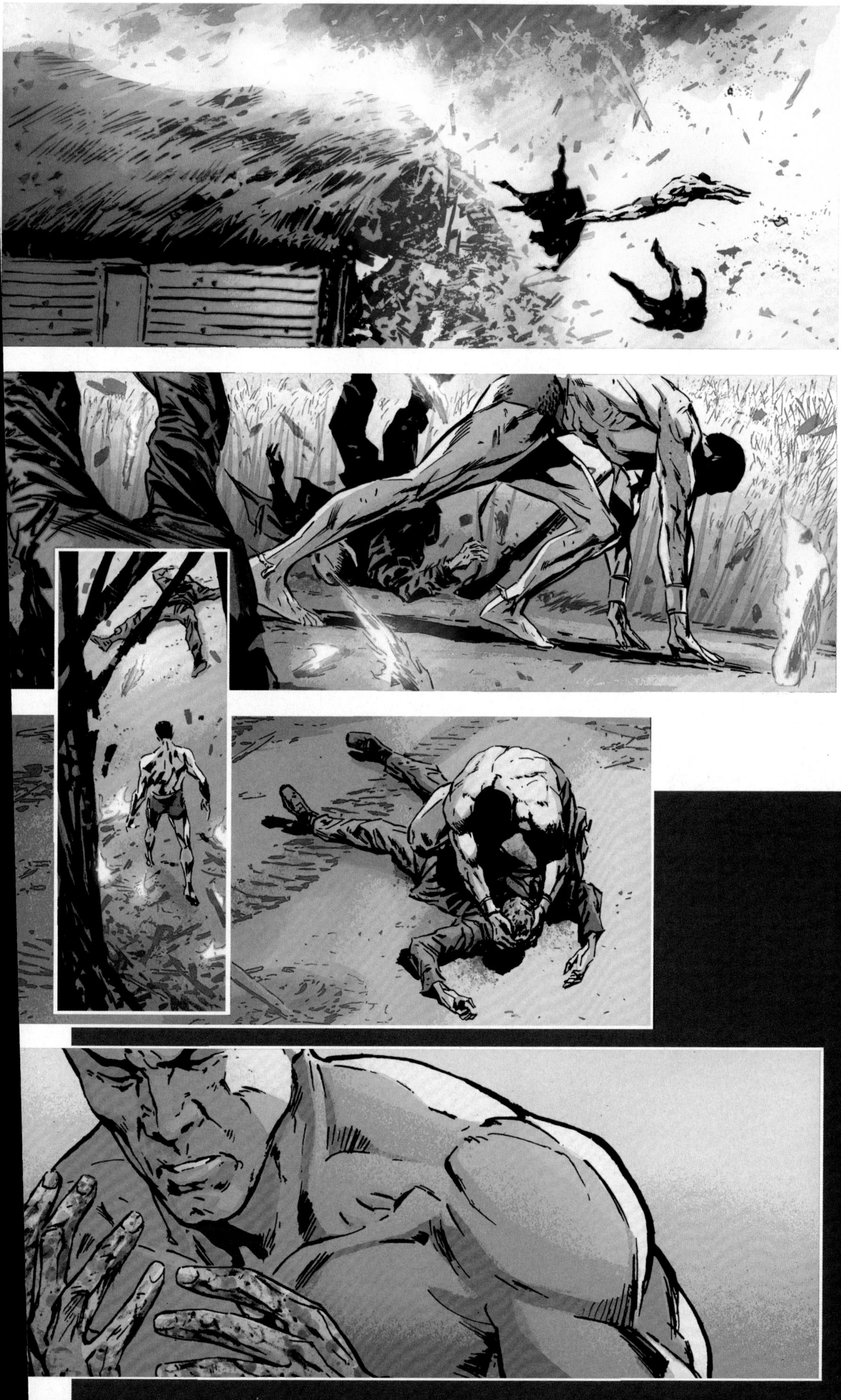

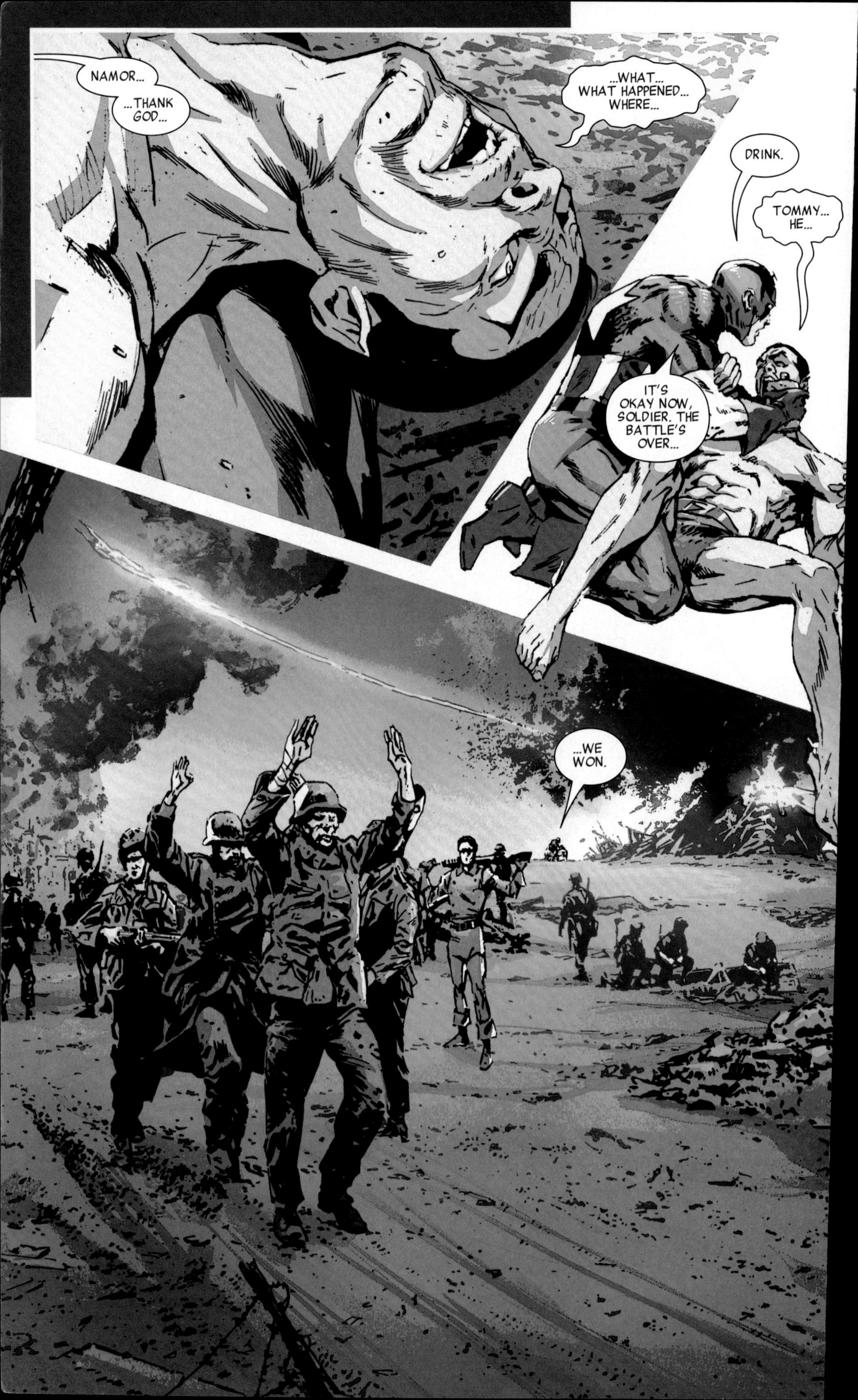
NAMOR...
...THANK GOD...
...WHAT... WHAT HAPPENED... WHERE...
DRINK.
TOMMY... HE...
IT'S OKAY NOW, SOLDIER. THE BATTLE'S OVER...
...WE WON.

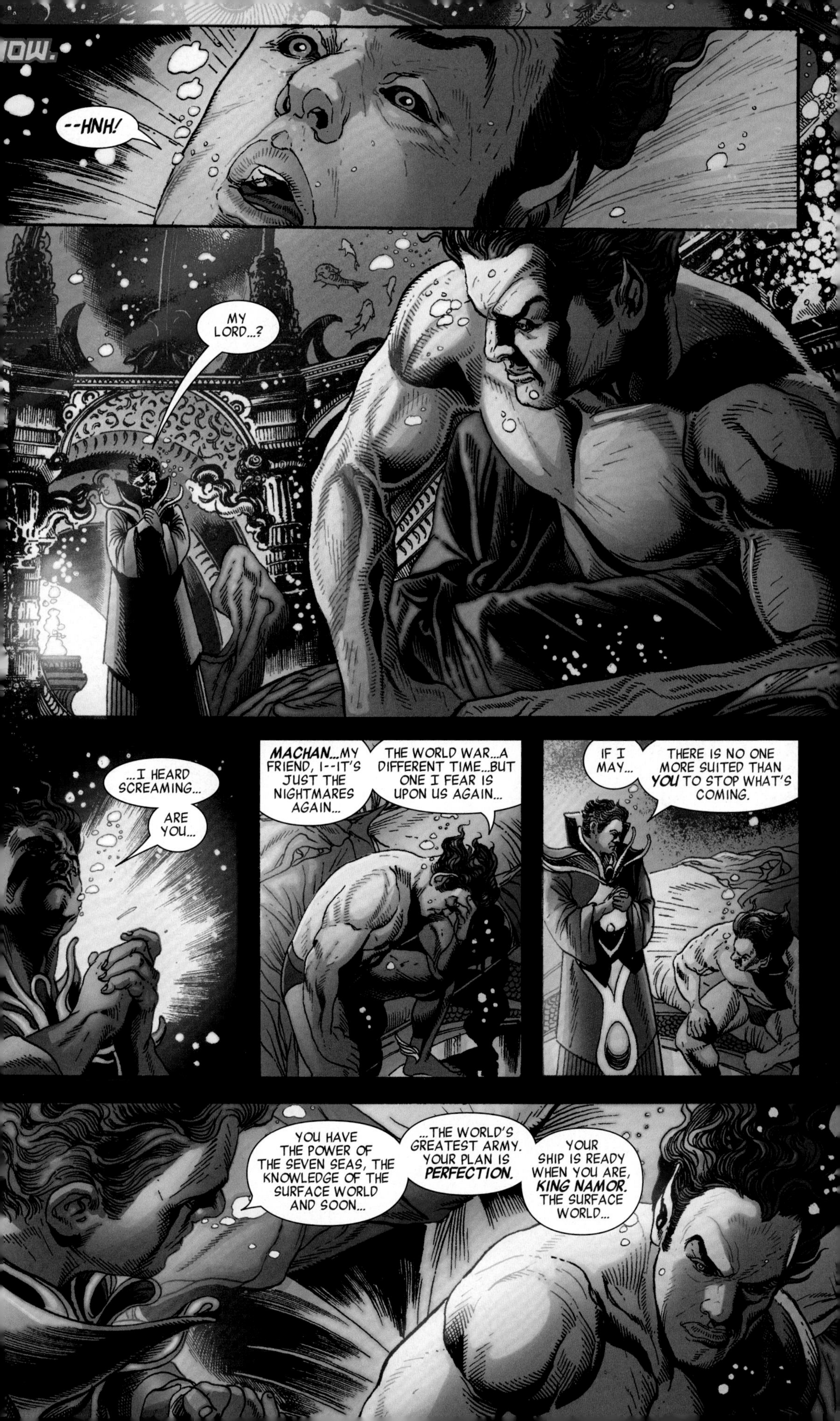
NOW.
--HNH!
MY LORD...?
...I HEARD SCREAMING...
ARE YOU...
MACHAN...MY FRIEND, I--IT'S JUST THE NIGHTMARES AGAIN...
THE WORLD WAR...A DIFFERENT TIME...BUT ONE I FEAR IS UPON US AGAIN...
IF I MAY...
THERE IS NO ONE MORE SUITED THAN YOU TO STOP WHAT'S COMING.
YOU HAVE THE POWER OF THE SEVEN SEAS, THE KNOWLEDGE OF THE SURFACE WORLD AND SOON...
...THE WORLD'S GREATEST ARMY. YOUR PLAN IS PERFECTION.
YOUR SHIP IS READY WHEN YOU ARE, KING NAMOR. THE SURFACE WORLD...

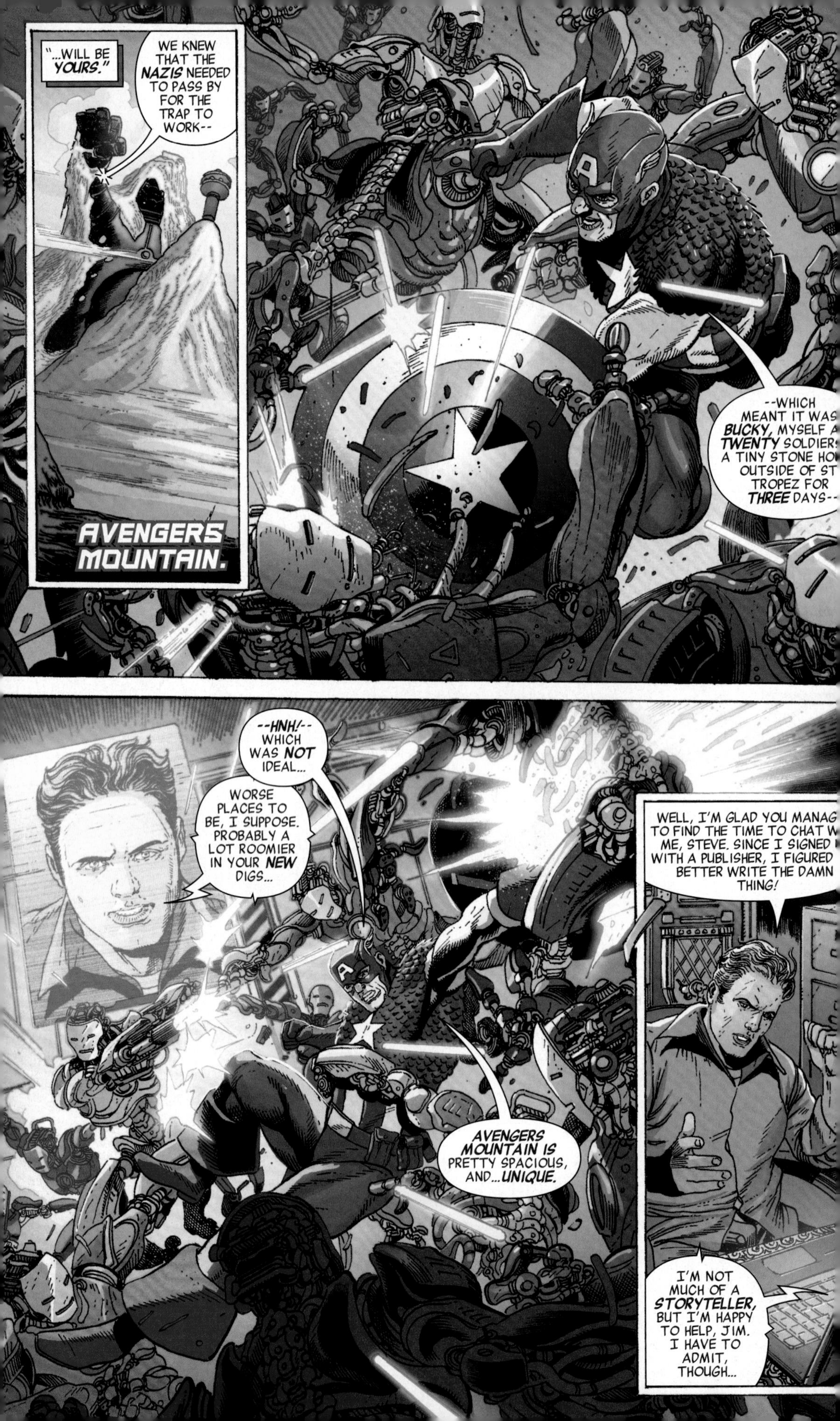
"...WILL BE *YOURS.*"
WE KNEW THAT THE ***NAZIS*** NEEDED TO PASS BY FOR THE TRAP TO WORK--
AVENGERS MOUNTAIN.
--WHICH MEANT IT WAS ***BUCKY,*** MYSELF A ***TWENTY*** SOLDIER A TINY STONE HO OUTSIDE OF ST TROPEZ FOR ***THREE*** DAYS--
--HNH!-- WHICH WAS ***NOT*** IDEAL...
WORSE PLACES TO BE, I SUPPOSE. PROBABLY A LOT ROOMIER IN YOUR ***NEW*** DIGS...
WELL, I'M GLAD YOU MANAG TO FIND THE TIME TO CHAT W ME, STEVE. SINCE I SIGNED WITH A PUBLISHER, I FIGURED BETTER WRITE THE DAMN *THING!*
AVENGERS MOUNTAIN IS PRETTY SPACIOUS, AND...***UNIQUE.***
I'M NOT MUCH OF A ***STORYTELLER,*** BUT I'M HAPPY TO HELP, JIM. I HAVE TO ADMIT, THOUGH...

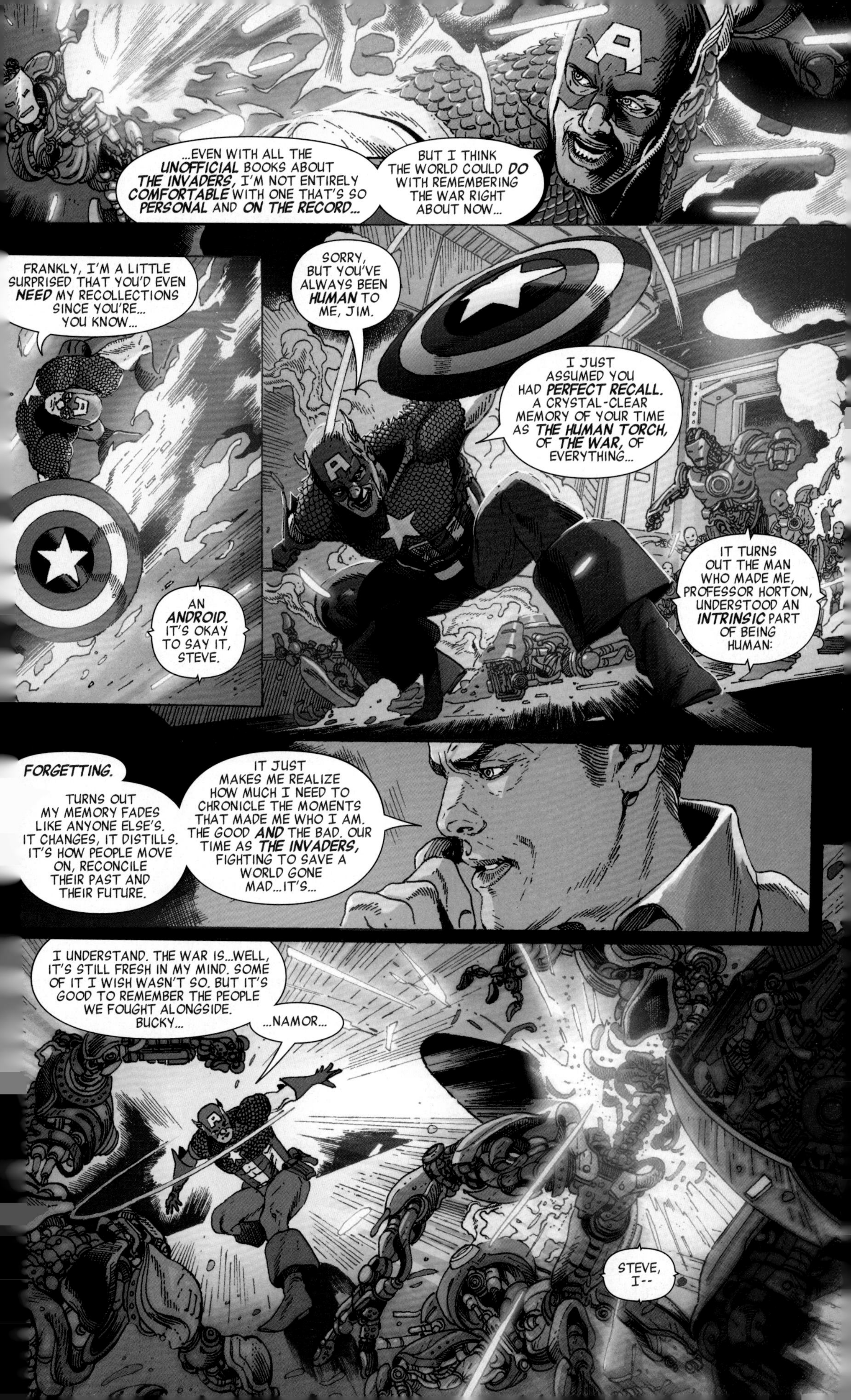
...EVEN WITH ALL THE UNOFFICIAL BOOKS ABOUT THE INVADERS, I'M NOT ENTIRELY COMFORTABLE WITH ONE THAT'S SO PERSONAL AND ON THE RECORD...
BUT I THINK THE WORLD COULD DO WITH REMEMBERING THE WAR RIGHT ABOUT NOW...
FRANKLY, I'M A LITTLE SURPRISED THAT YOU'D EVEN NEED MY RECOLLECTIONS SINCE YOU'RE... YOU KNOW...
AN ANDROID. IT'S OKAY TO SAY IT, STEVE.
SORRY, BUT YOU'VE ALWAYS BEEN HUMAN TO ME, JIM.
I JUST ASSUMED YOU HAD PERFECT RECALL. A CRYSTAL-CLEAR MEMORY OF YOUR TIME AS THE HUMAN TORCH, OF THE WAR, OF EVERYTHING...
IT TURNS OUT THE MAN WHO MADE ME, PROFESSOR HORTON, UNDERSTOOD AN INTRINSIC PART OF BEING HUMAN:
FORGETTING.
TURNS OUT MY MEMORY FADES LIKE ANYONE ELSE'S. IT CHANGES, IT DISTILLS. IT'S HOW PEOPLE MOVE ON, RECONCILE THEIR PAST AND THEIR FUTURE.
IT JUST MAKES ME REALIZE HOW MUCH I NEED TO CHRONICLE THE MOMENTS THAT MADE ME WHO I AM. THE GOOD AND THE BAD. OUR TIME AS THE INVADERS, FIGHTING TO SAVE A WORLD GONE MAD...IT'S...
I UNDERSTAND. THE WAR IS...WELL, IT'S STILL FRESH IN MY MIND. SOME OF IT I WISH WASN'T SO. BUT IT'S GOOD TO REMEMBER THE PEOPLE WE FOUGHT ALONGSIDE. BUCKY...
...NAMOR...
STEVE, I--

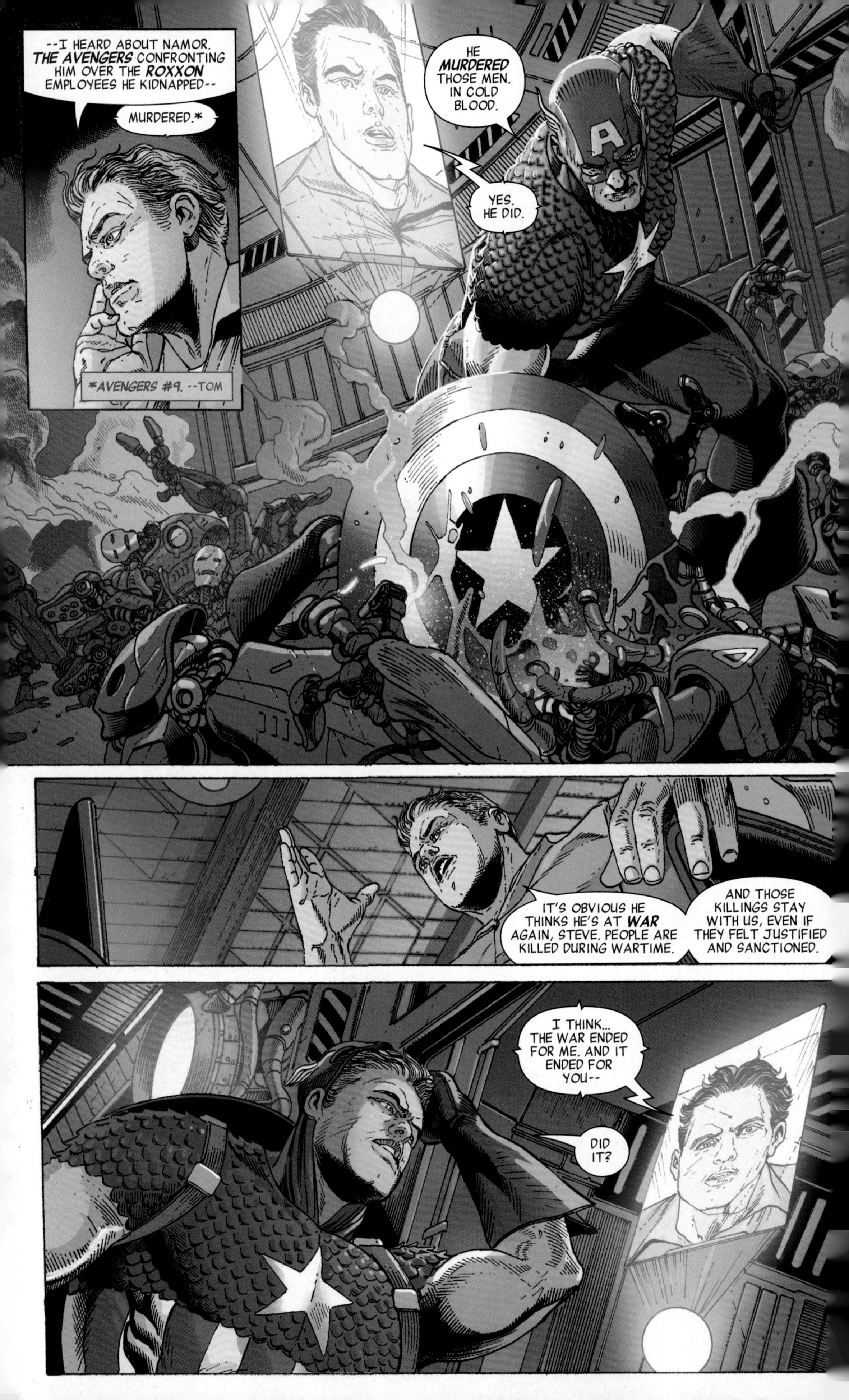
--I HEARD ABOUT NAMOR. THE AVENGERS CONFRONTING HIM OVER THE ROXXON EMPLOYEES HE KIDNAPPED--
MURDERED.*
*AVENGERS #9. --TOM
HE MURDERED THOSE MEN. IN COLD BLOOD.
YES. HE DID.
IT'S OBVIOUS HE THINKS HE'S AT WAR AGAIN, STEVE. PEOPLE ARE KILLED DURING WARTIME.
AND THOSE KILLINGS STAY WITH US, EVEN IF THEY FELT JUSTIFIED AND SANCTIONED.
I THINK... THE WAR ENDED FOR ME. AND IT ENDED FOR YOU--
DID IT?

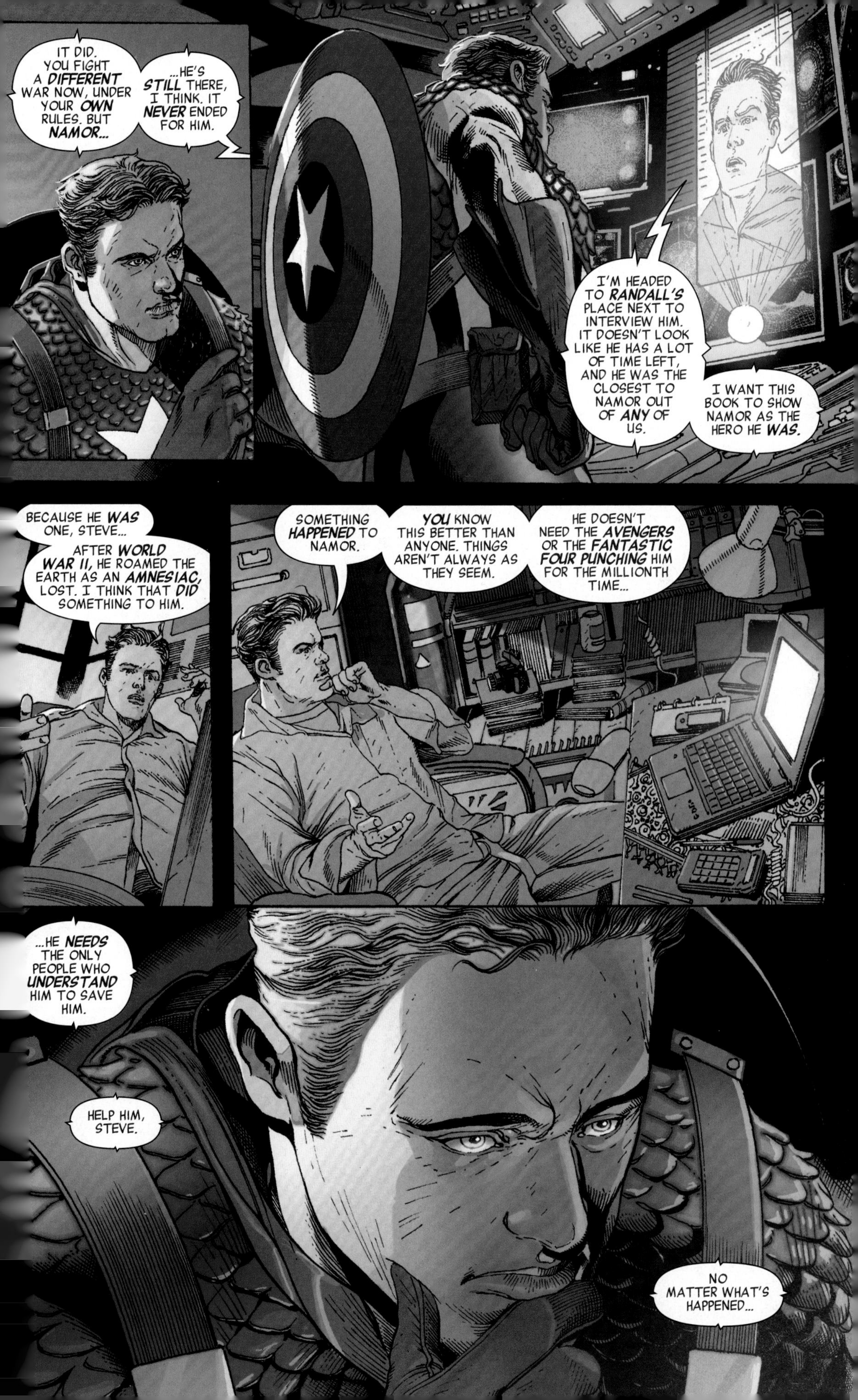
IT DID. YOU FIGHT A DIFFERENT WAR NOW, UNDER YOUR OWN RULES. BUT NAMOR...
...HE'S STILL THERE, I THINK. IT NEVER ENDED FOR HIM.
I'M HEADED TO RANDALL'S PLACE NEXT TO INTERVIEW HIM. IT DOESN'T LOOK LIKE HE HAS A LOT OF TIME LEFT, AND HE WAS THE CLOSEST TO NAMOR OUT OF ANY OF US.
I WANT THIS BOOK TO SHOW NAMOR AS THE HERO HE WAS.
BECAUSE HE WAS ONE, STEVE...
AFTER WORLD WAR II, HE ROAMED THE EARTH AS AN AMNESIAC, LOST. I THINK THAT DID SOMETHING TO HIM.
SOMETHING HAPPENED TO NAMOR.
YOU KNOW THIS BETTER THAN ANYONE. THINGS AREN'T ALWAYS AS THEY SEEM.
HE DOESN'T NEED THE AVENGERS OR THE FANTASTIC FOUR PUNCHING HIM FOR THE MILLIONTH TIME...
...HE NEEDS THE ONLY PEOPLE WHO UNDERSTAND HIM TO SAVE HIM.
HELP HIM, STEVE.
NO MATTER WHAT'S HAPPENED...

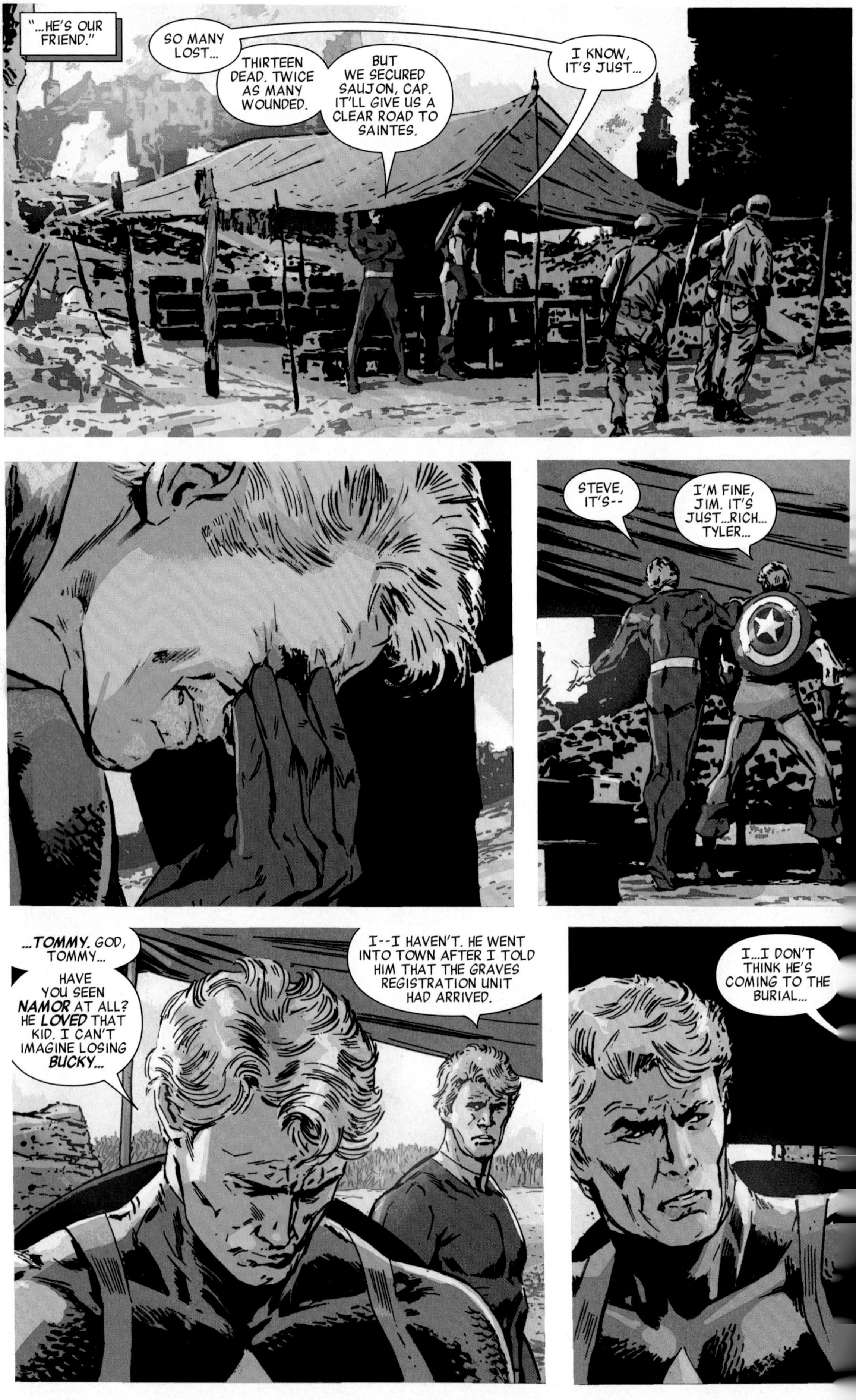
"...HE'S OUR FRIEND."
SO MANY LOST...
THIRTEEN DEAD. TWICE AS MANY WOUNDED.
BUT WE SECURED SAUJON, CAP. IT'LL GIVE US A CLEAR ROAD TO SAINTES.
I KNOW, IT'S JUST...
STEVE, IT'S--
I'M FINE, JIM. IT'S JUST...RICH... TYLER...
...TOMMY. GOD, TOMMY...
HAVE YOU SEEN NAMOR AT ALL? HE LOVED THAT KID. I CAN'T IMAGINE LOSING BUCKY...
I--I HAVEN'T. HE WENT INTO TOWN AFTER I TOLD HIM THAT THE GRAVES REGISTRATION UNIT HAD ARRIVED.
I...I DON'T THINK HE'S COMING TO THE BURIAL...

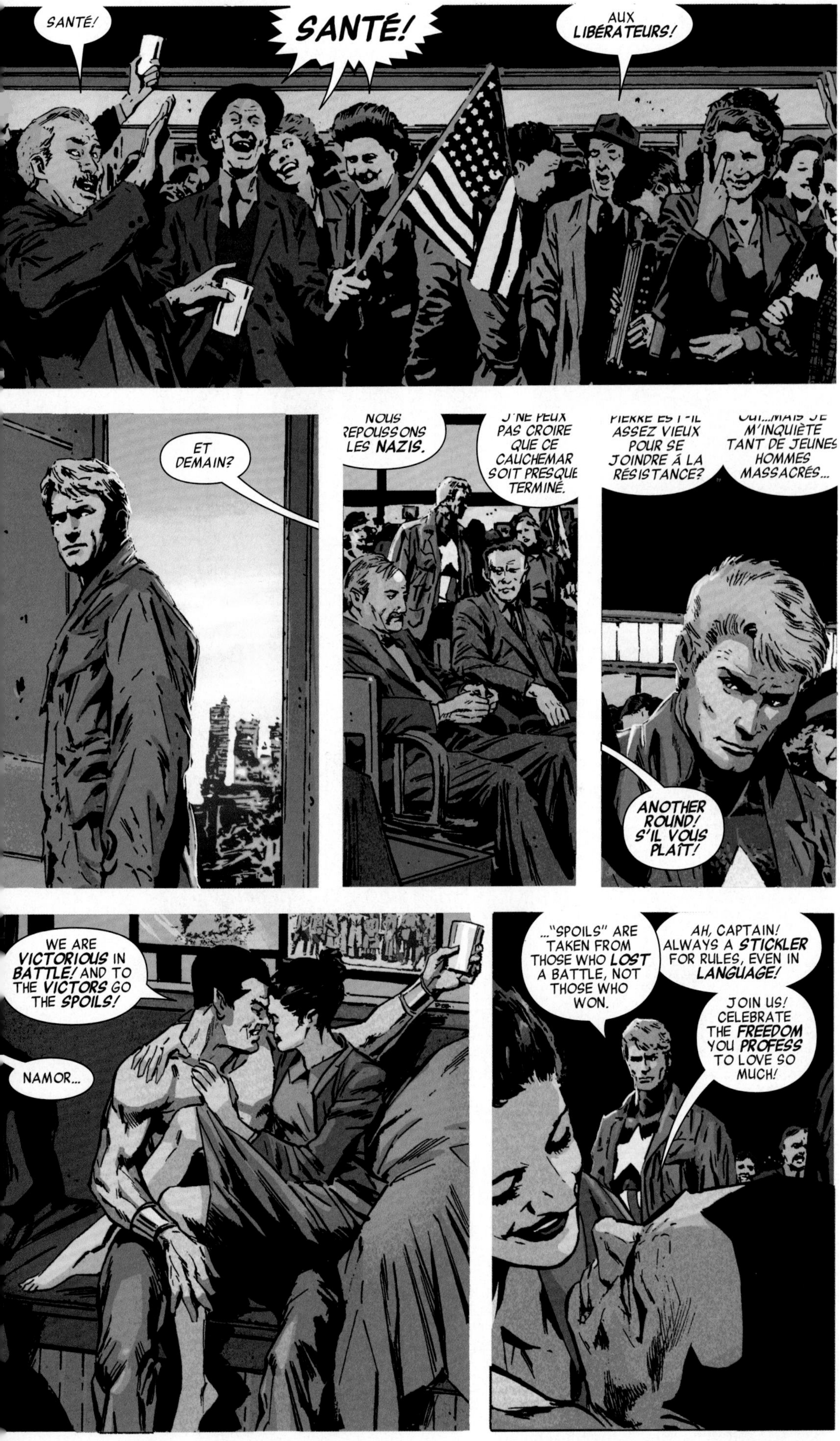
SANTÉ!
SANTÉ!
AUX LIBÉRATEURS!
ET DEMAIN?
NOUS REPOUSSONS LES NAZIS.
J'NE PEUX PAS CROIRE QUE CE CAUCHEMAR SOIT PRESQUE TERMINÉ.
PIERRE EST-IL ASSEZ VIEUX POUR SE JOINDRE À LA RÉSISTANCE?
OUI...MAIS JE M'INQUIÈTE TANT DE JEUNES HOMMES MASSACRÉS...
ANOTHER ROUND! S'IL VOUS PLAÎT!
WE ARE VICTORIOUS IN BATTLE! AND TO THE VICTORS GO THE SPOILS!
NAMOR...
..."SPOILS" ARE TAKEN FROM THOSE WHO LOST A BATTLE, NOT THOSE WHO WON.
AH, CAPTAIN! ALWAYS A STICKLER FOR RULES, EVEN IN LANGUAGE!
JOIN US! CELEBRATE THE FREEDOM YOU PROFESS TO LOVE SO MUCH!

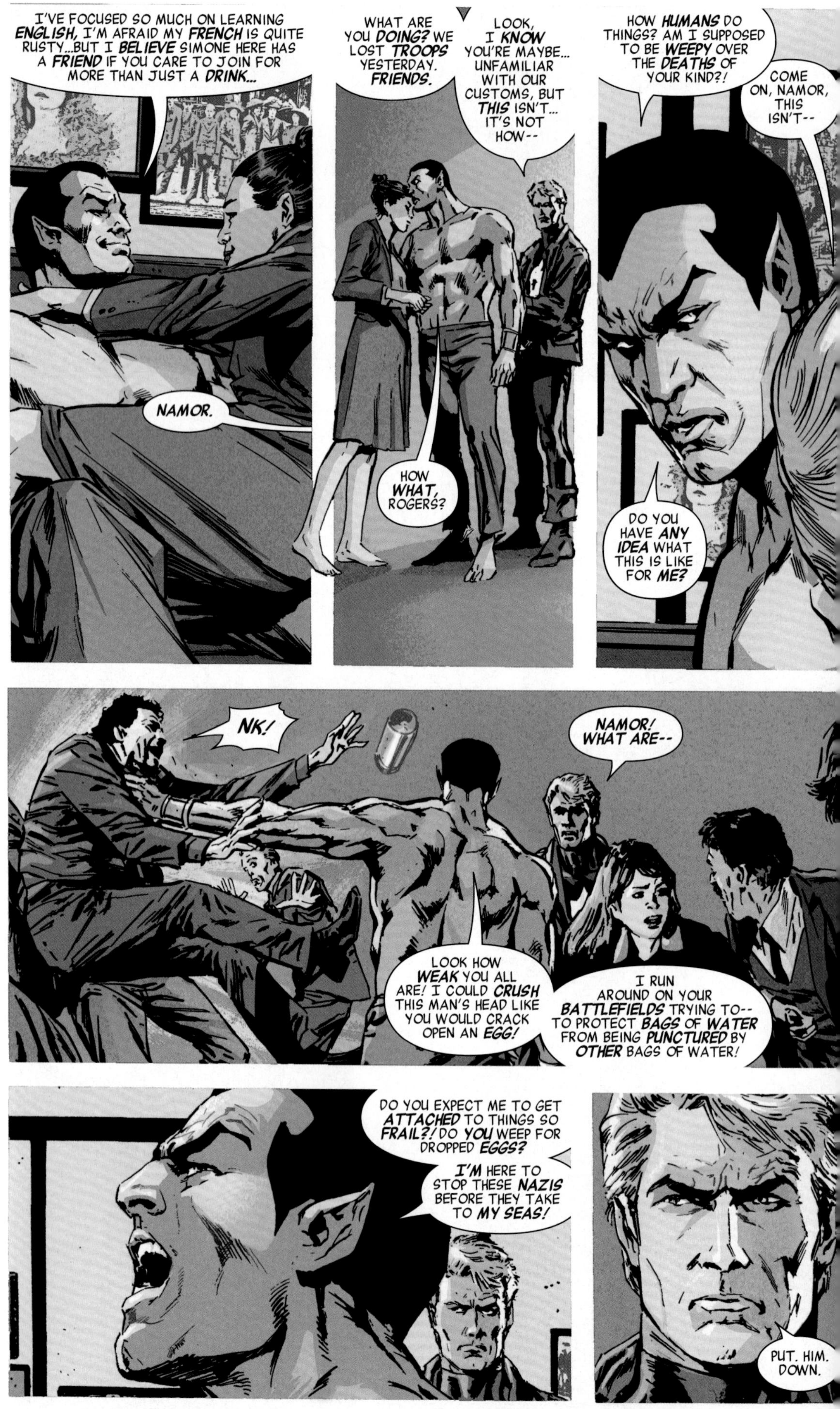
I'VE FOCUSED SO MUCH ON LEARNING ENGLISH, I'M AFRAID MY FRENCH IS QUITE RUSTY...BUT I BELIEVE SIMONE HERE HAS A FRIEND IF YOU CARE TO JOIN FOR MORE THAN JUST A DRINK...
NAMOR.
WHAT ARE YOU DOING? WE LOST TROOPS YESTERDAY. FRIENDS.
LOOK, I KNOW YOU'RE MAYBE... UNFAMILIAR WITH OUR CUSTOMS, BUT THIS ISN'T... IT'S NOT HOW--
HOW WHAT, ROGERS?
HOW HUMANS DO THINGS? AM I SUPPOSED TO BE WEEPY OVER THE DEATHS OF YOUR KIND?!
COME ON, NAMOR, THIS ISN'T--
DO YOU HAVE ANY IDEA WHAT THIS IS LIKE FOR ME?
NK!
NAMOR! WHAT ARE--
LOOK HOW WEAK YOU ALL ARE! I COULD CRUSH THIS MAN'S HEAD LIKE YOU WOULD CRACK OPEN AN EGG!
I RUN AROUND ON YOUR BATTLEFIELDS TRYING TO-- TO PROTECT BAGS OF WATER FROM BEING PUNCTURED BY OTHER BAGS OF WATER!
DO YOU EXPECT ME TO GET ATTACHED TO THINGS SO FRAIL?! DO YOU WEEP FOR DROPPED EGGS?
I'M HERE TO STOP THESE NAZIS BEFORE THEY TAKE TO MY SEAS!
PUT. HIM. DOWN.

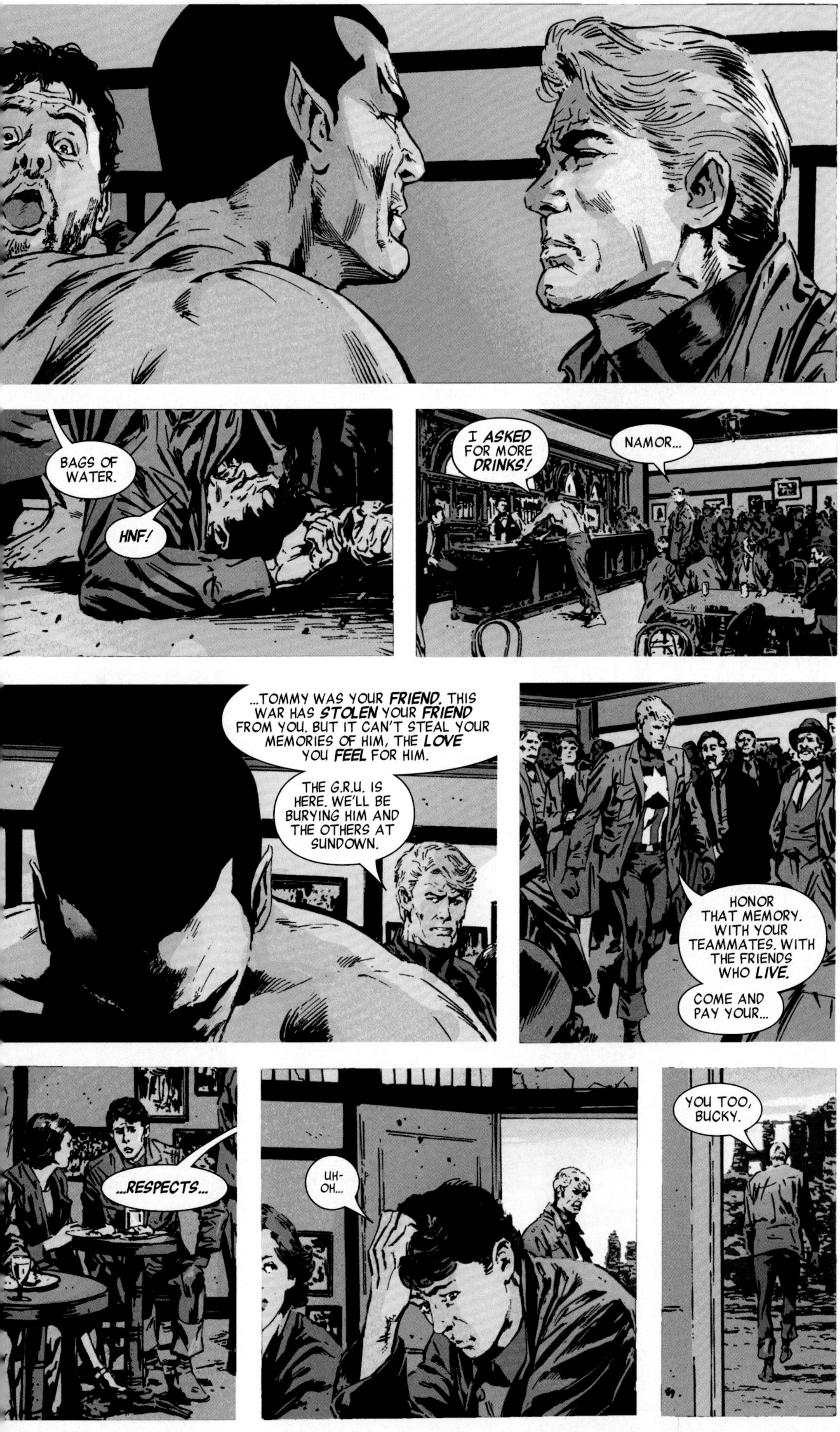
BAGS OF WATER.
HNF!
I ASKED FOR MORE DRINKS!
NAMOR...
...TOMMY WAS YOUR FRIEND. THIS WAR HAS STOLEN YOUR FRIEND FROM YOU. BUT IT CAN'T STEAL YOUR MEMORIES OF HIM, THE LOVE YOU FEEL FOR HIM.
THE G.R.U. IS HERE. WE'LL BE BURYING HIM AND THE OTHERS AT SUNDOWN.
HONOR THAT MEMORY. WITH YOUR TEAMMATES. WITH THE FRIENDS WHO LIVE.
COME AND PAY YOUR...
...RESPECTS...
UH-OH...
YOU TOO, BUCKY.

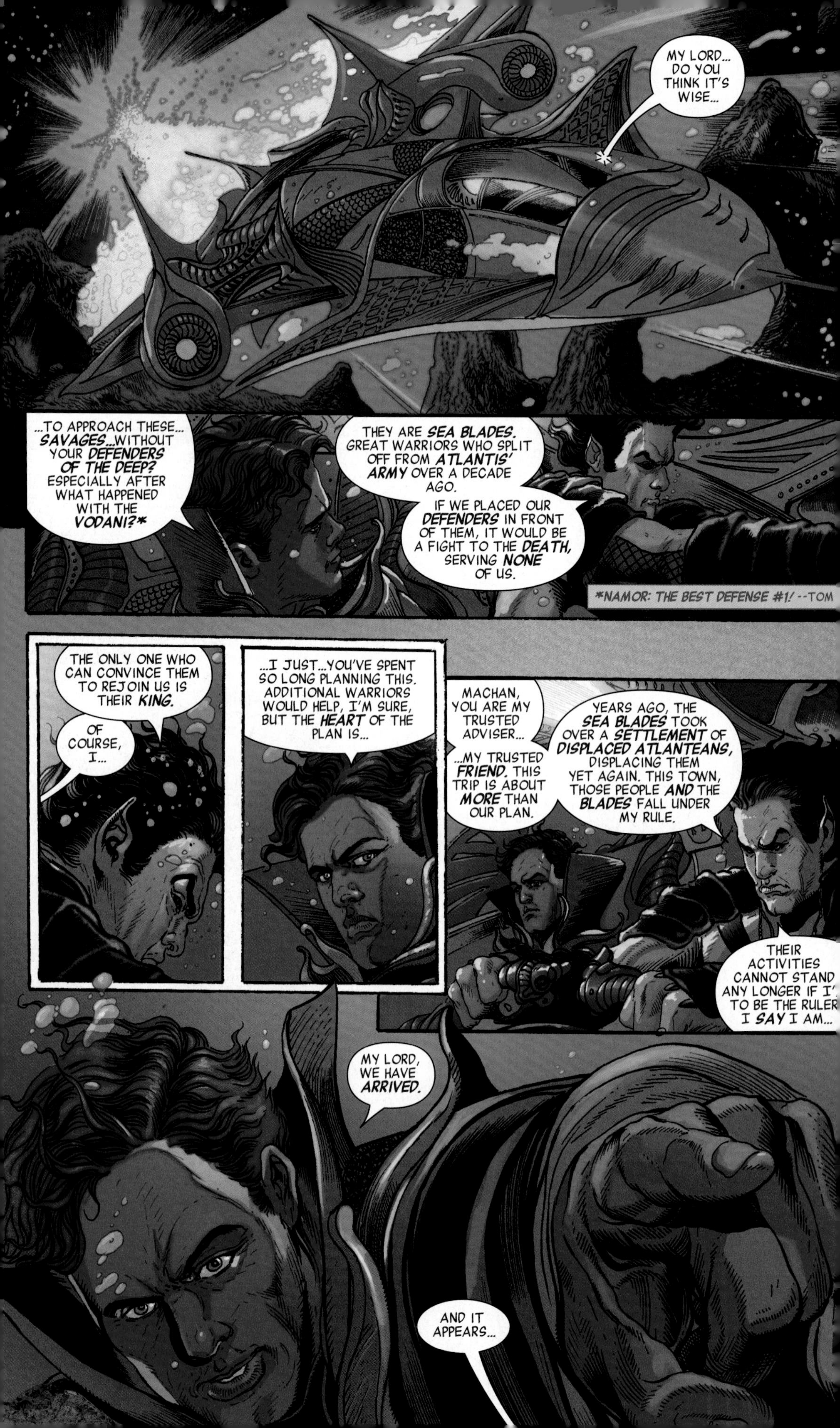
MY LORD... DO YOU THINK IT'S WISE...
...TO APPROACH THESE... SAVAGES...WITHOUT YOUR DEFENDERS OF THE DEEP? ESPECIALLY AFTER WHAT HAPPENED WITH THE VODANI?*
THEY ARE SEA BLADES. GREAT WARRIORS WHO SPLIT OFF FROM ATLANTIS' ARMY OVER A DECADE AGO.
IF WE PLACED OUR DEFENDERS IN FRONT OF THEM, IT WOULD BE A FIGHT TO THE DEATH, SERVING NONE OF US.
*NAMOR: THE BEST DEFENSE #1! --TOM
THE ONLY ONE WHO CAN CONVINCE THEM TO REJOIN US IS THEIR KING.
OF COURSE, I...
...I JUST...YOU'VE SPENT SO LONG PLANNING THIS. ADDITIONAL WARRIORS WOULD HELP, I'M SURE, BUT THE HEART OF THE PLAN IS...
MACHAN, YOU ARE MY TRUSTED ADVISER...
...MY TRUSTED FRIEND. THIS TRIP IS ABOUT MORE THAN OUR PLAN.
YEARS AGO, THE SEA BLADES TOOK OVER A SETTLEMENT OF DISPLACED ATLANTEANS, DISPLACING THEM YET AGAIN. THIS TOWN, THOSE PEOPLE AND THE BLADES FALL UNDER MY RULE.
THEIR ACTIVITIES CANNOT STAND ANY LONGER IF I' TO BE THE RULER I SAY I AM...
MY LORD, WE HAVE ARRIVED.
AND IT APPEARS...

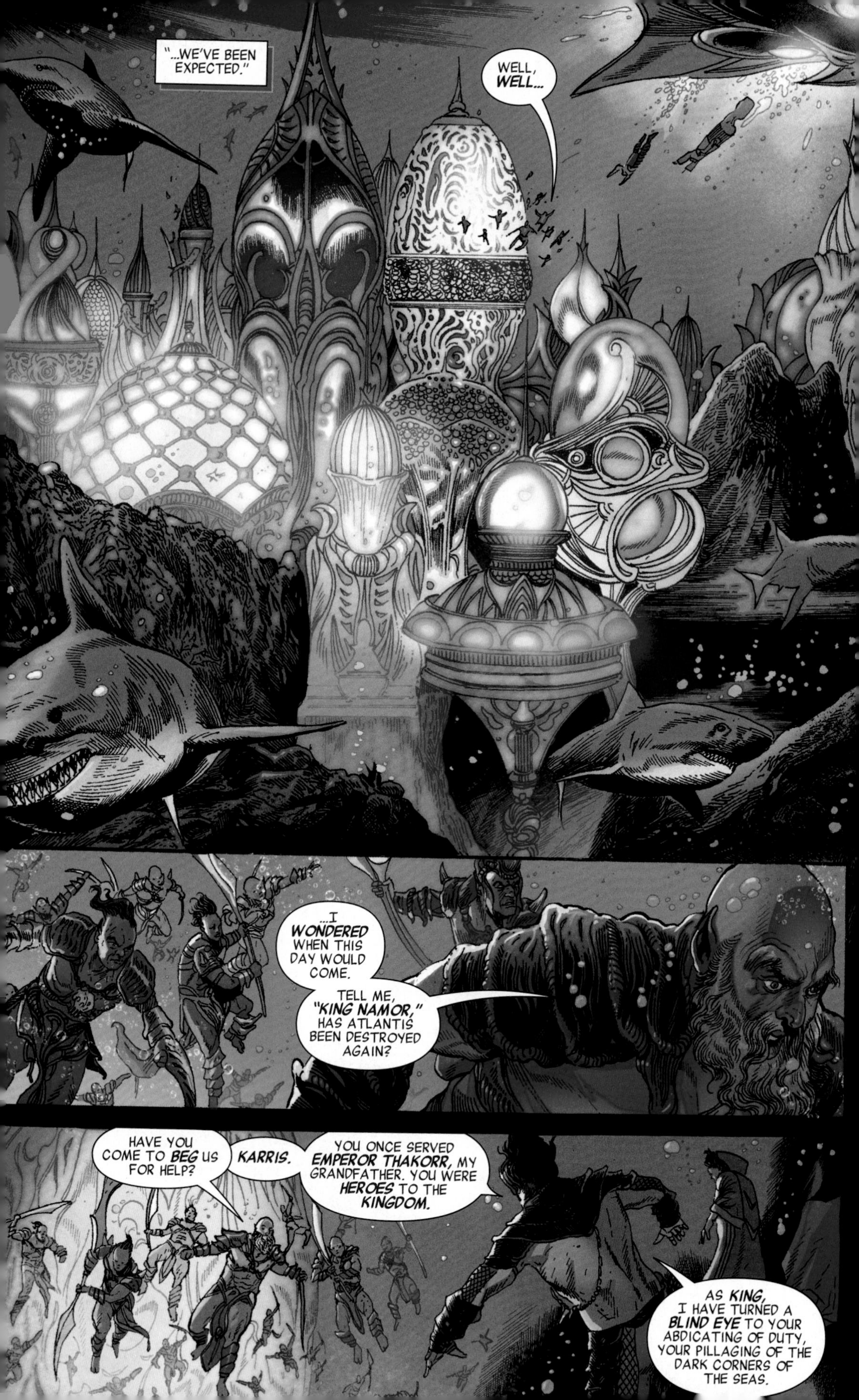
"...WE'VE BEEN EXPECTED."
WELL, WELL...
...I WONDERED WHEN THIS DAY WOULD COME.
TELL ME, "KING NAMOR," HAS ATLANTIS BEEN DESTROYED AGAIN?
HAVE YOU COME TO BEG US FOR HELP?
KARRIS.
YOU ONCE SERVED EMPEROR THAKORR, MY GRANDFATHER. YOU WERE HEROES TO THE KINGDOM.
AS KING, I HAVE TURNED A BLIND EYE TO YOUR ABDICATING OF DUTY, YOUR PILLAGING OF THE DARK CORNERS OF THE SEAS.

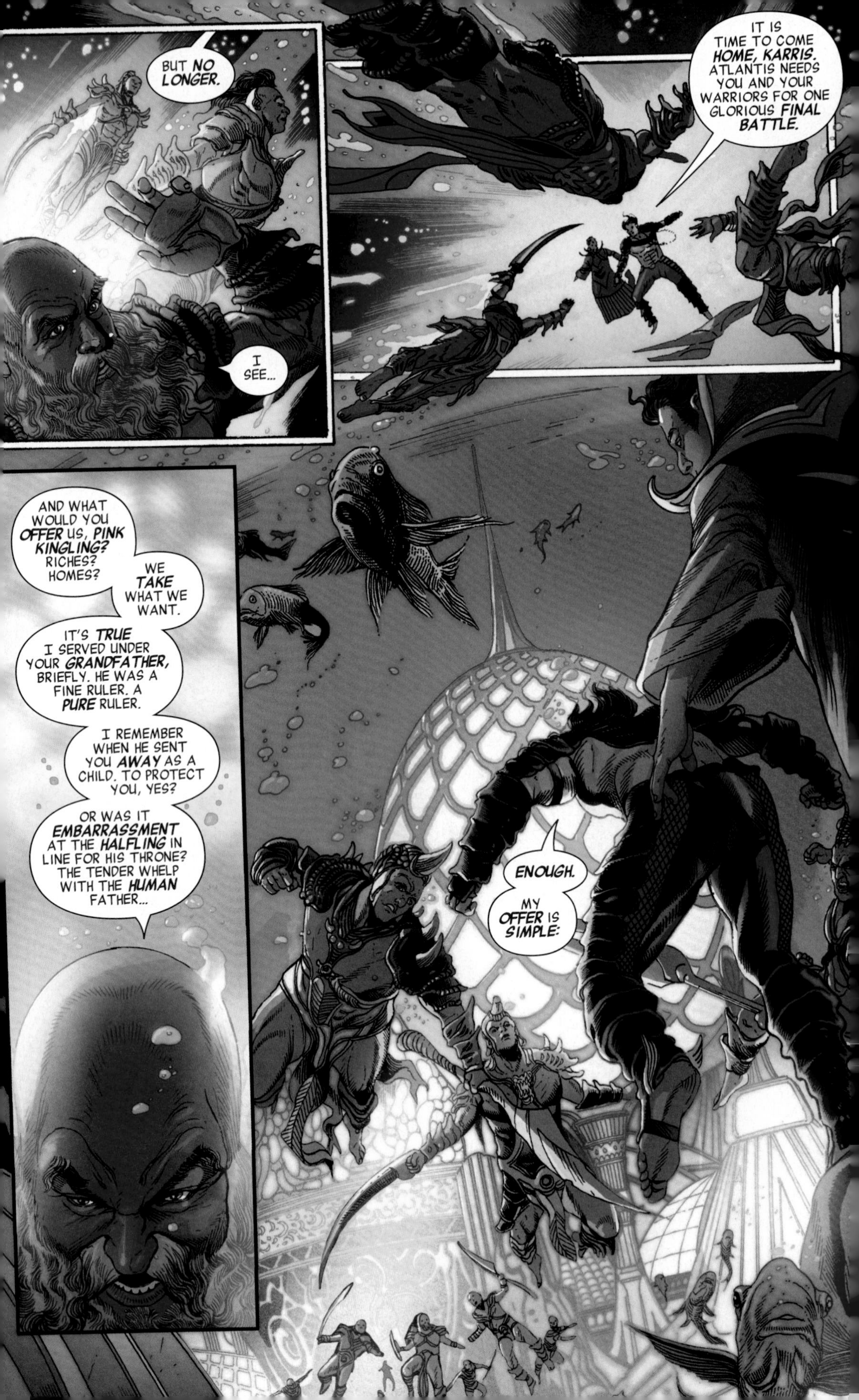

BUT NO LONGER.
I SEE...
IT IS TIME TO COME HOME, KARRIS. ATLANTIS NEEDS YOU AND YOUR WARRIORS FOR ONE GLORIOUS FINAL BATTLE.
AND WHAT WOULD YOU OFFER US, PINK KINGLING? RICHES? HOMES?
WE TAKE WHAT WE WANT.
IT'S TRUE I SERVED UNDER YOUR GRANDFATHER, BRIEFLY. HE WAS A FINE RULER. A PURE RULER.
I REMEMBER WHEN HE SENT YOU AWAY AS A CHILD. TO PROTECT YOU, YES?
OR WAS IT EMBARRASSMENT AT THE HALFLING IN LINE FOR HIS THRONE? THE TENDER WHELP WITH THE HUMAN FATHER...
ENOUGH.
MY OFFER IS SIMPLE:

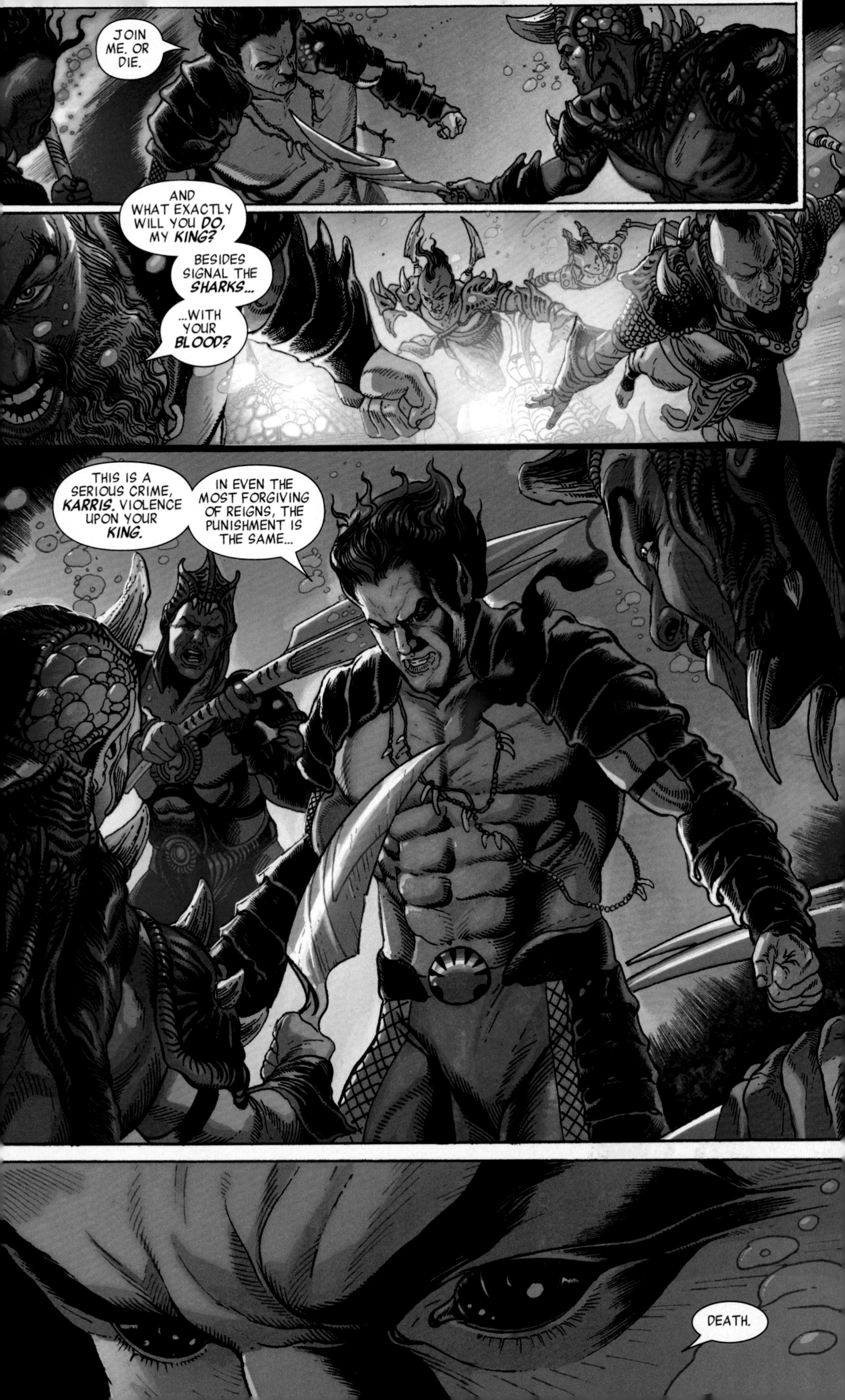
JOIN ME. OR DIE.
AND WHAT EXACTLY WILL YOU DO, MY KING?
BESIDES SIGNAL THE SHARKS...
...WITH YOUR BLOOD?
THIS IS A SERIOUS CRIME, KARRIS. VIOLENCE UPON YOUR KING.
IN EVEN THE MOST FORGIVING OF REIGNS, THE PUNISHMENT IS THE SAME...
DEATH.

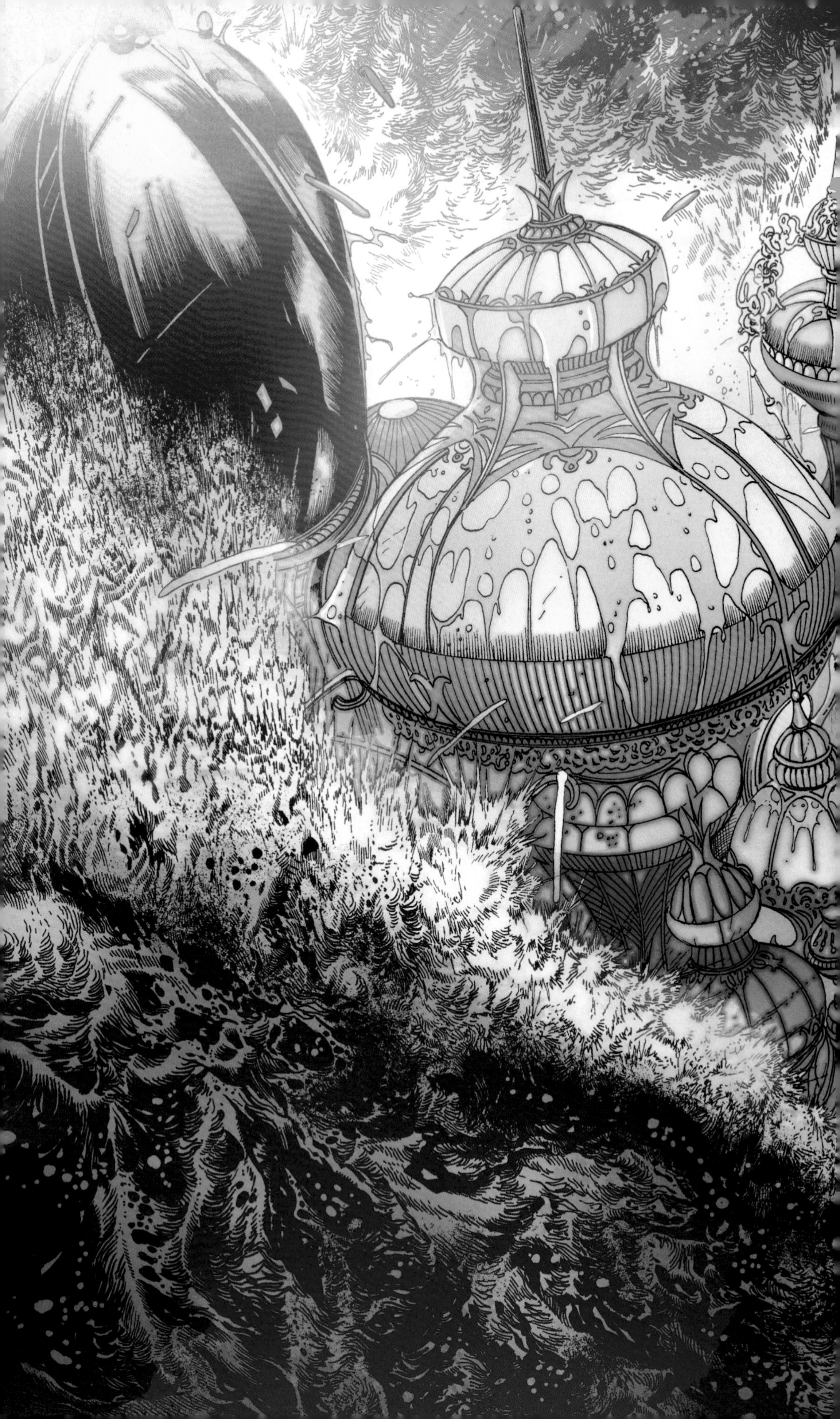

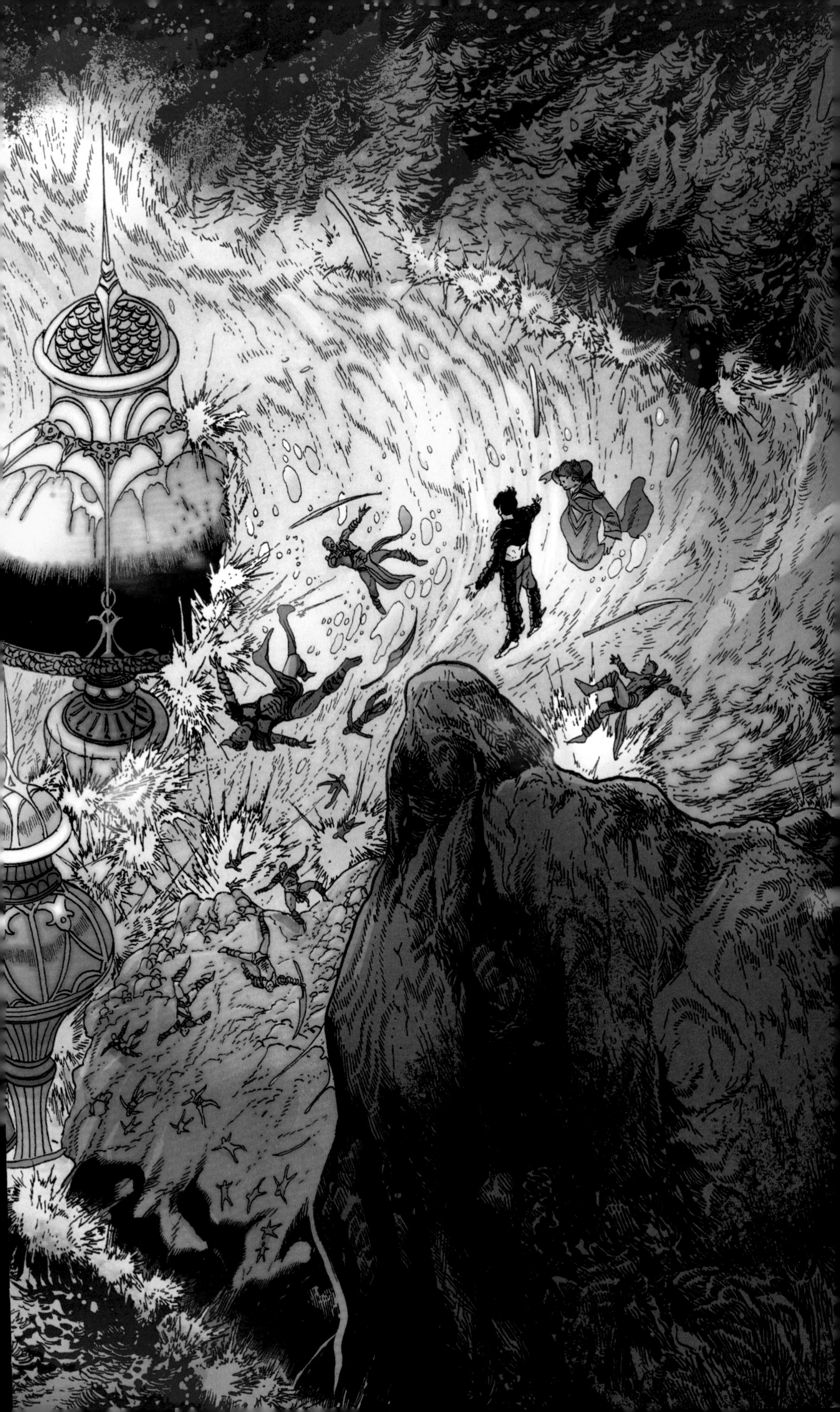

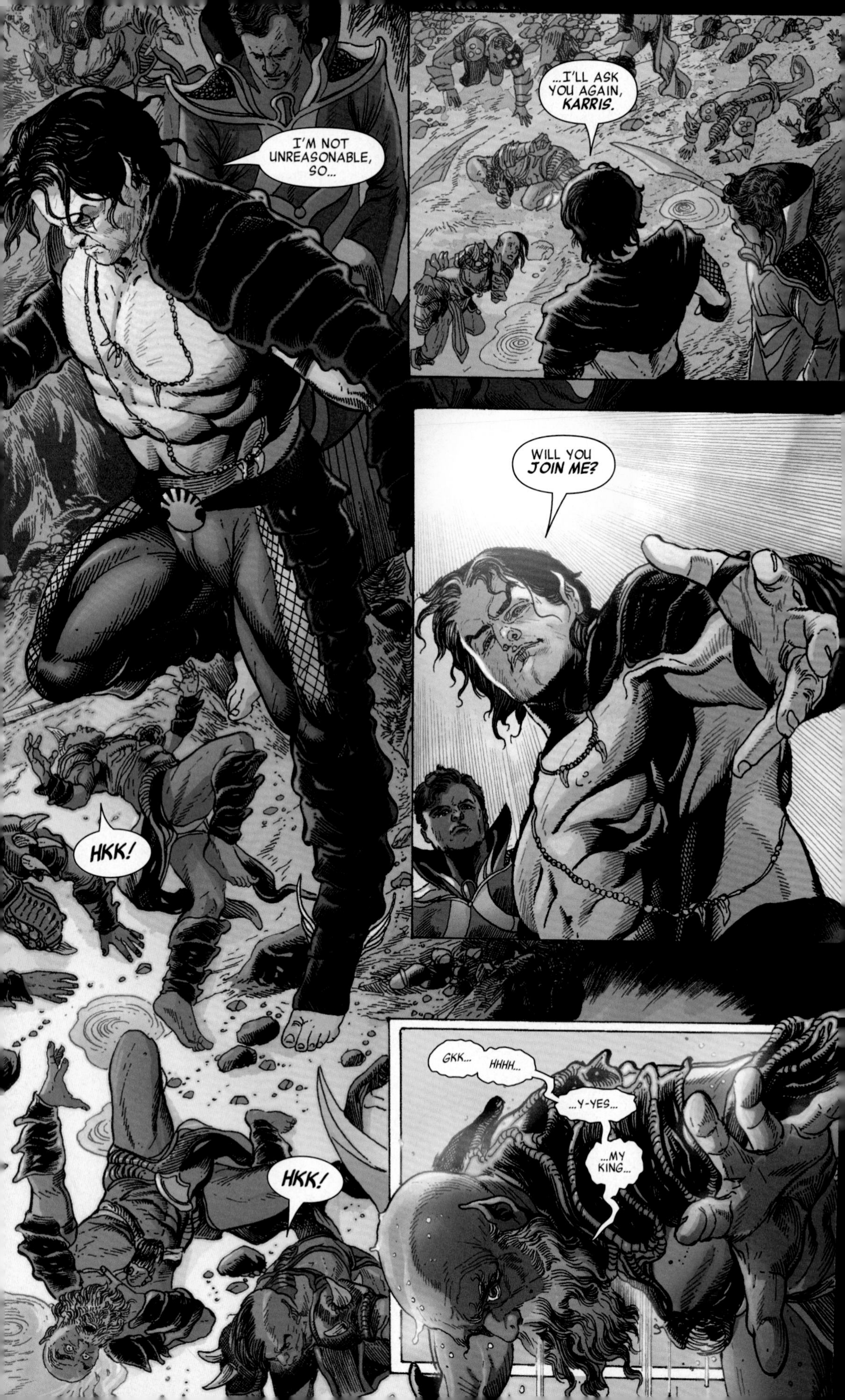
I'M NOT UNREASONABLE, SO...
...I'LL ASK YOU AGAIN, KARRIS.
WILL YOU JOIN ME?
HKK!
HKK!
GKK...
HHHH...
...Y-YES...
...MY KING...

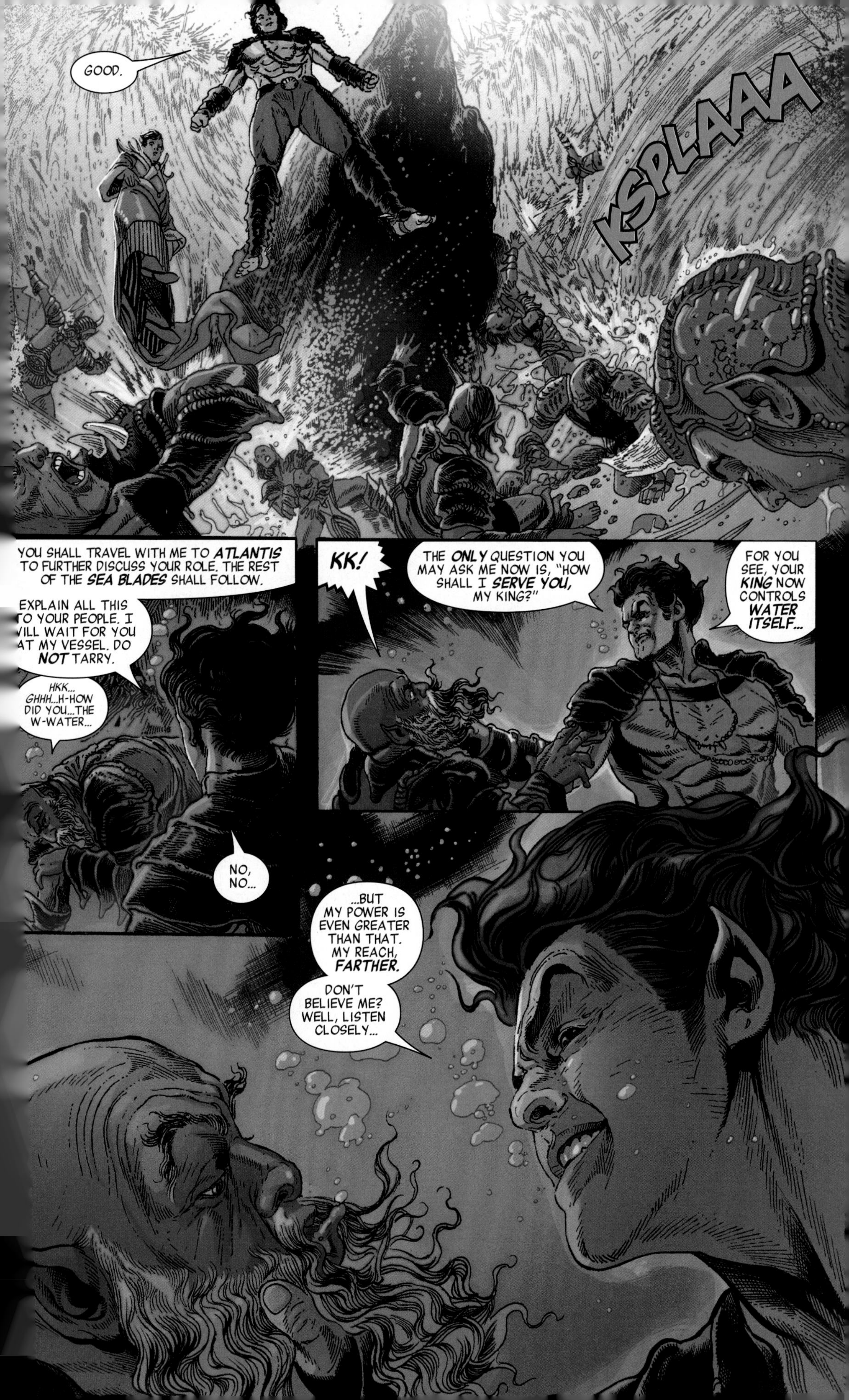
GOOD.
KSPLAAA
YOU SHALL TRAVEL WITH ME TO ATLANTIS TO FURTHER DISCUSS YOUR ROLE. THE REST OF THE SEA BLADES SHALL FOLLOW.
EXPLAIN ALL THIS TO YOUR PEOPLE. I WILL WAIT FOR YOU AT MY VESSEL. DO NOT TARRY.
HKK... GHHH...H-HOW DID YOU...THE W-WATER...
NO, NO...
KK!
THE ONLY QUESTION YOU MAY ASK ME NOW IS, "HOW SHALL I SERVE YOU, MY KING?"
FOR YOU SEE, YOUR KING NOW CONTROLS WATER ITSELF...
...BUT MY POWER IS EVEN GREATER THAN THAT. MY REACH, FARTHER.
DON'T BELIEVE ME? WELL, LISTEN CLOSELY...

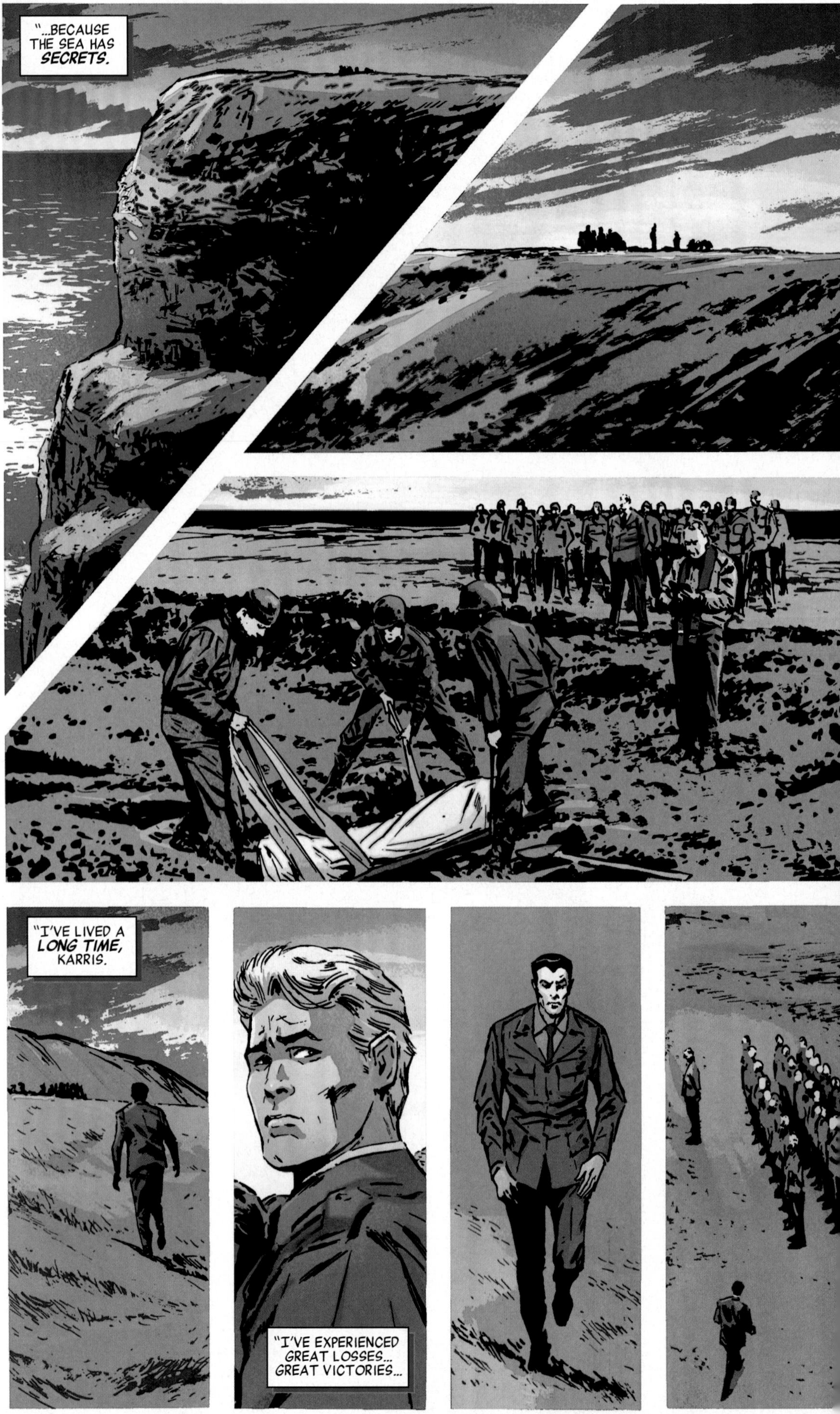
"...BECAUSE THE SEA HAS *SECRETS.*
"I'VE LIVED A *LONG TIME,* KARRIS.
"I'VE EXPERIENCED GREAT LOSSES... GREAT VICTORIES...

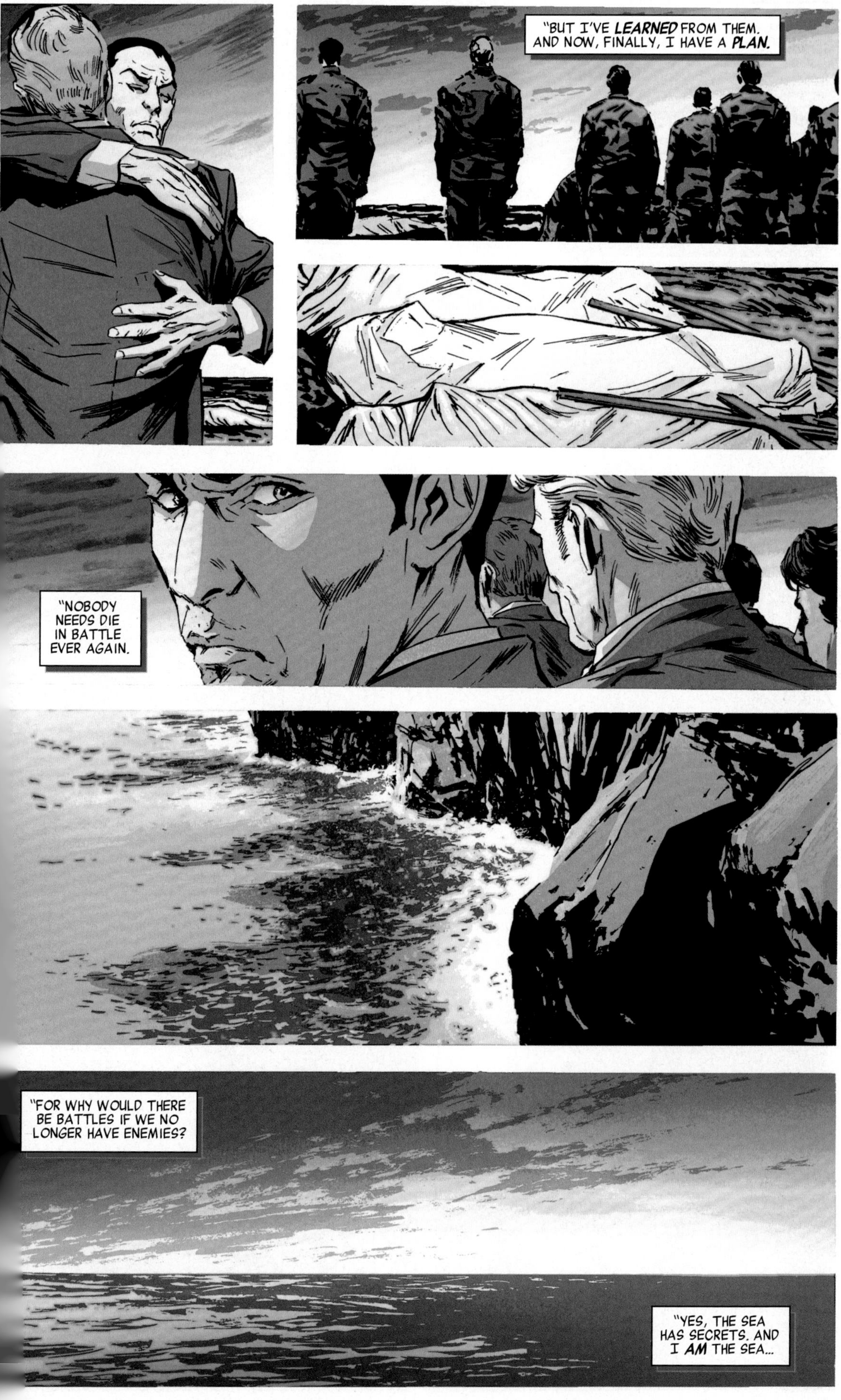
"BUT I'VE LEARNED FROM THEM. AND NOW, FINALLY, I HAVE A PLAN.
"NOBODY NEEDS DIE IN BATTLE EVER AGAIN.
"FOR WHY WOULD THERE BE BATTLES IF WE NO LONGER HAVE ENEMIES?
"YES, THE SEA HAS SECRETS. AND I AM THE SEA...

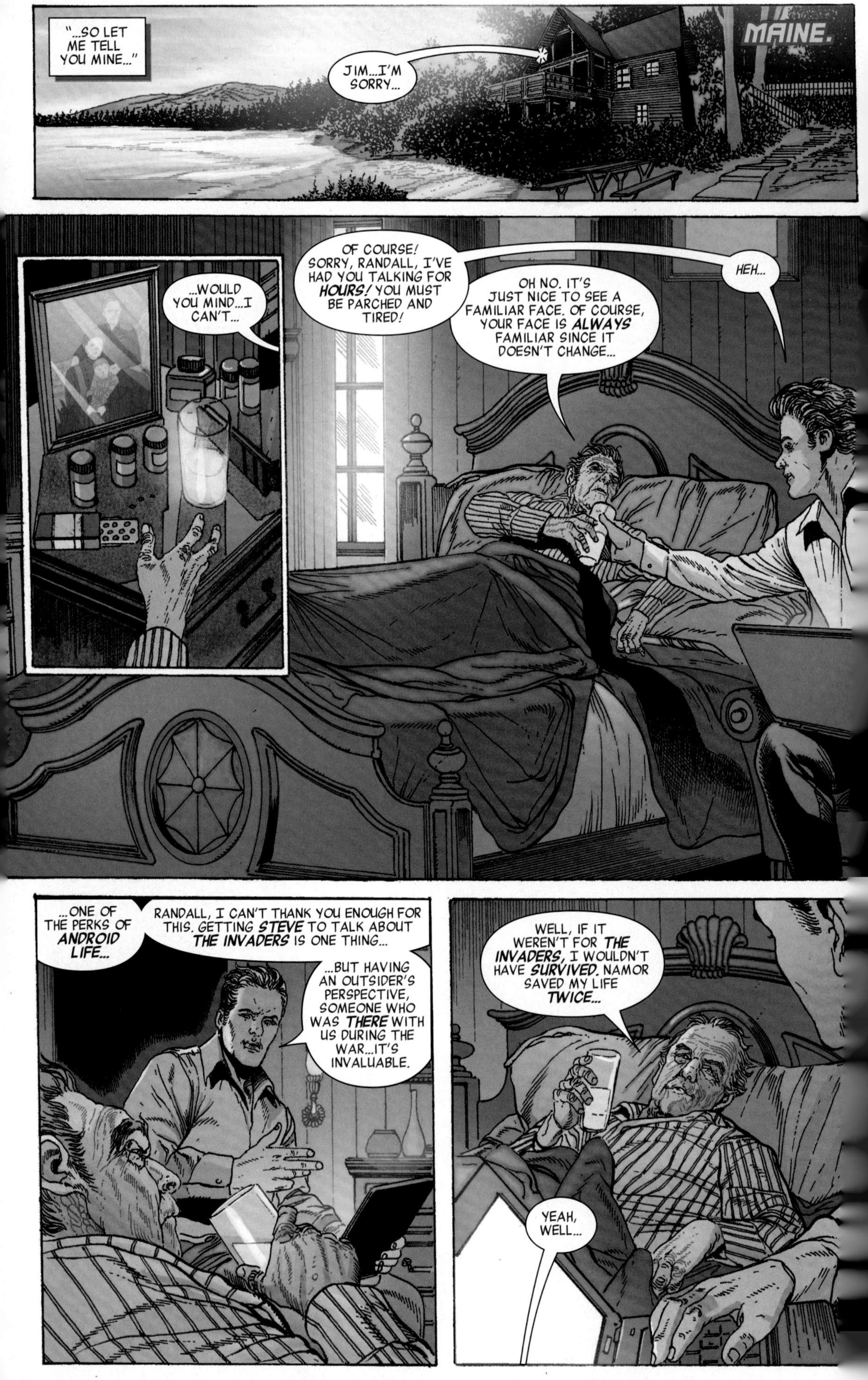
"...SO LET ME TELL YOU MINE..."
MAINE.
JIM...I'M SORRY...
...WOULD YOU MIND...I CAN'T...
OF COURSE! SORRY, RANDALL, I'VE HAD YOU TALKING FOR HOURS! YOU MUST BE PARCHED AND TIRED!
HEH...
OH NO. IT'S JUST NICE TO SEE A FAMILIAR FACE. OF COURSE, YOUR FACE IS ALWAYS FAMILIAR SINCE IT DOESN'T CHANGE...
...ONE OF THE PERKS OF ANDROID LIFE...
RANDALL, I CAN'T THANK YOU ENOUGH FOR THIS. GETTING STEVE TO TALK ABOUT THE INVADERS IS ONE THING...
...BUT HAVING AN OUTSIDER'S PERSPECTIVE, SOMEONE WHO WAS THERE WITH US DURING THE WAR...IT'S INVALUABLE.
WELL, IF IT WEREN'T FOR THE INVADERS, I WOULDN'T HAVE SURVIVED. NAMOR SAVED MY LIFE TWICE...
YEAH, WELL...

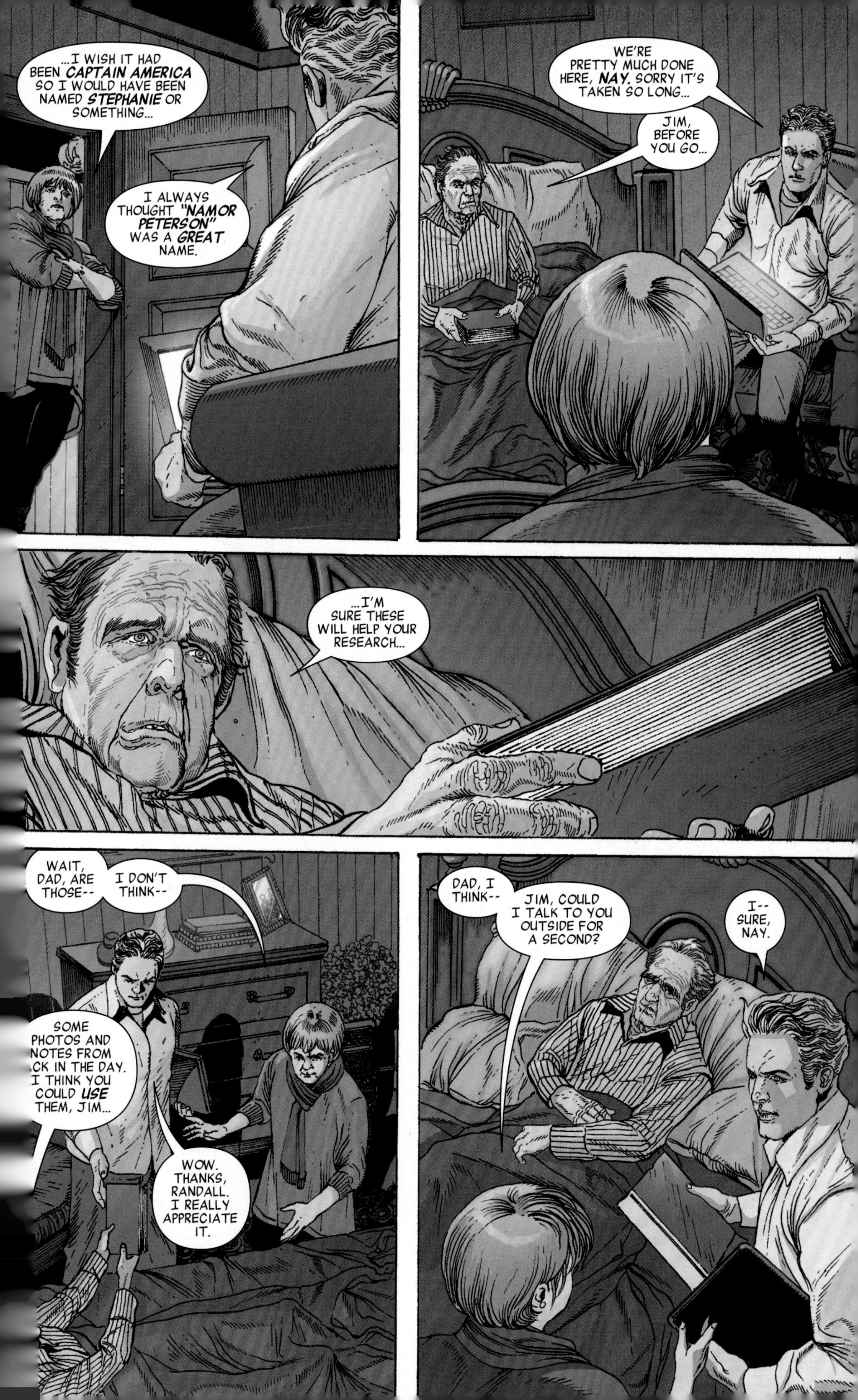
...I WISH IT HAD BEEN CAPTAIN AMERICA SO I WOULD HAVE BEEN NAMED STEPHANIE OR SOMETHING...
I ALWAYS THOUGHT "NAMOR PETERSON" WAS A GREAT NAME.
WE'RE PRETTY MUCH DONE HERE, NAY. SORRY IT'S TAKEN SO LONG...
JIM, BEFORE YOU GO...
...I'M SURE THESE WILL HELP YOUR RESEARCH...
WAIT, DAD, ARE THOSE--
I DON'T THINK--
SOME PHOTOS AND NOTES FROM CK IN THE DAY. I THINK YOU COULD USE THEM, JIM...
WOW. THANKS, RANDALL. I REALLY APPRECIATE IT.
DAD, I THINK--
JIM, COULD I TALK TO YOU OUTSIDE FOR A SECOND?
I-- SURE, NAY.

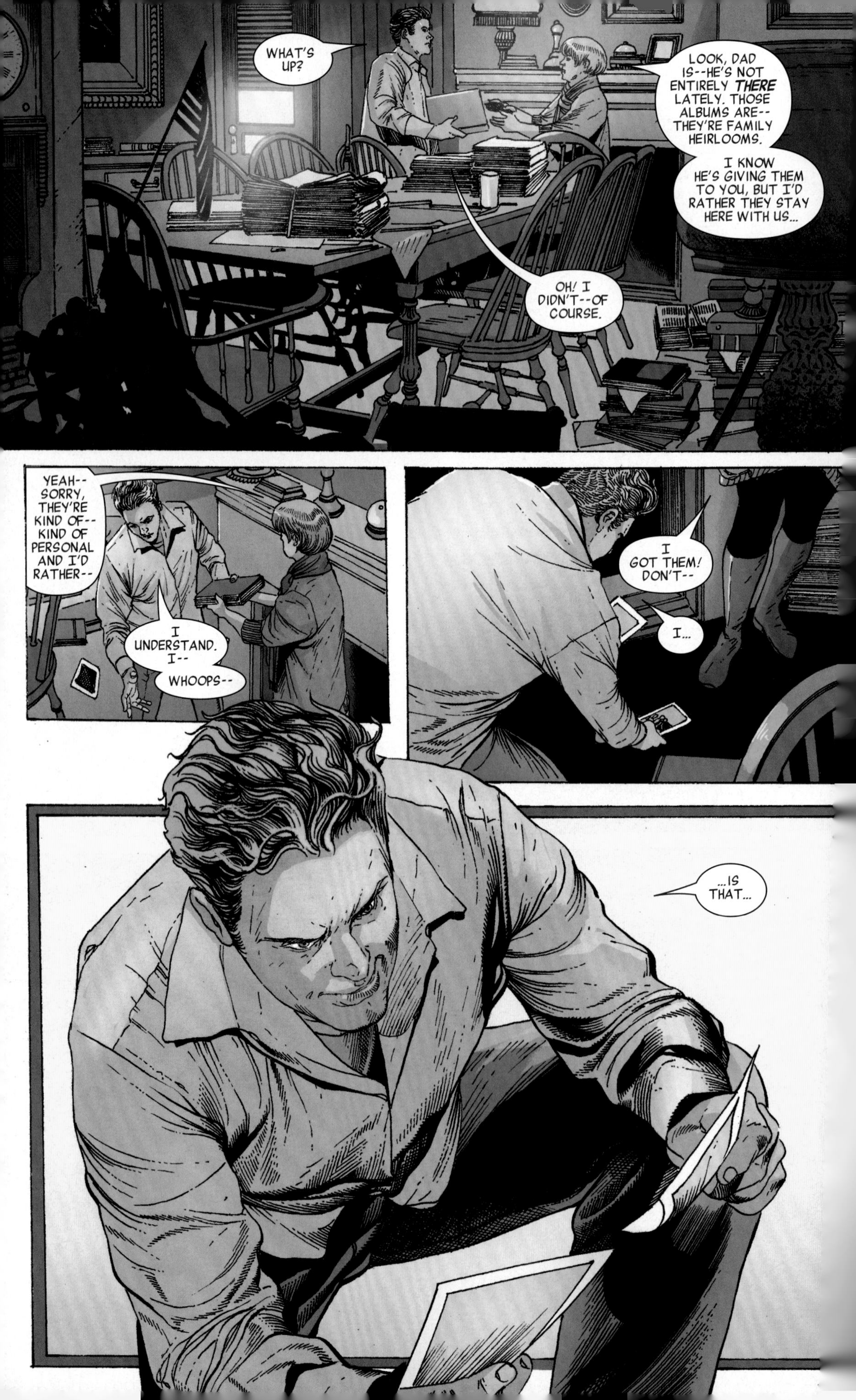
WHAT'S UP?
LOOK, DAD IS--HE'S NOT ENTIRELY THERE LATELY. THOSE ALBUMS ARE--THEY'RE FAMILY HEIRLOOMS.
I KNOW HE'S GIVING THEM TO YOU, BUT I'D RATHER THEY STAY HERE WITH US...
OH! I DIDN'T--OF COURSE.
YEAH--SORRY, THEY'RE KIND OF--KIND OF PERSONAL AND I'D RATHER--
I UNDERSTAND. I--
WHOOPS--
I GOT THEM! DON'T--
I...
...IS THAT...

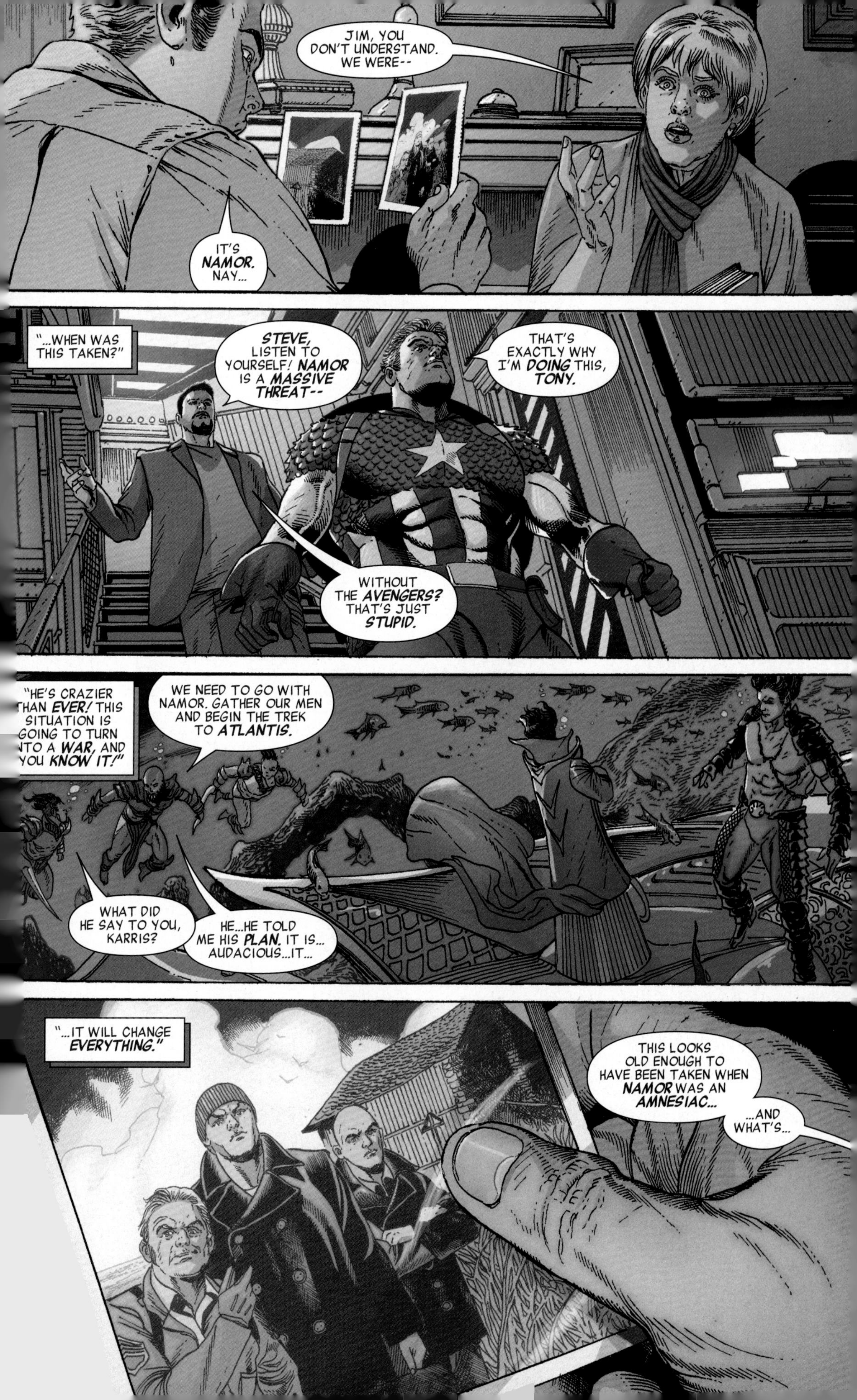
JIM, YOU DON'T UNDERSTAND. WE WERE--
IT'S NAMOR. NAY...
"...WHEN WAS THIS TAKEN?"
STEVE, LISTEN TO YOURSELF! NAMOR IS A MASSIVE THREAT--
THAT'S EXACTLY WHY I'M DOING THIS, TONY.
WITHOUT THE AVENGERS? THAT'S JUST STUPID.
"HE'S CRAZIER THAN EVER! THIS SITUATION IS GOING TO TURN INTO A WAR, AND YOU KNOW IT!"
WE NEED TO GO WITH NAMOR. GATHER OUR MEN AND BEGIN THE TREK TO ATLANTIS.
WHAT DID HE SAY TO YOU, KARRIS?
HE...HE TOLD ME HIS PLAN. IT IS... AUDACIOUS...IT...
"...IT WILL CHANGE EVERYTHING."
THIS LOOKS OLD ENOUGH TO HAVE BEEN TAKEN WHEN NAMOR WAS AN AMNESIAC...
...AND WHAT'S...

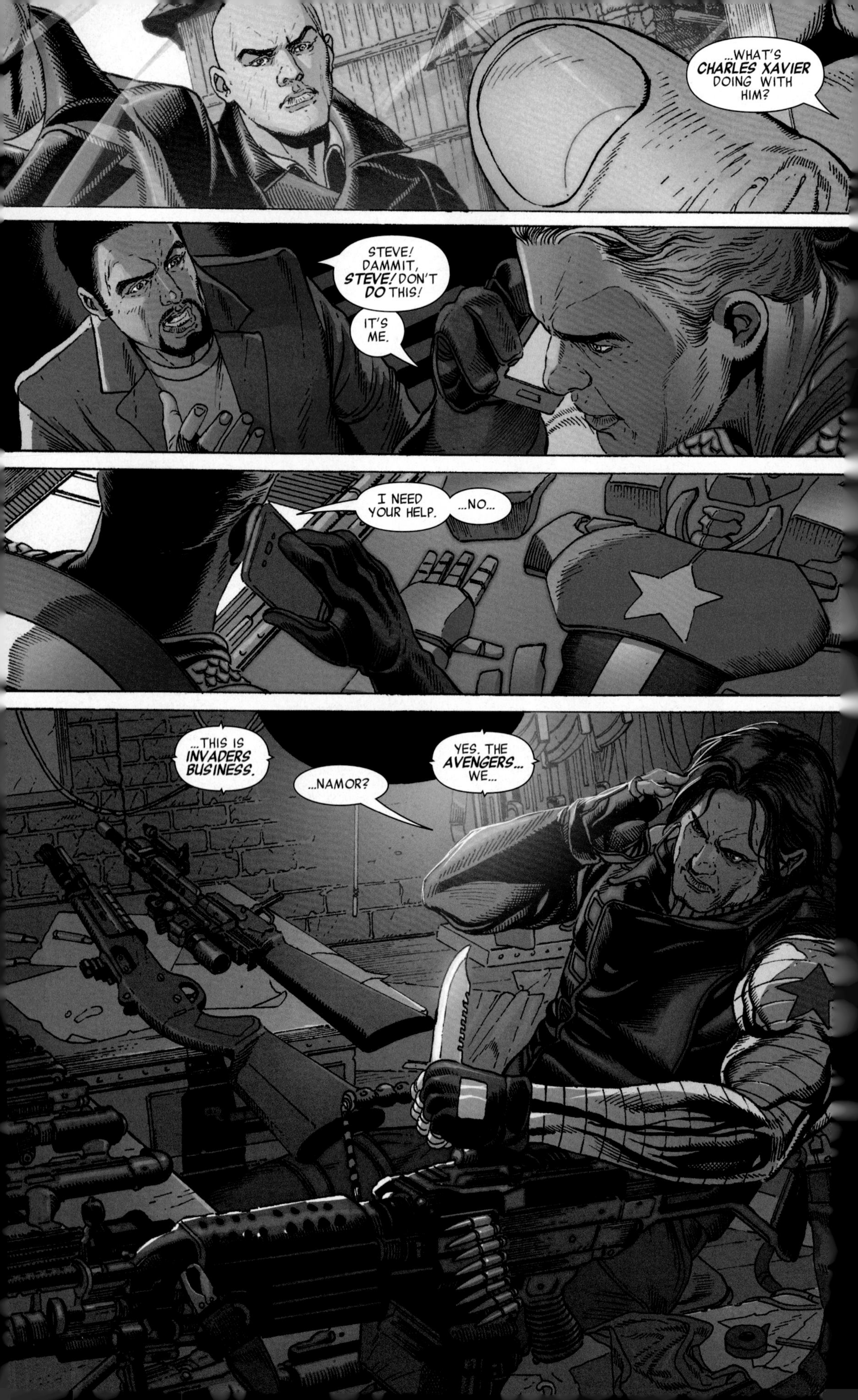
...WHAT'S CHARLES XAVIER DOING WITH HIM?
STEVE! DAMMIT, STEVE! DON'T DO THIS!
IT'S ME.
I NEED YOUR HELP.
...NO...
...THIS IS INVADERS BUSINESS.
...NAMOR?
YES. THE AVENGERS... WE...

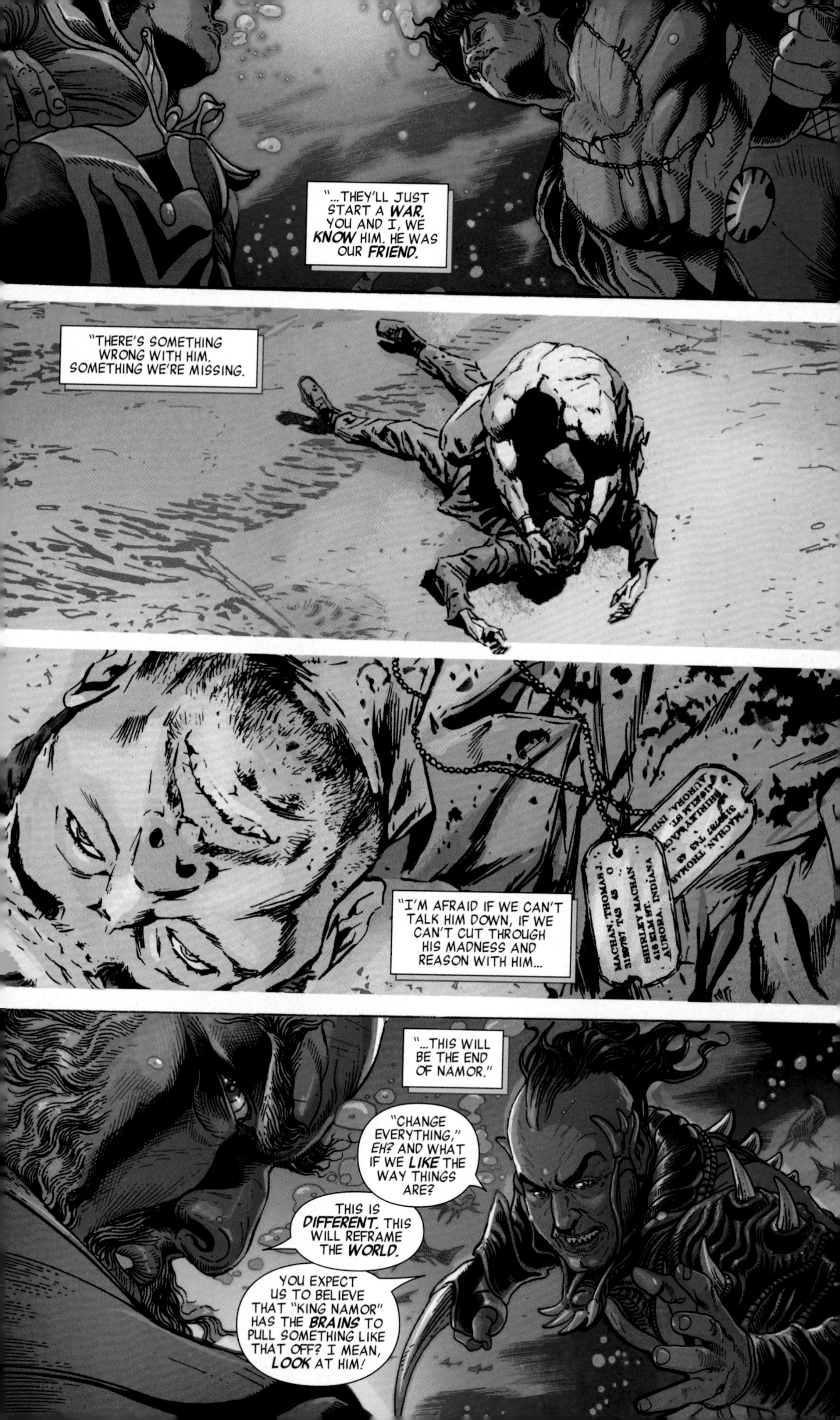
"...THEY'LL JUST START A **WAR**. YOU AND I, WE **KNOW** HIM. HE WAS OUR **FRIEND**.
"THERE'S SOMETHING WRONG WITH HIM. SOMETHING WE'RE MISSING.
MACHAN, THOMAS J.
SHIRLEY MACHAN
416 ELM ST.
AURORA, INDIANA
"I'M AFRAID IF WE CAN'T TALK HIM DOWN, IF WE CAN'T CUT THROUGH HIS MADNESS AND REASON WITH HIM...
"...THIS WILL BE THE END OF NAMOR."
"CHANGE EVERYTHING," *EH?* AND WHAT IF WE **LIKE** THE WAY THINGS ARE?
THIS IS **DIFFERENT**. THIS WILL REFRAME THE **WORLD**.
YOU EXPECT US TO BELIEVE THAT "KING NAMOR" HAS THE **BRAINS** TO PULL SOMETHING LIKE THAT OFF? I MEAN, **LOOK** AT HIM!

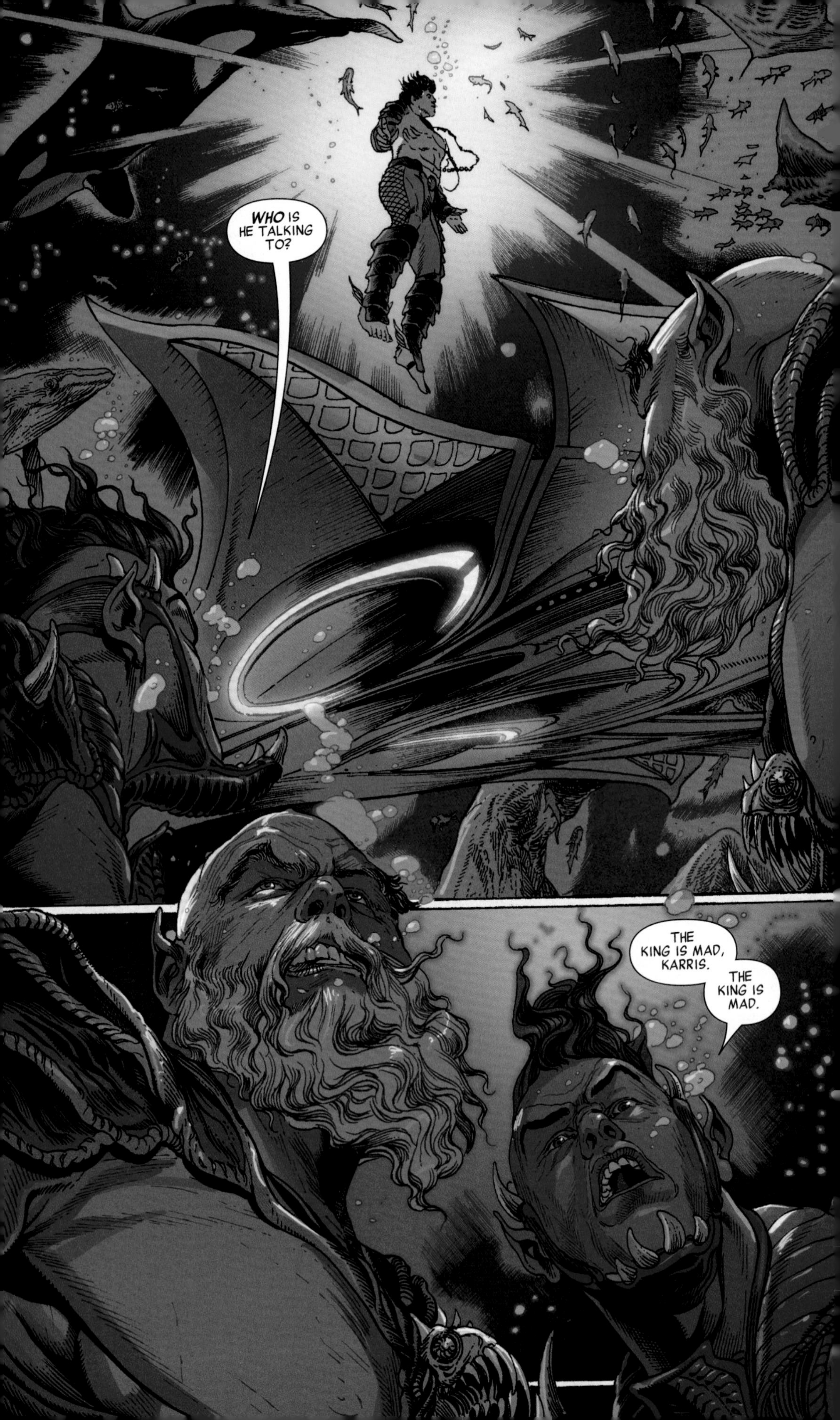
WHO IS HE TALKING TO?
THE KING IS MAD, KARRIS.
THE KING IS MAD.

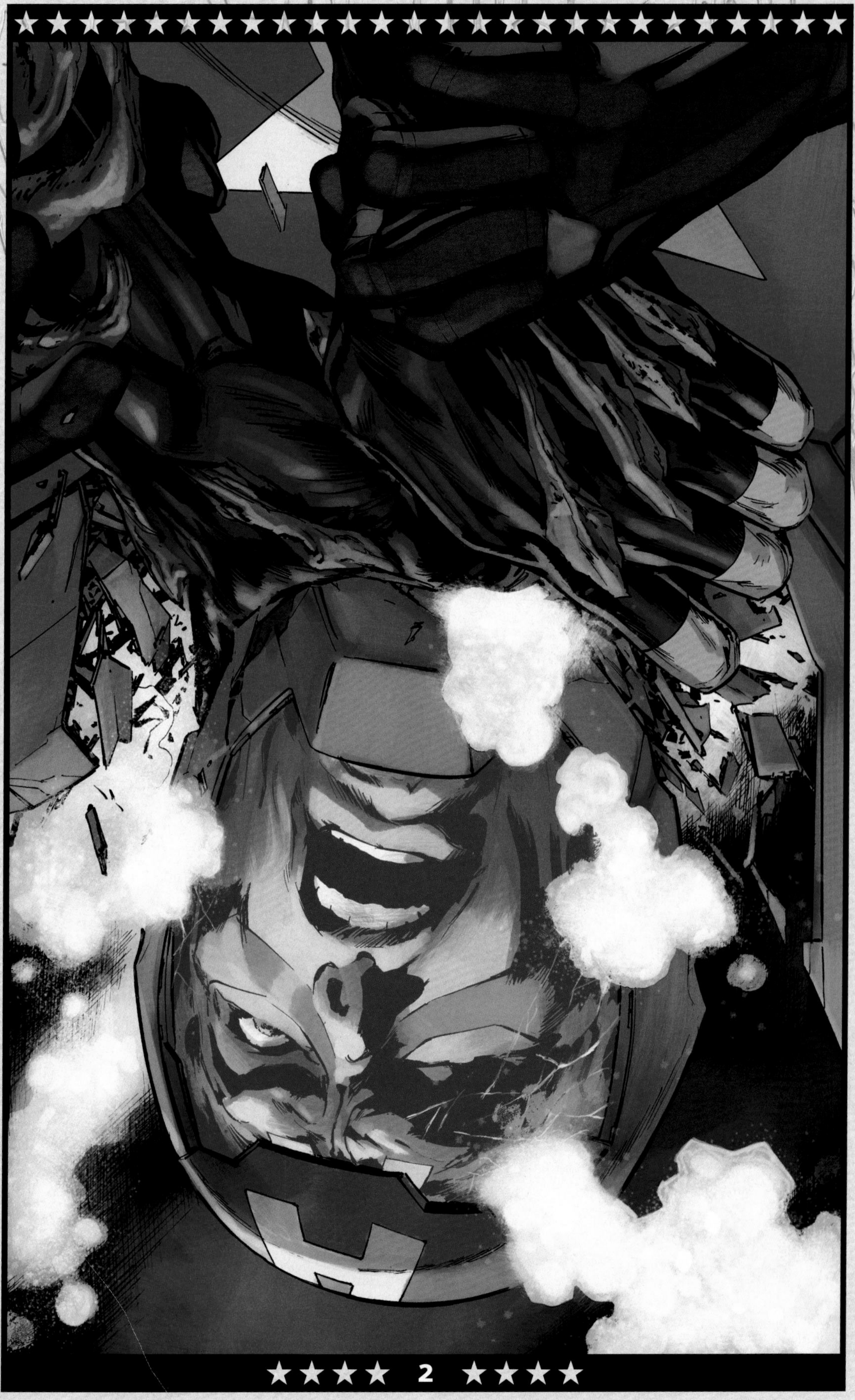

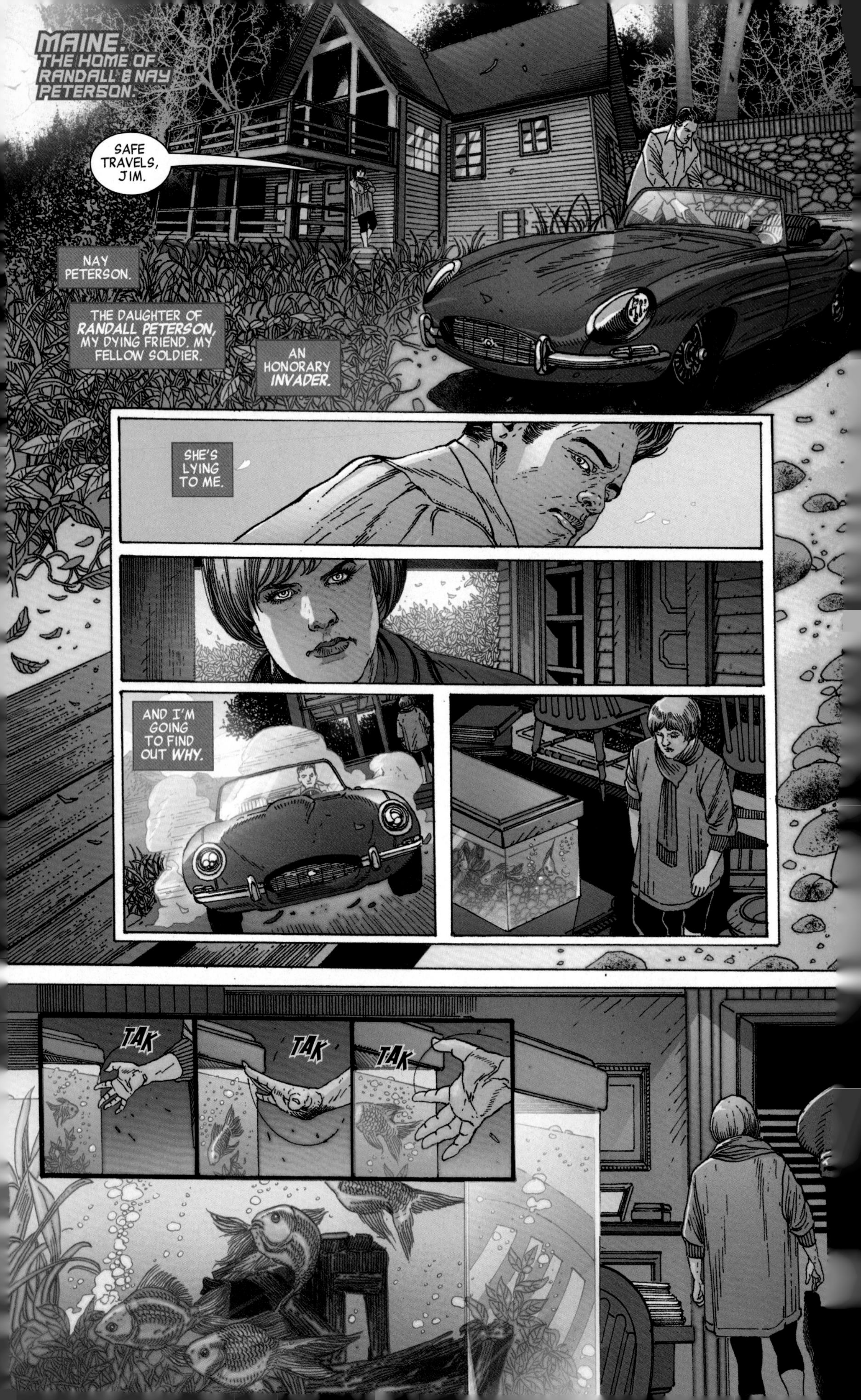
MAINE. THE HOME OF RANDALL & NAY PETERSON.
SAFE TRAVELS, JIM.
NAY PETERSON.
THE DAUGHTER OF RANDALL PETERSON, MY DYING FRIEND. MY FELLOW SOLDIER.
AN HONORARY INVADER.
SHE'S LYING TO ME.
AND I'M GOING TO FIND OUT WHY.
TAK
TAK
TAK

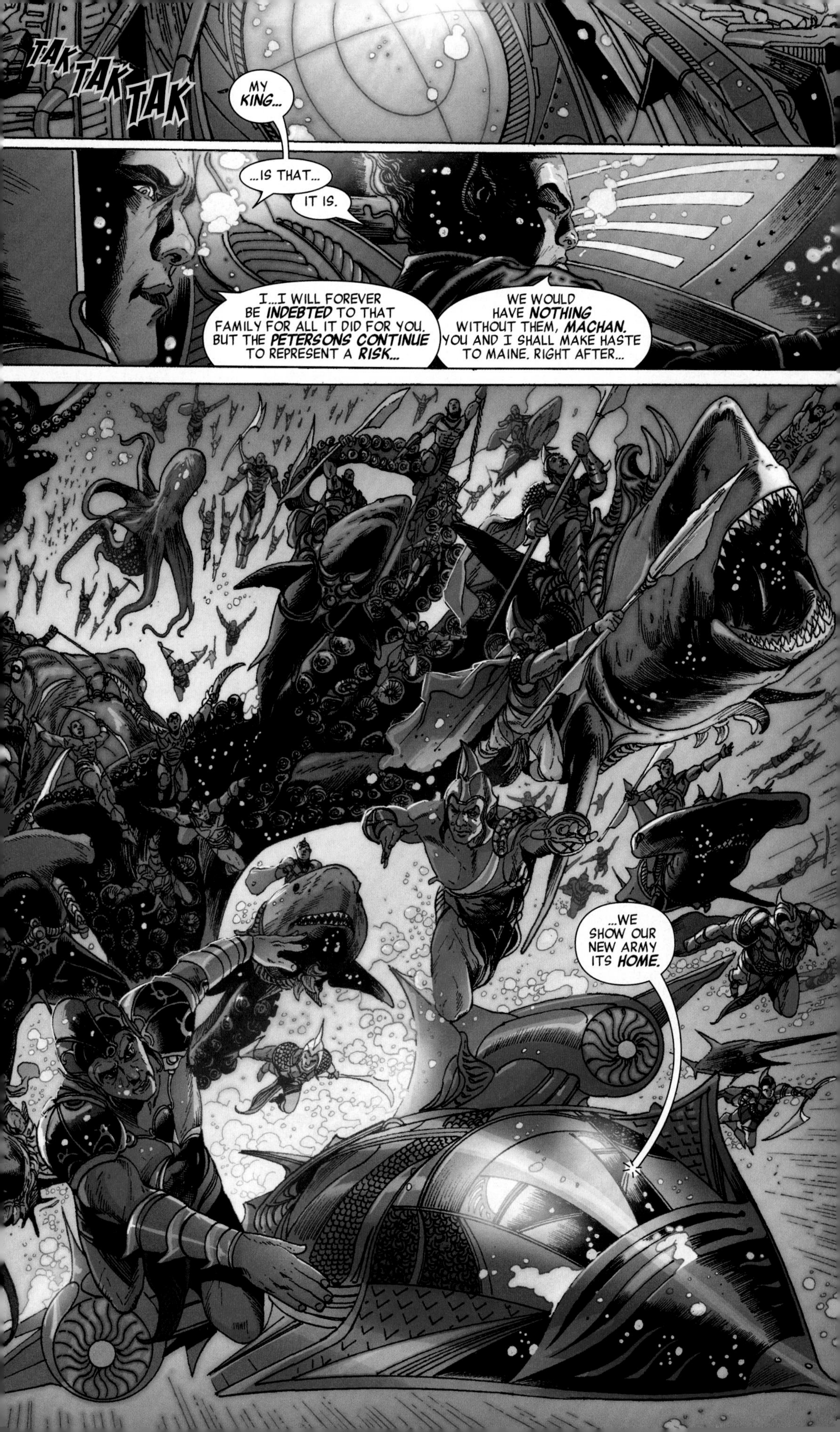
TAK TAK TAK
MY KING...
...IS THAT...
IT IS.
I...I WILL FOREVER BE INDEBTED TO THAT FAMILY FOR ALL IT DID FOR YOU. BUT THE PETERSONS CONTINUE TO REPRESENT A RISK...
WE WOULD HAVE NOTHING WITHOUT THEM, MACHAN. YOU AND I SHALL MAKE HASTE TO MAINE. RIGHT AFTER...
...WE SHOW OUR NEW ARMY ITS HOME.

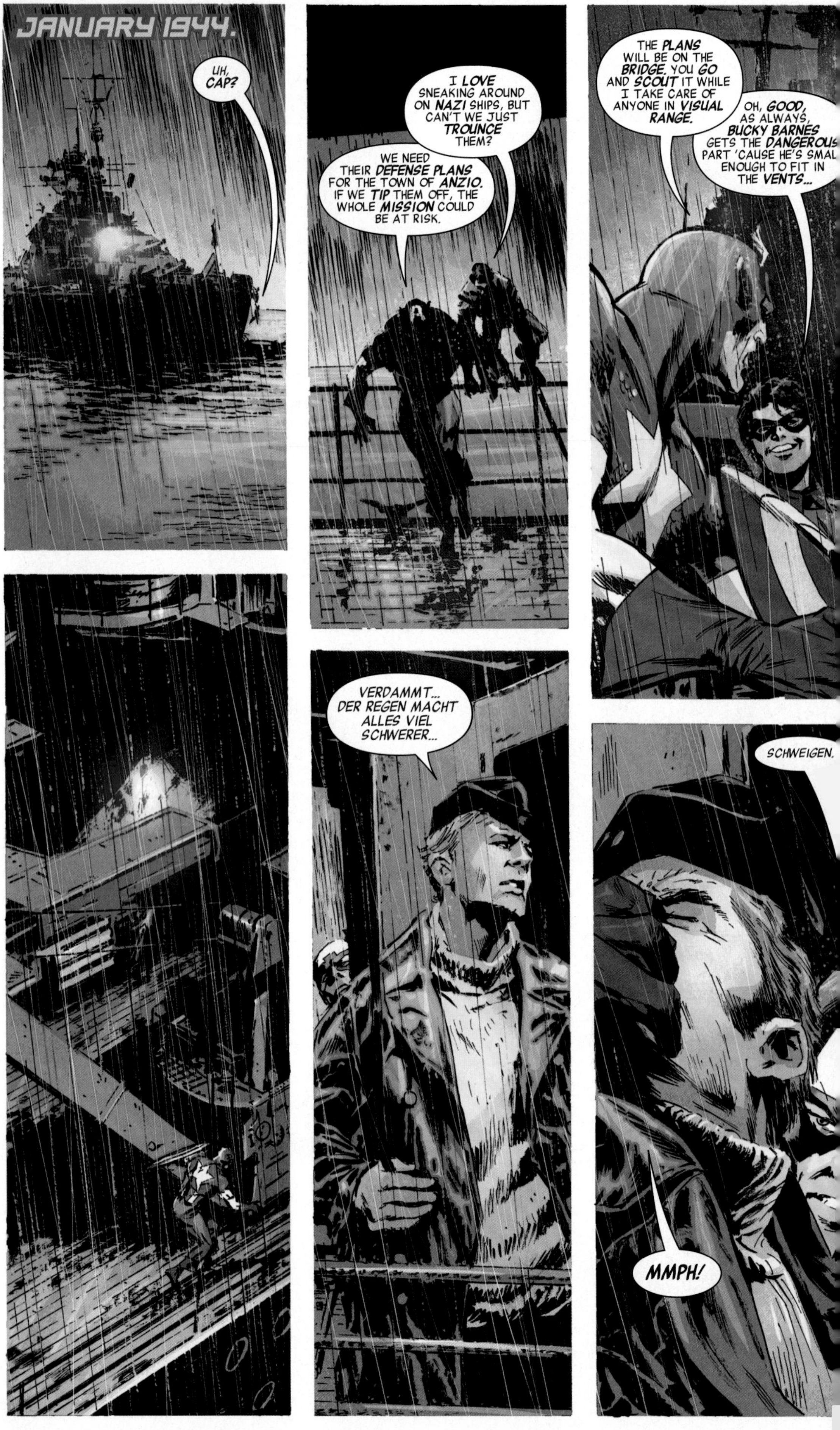
JANUARY 1944.
UH, CAP?
I LOVE SNEAKING AROUND ON NAZI SHIPS, BUT CAN'T WE JUST TROUNCE THEM?
WE NEED THEIR DEFENSE PLANS FOR THE TOWN OF ANZIO. IF WE TIP THEM OFF, THE WHOLE MISSION COULD BE AT RISK.
THE PLANS WILL BE ON THE BRIDGE. YOU GO AND SCOUT IT WHILE I TAKE CARE OF ANYONE IN VISUAL RANGE.
OH, GOOD, AS ALWAYS, BUCKY BARNES GETS THE DANGEROUS PART 'CAUSE HE'S SMAL ENOUGH TO FIT IN THE VENTS...
VERDAMMT... DER REGEN MACHT ALLES VIEL SCHWERER...
SCHWEIGEN.
MMPH!

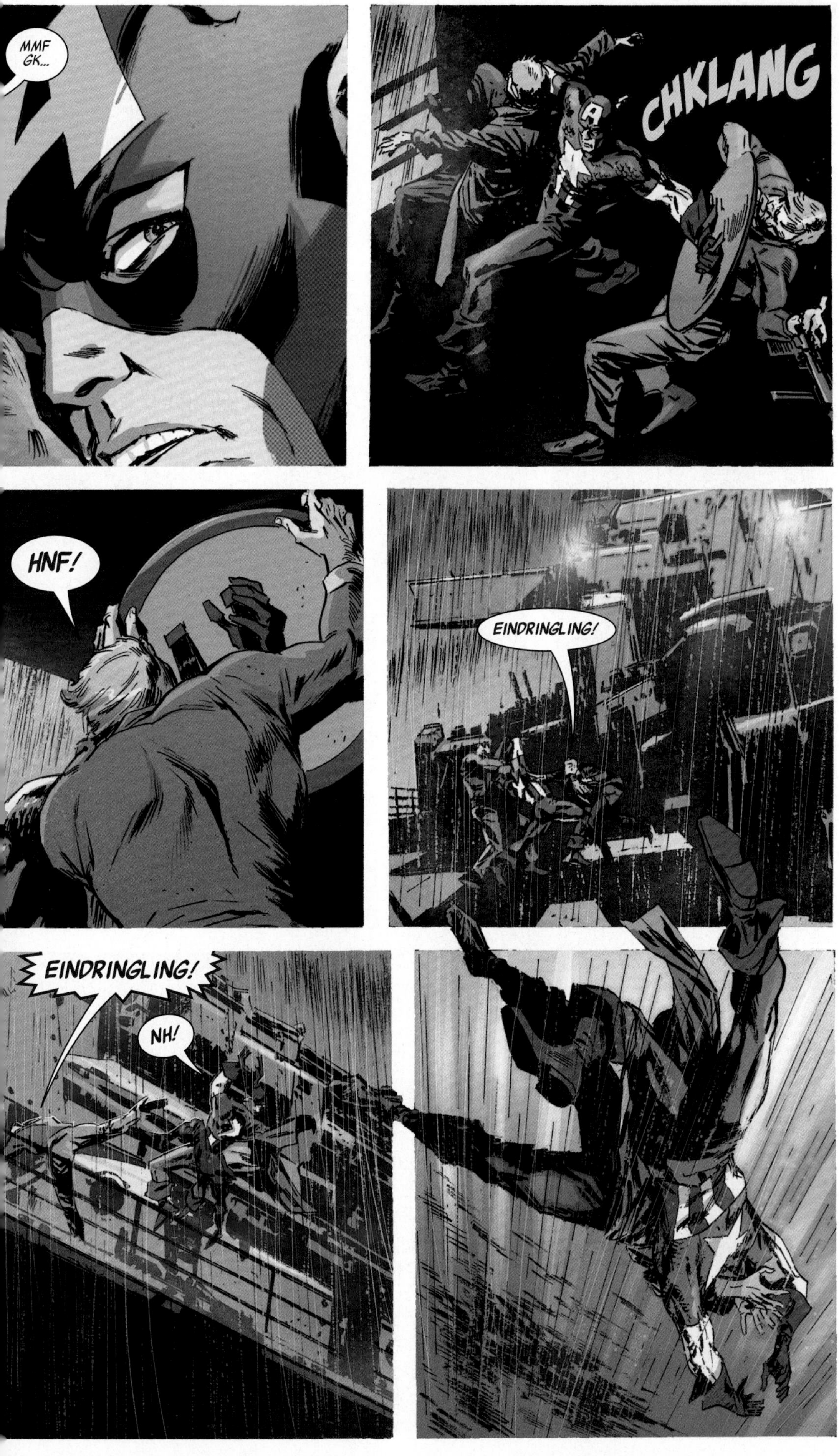
MMF GK...
CHKLANG
HNF!
EINDRINGLING!
EINDRINGLING!
NH!

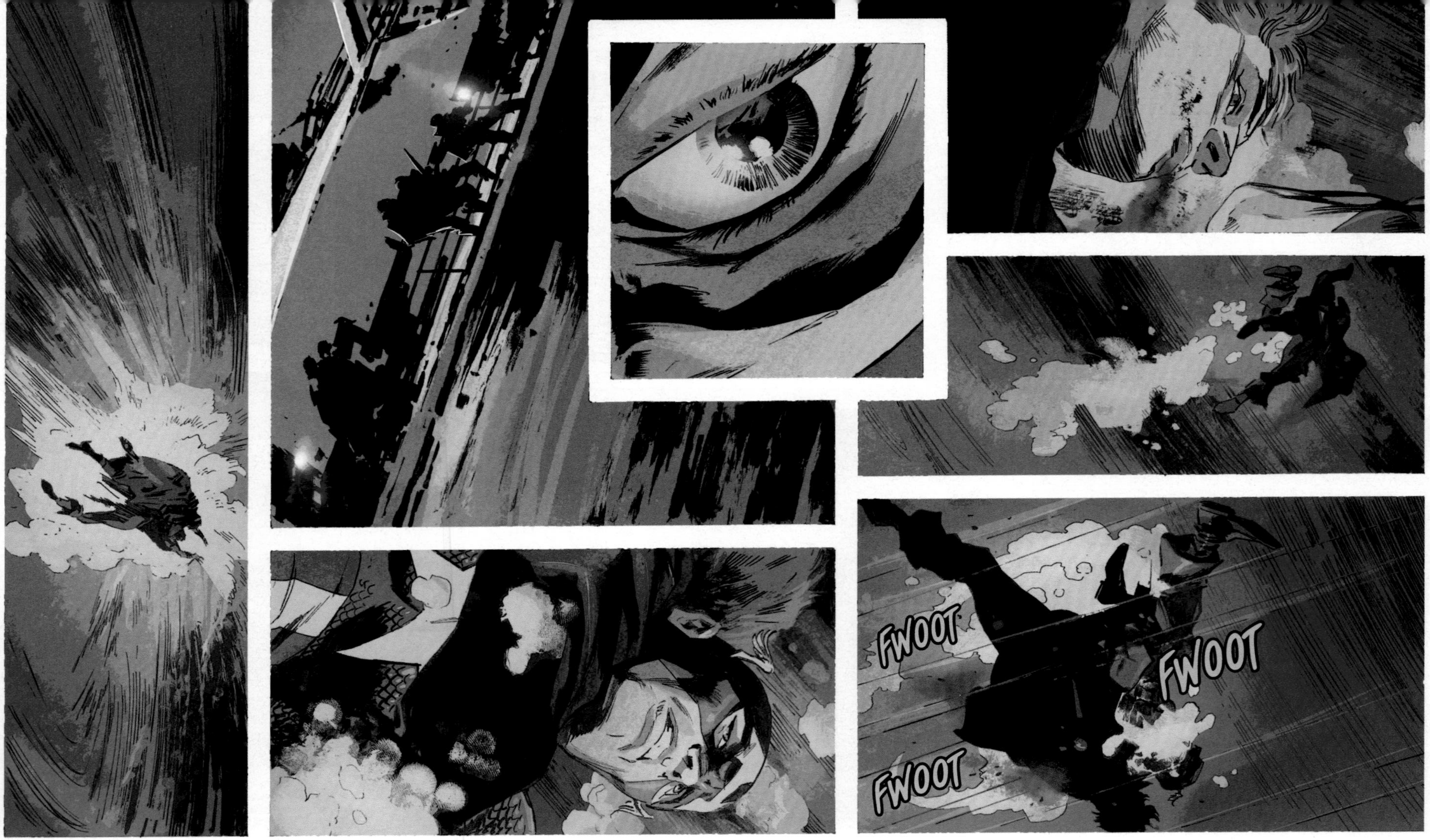
FWOOT
FWOOT
FWOOT

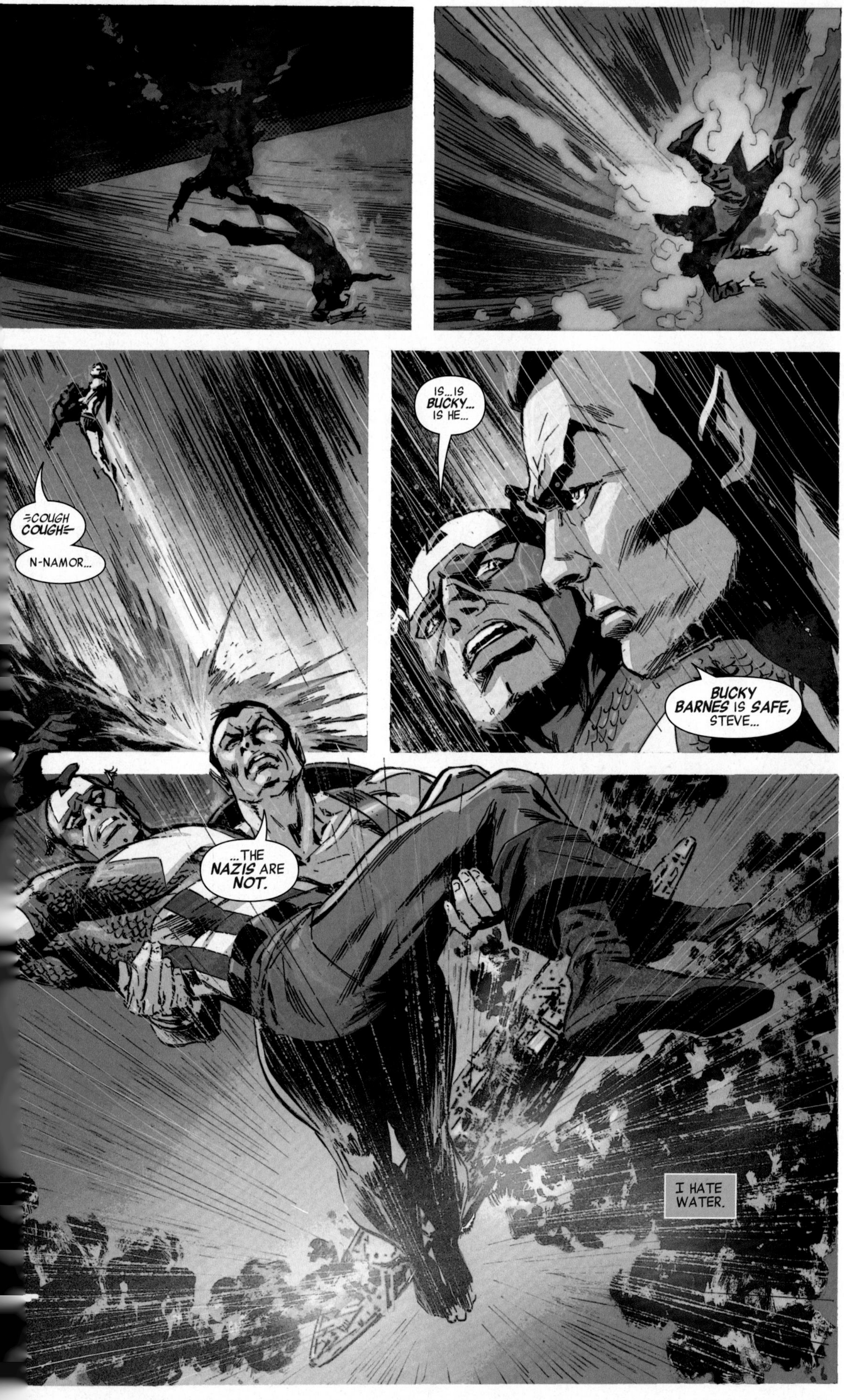
=COUGH COUGH=
N-NAMOR...
IS...IS BUCKY... IS HE...
BUCKY BARNES IS SAFE, STEVE...
...THE NAZIS ARE NOT.
I HATE WATER.

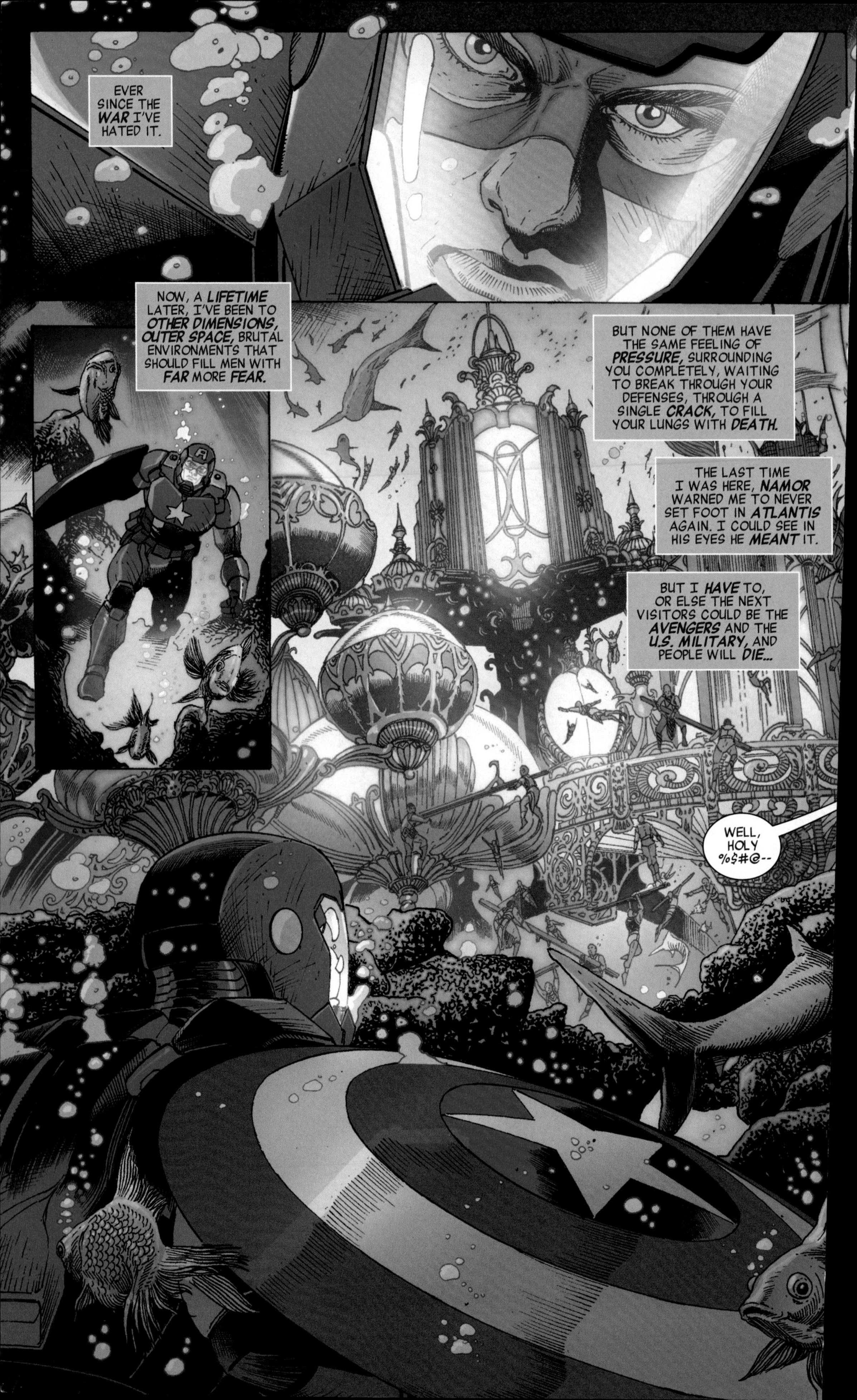
EVER SINCE THE WAR I'VE HATED IT.
NOW, A LIFETIME LATER, I'VE BEEN TO OTHER DIMENSIONS, OUTER SPACE, BRUTAL ENVIRONMENTS THAT SHOULD FILL MEN WITH FAR MORE FEAR.
BUT NONE OF THEM HAVE THE SAME FEELING OF PRESSURE, SURROUNDING YOU COMPLETELY, WAITING TO BREAK THROUGH YOUR DEFENSES, THROUGH A SINGLE CRACK, TO FILL YOUR LUNGS WITH DEATH.
THE LAST TIME I WAS HERE, NAMOR WARNED ME TO NEVER SET FOOT IN ATLANTIS AGAIN. I COULD SEE IN HIS EYES HE MEANT IT.
BUT I HAVE TO, OR ELSE THE NEXT VISITORS COULD BE THE AVENGERS AND THE U.S. MILITARY, AND PEOPLE WILL DIE...
WELL, HOLY %$#@--

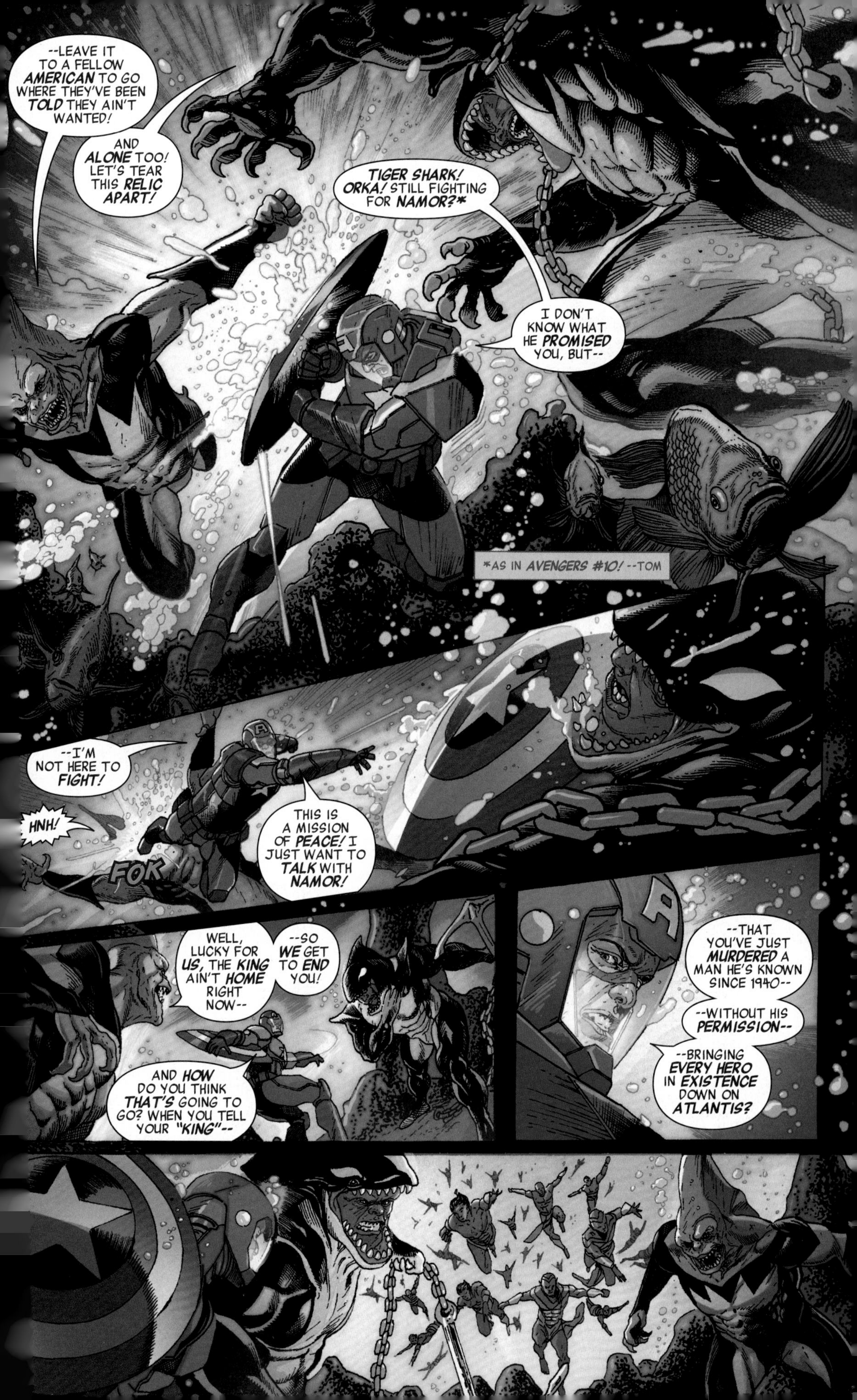
--LEAVE IT TO A FELLOW AMERICAN TO GO WHERE THEY'VE BEEN TOLD THEY AIN'T WANTED!
AND ALONE TOO! LET'S TEAR THIS RELIC APART!
TIGER SHARK! ORKA! STILL FIGHTING FOR NAMOR?*
I DON'T KNOW WHAT HE PROMISED YOU, BUT--
*AS IN AVENGERS #10! --TOM
--I'M NOT HERE TO FIGHT!
HNH!
FOK
THIS IS A MISSION OF PEACE! I JUST WANT TO TALK WITH NAMOR!
WELL, LUCKY FOR US, THE KING AIN'T HOME RIGHT NOW--
--SO WE GET TO END YOU!
AND HOW DO YOU THINK THAT'S GOING TO GO? WHEN YOU TELL YOUR "KING"--
--THAT YOU'VE JUST MURDERED A MAN HE'S KNOWN SINCE 1940--
--WITHOUT HIS PERMISSION--
--BRINGING EVERY HERO IN EXISTENCE DOWN ON ATLANTIS?

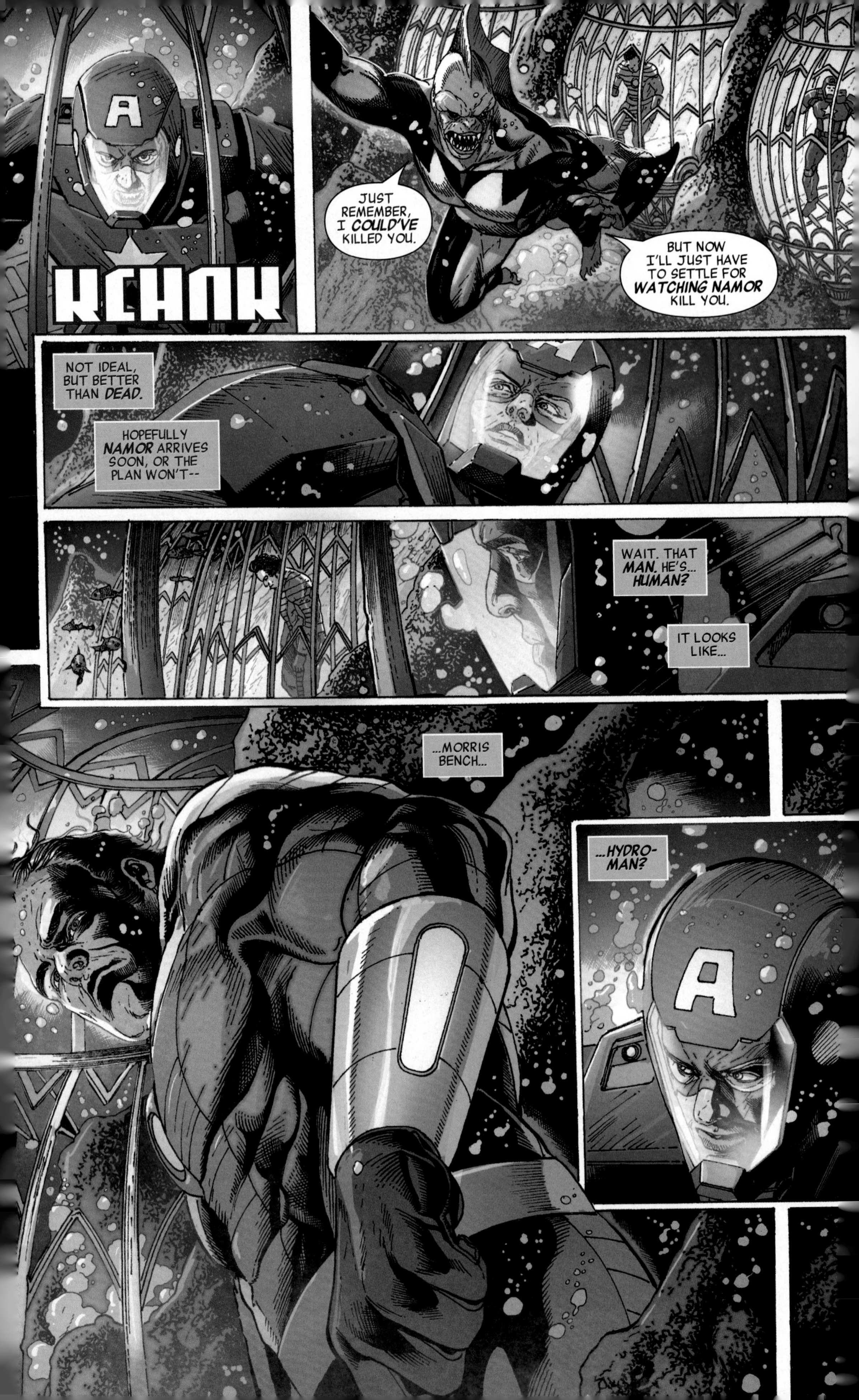
KCHAK
JUST REMEMBER, I COULD'VE KILLED YOU.
BUT NOW I'LL JUST HAVE TO SETTLE FOR WATCHING NAMOR KILL YOU.
NOT IDEAL, BUT BETTER THAN DEAD.
HOPEFULLY NAMOR ARRIVES SOON, OR THE PLAN WON'T--
WAIT. THAT MAN. HE'S... HUMAN?
IT LOOKS LIKE...
...MORRIS BENCH...
...HYDRO-MAN?

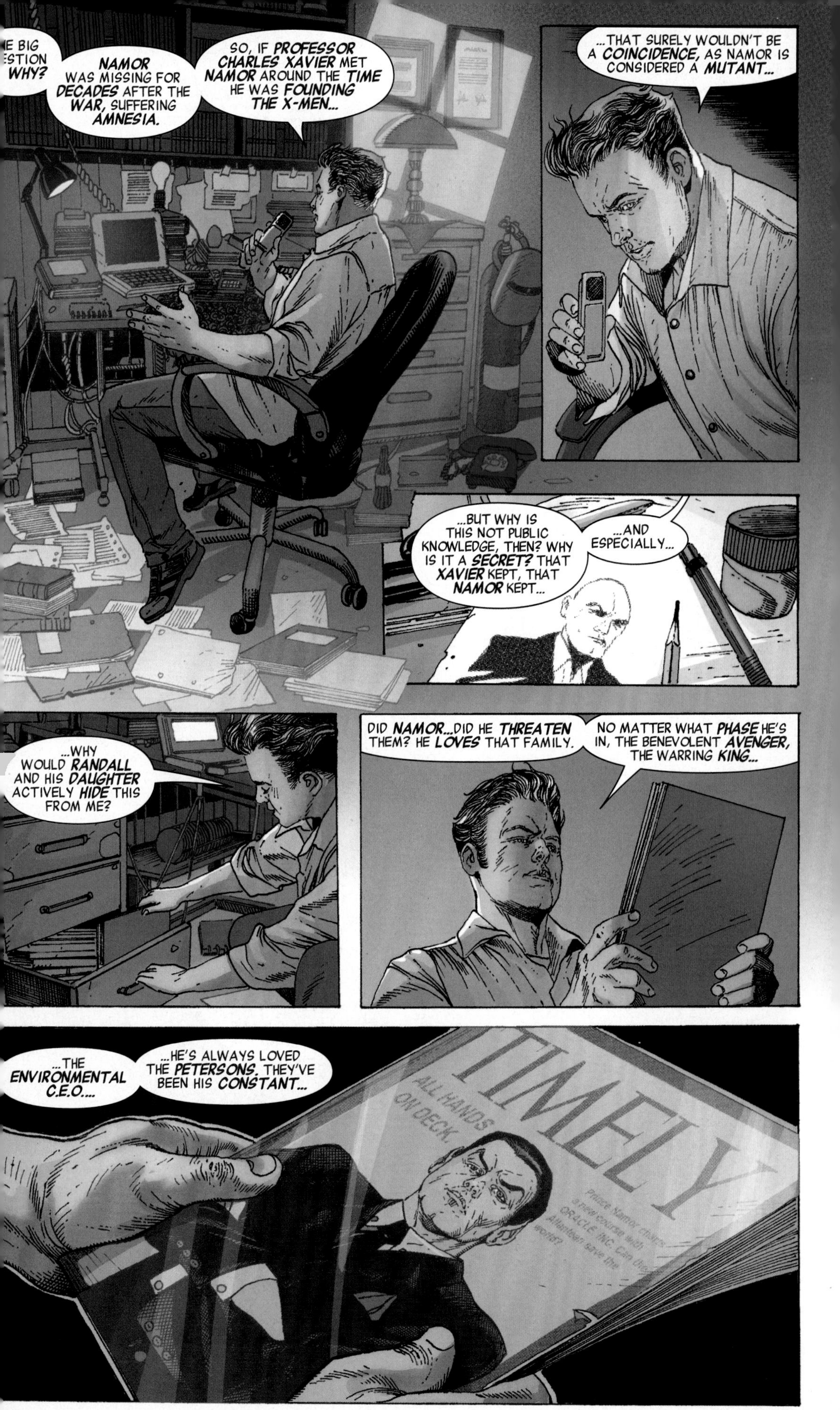

E BIG
ESTION
WHY?
NAMOR WAS MISSING FOR DECADES AFTER THE WAR, SUFFERING AMNESIA.
SO, IF PROFESSOR CHARLES XAVIER MET NAMOR AROUND THE TIME HE WAS FOUNDING THE X-MEN...
...THAT SURELY WOULDN'T BE A COINCIDENCE, AS NAMOR IS CONSIDERED A MUTANT...
...BUT WHY IS THIS NOT PUBLIC KNOWLEDGE, THEN? WHY IS IT A SECRET? THAT XAVIER KEPT, THAT NAMOR KEPT...
...AND ESPECIALLY...
...WHY WOULD RANDALL AND HIS DAUGHTER ACTIVELY HIDE THIS FROM ME?
DID NAMOR...DID HE THREATEN THEM? HE LOVES THAT FAMILY.
NO MATTER WHAT PHASE HE'S IN, THE BENEVOLENT AVENGER, THE WARRING KING...
...THE ENVIRONMENTAL C.E.O....
...HE'S ALWAYS LOVED THE PETERSONS. THEY'VE BEEN HIS CONSTANT...
TIMELY
ALL HANDS ON DECK.

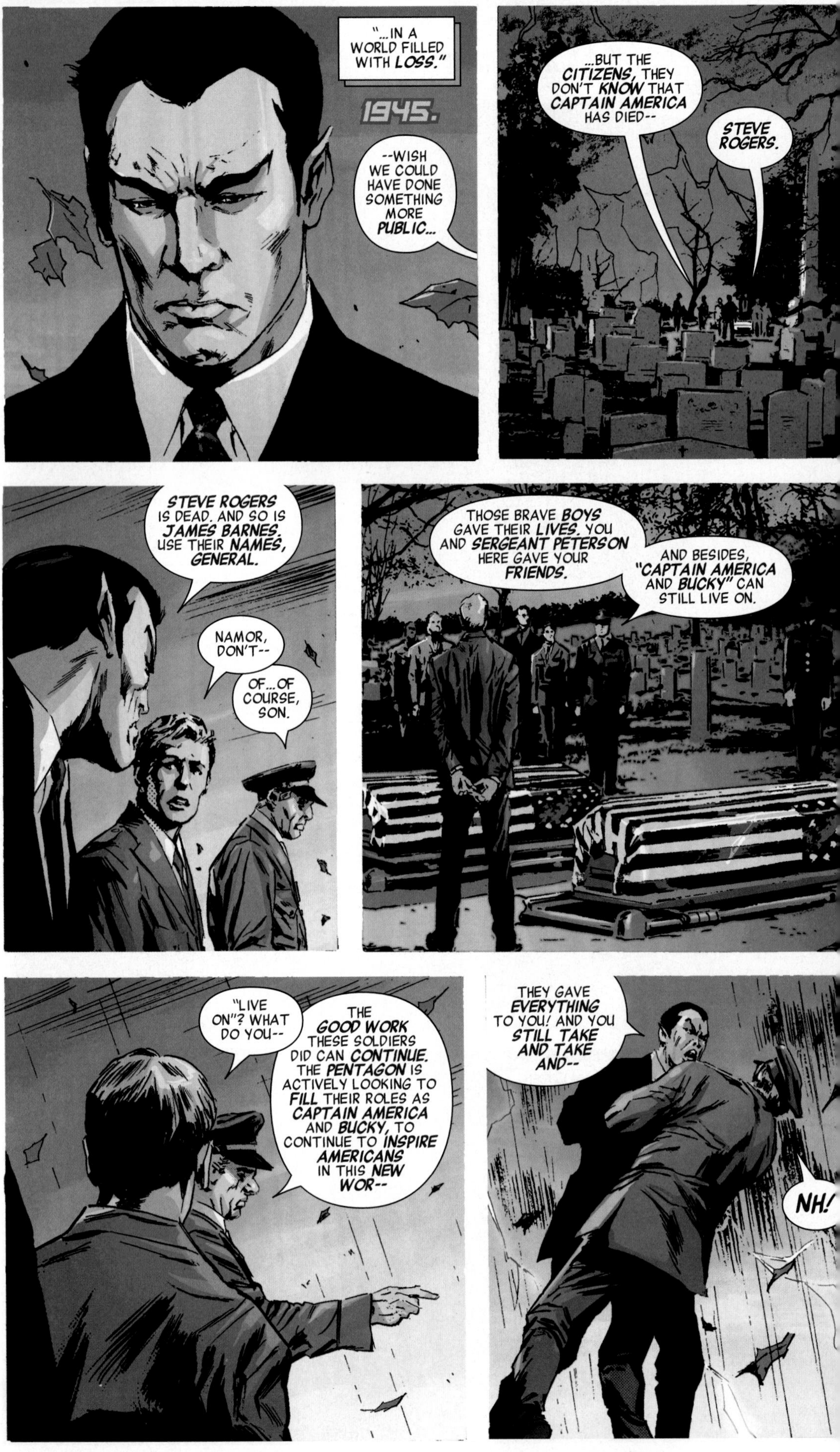
"...IN A WORLD FILLED WITH LOSS."
1945.
--WISH WE COULD HAVE DONE SOMETHING MORE PUBLIC...
...BUT THE CITIZENS, THEY DON'T KNOW THAT CAPTAIN AMERICA HAS DIED--
STEVE ROGERS.
STEVE ROGERS IS DEAD. AND SO IS JAMES BARNES. USE THEIR NAMES, GENERAL.
NAMOR, DON'T--
OF...OF COURSE, SON.
THOSE BRAVE BOYS GAVE THEIR LIVES. YOU AND SERGEANT PETERSON HERE GAVE YOUR FRIENDS.
AND BESIDES, "CAPTAIN AMERICA AND BUCKY" CAN STILL LIVE ON.
"LIVE ON"? WHAT DO YOU--
THE GOOD WORK THESE SOLDIERS DID CAN CONTINUE. THE PENTAGON IS ACTIVELY LOOKING TO FILL THEIR ROLES AS CAPTAIN AMERICA AND BUCKY, TO CONTINUE TO INSPIRE AMERICANS IN THIS NEW WOR--
THEY GAVE EVERYTHING TO YOU! AND YOU STILL TAKE AND TAKE AND--
NH!

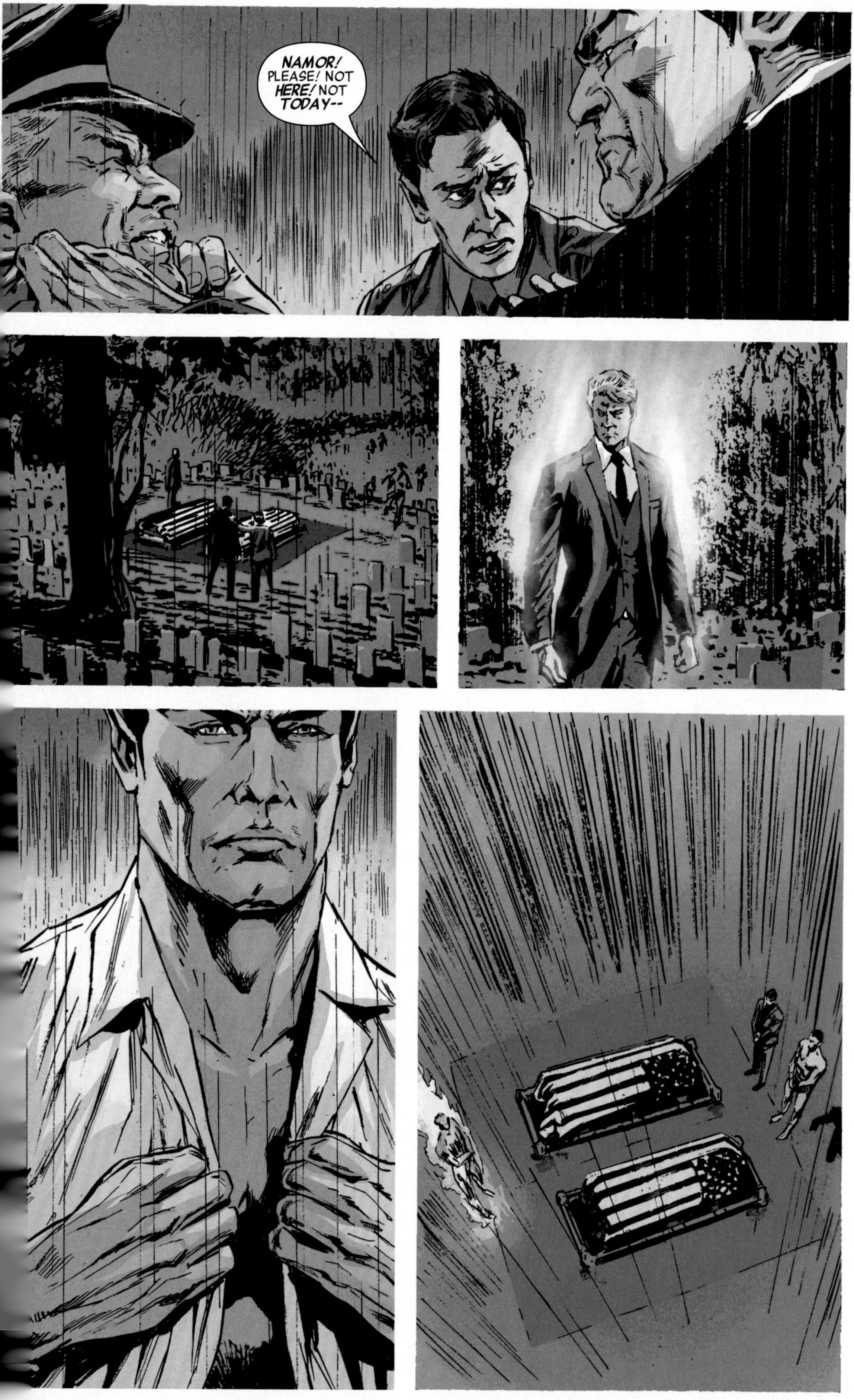
NAMOR! PLEASE! NOT HERE! NOT TODAY--

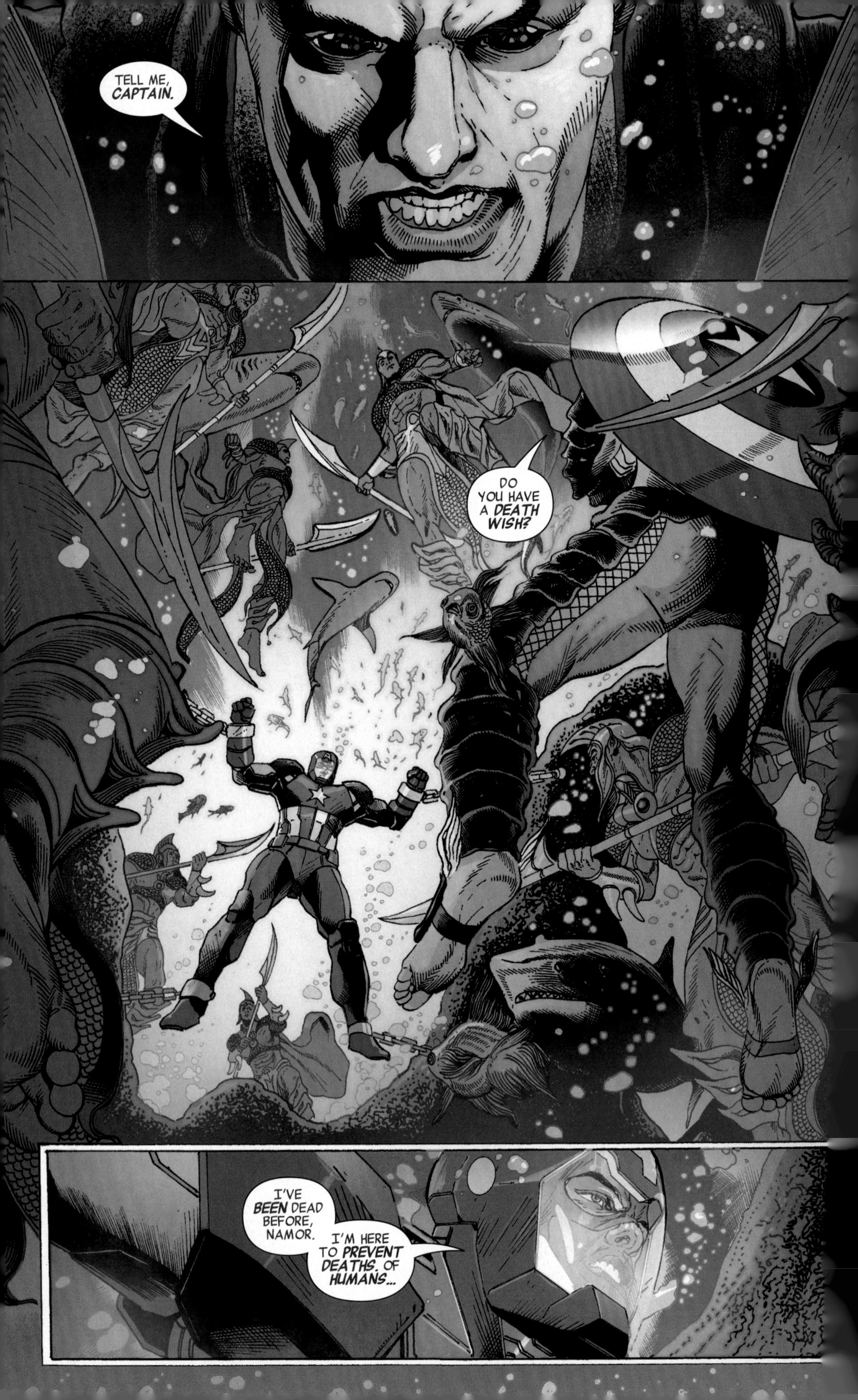
TELL ME, CAPTAIN.
DO YOU HAVE A DEATH WISH?
I'VE BEEN DEAD BEFORE, NAMOR.
I'M HERE TO PREVENT DEATHS. OF HUMANS...

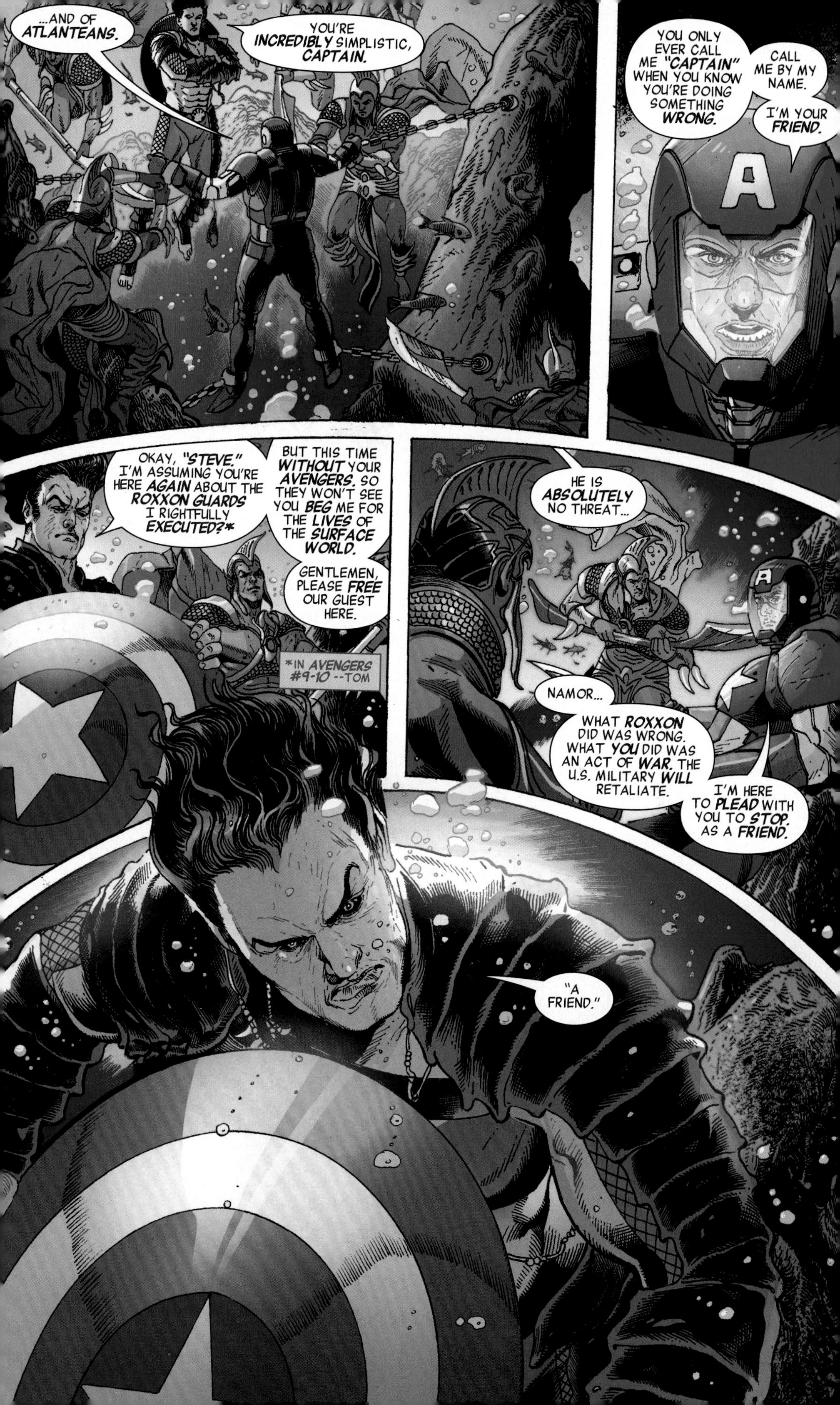
...AND OF ATLANTEANS.
YOU'RE INCREDIBLY SIMPLISTIC, CAPTAIN.
YOU ONLY EVER CALL ME "CAPTAIN" WHEN YOU KNOW YOU'RE DOING SOMETHING WRONG.
CALL ME BY MY NAME.
I'M YOUR FRIEND.
OKAY, "STEVE." I'M ASSUMING YOU'RE HERE AGAIN ABOUT THE ROXXON GUARDS I RIGHTFULLY EXECUTED?*
BUT THIS TIME WITHOUT YOUR AVENGERS. SO THEY WON'T SEE YOU BEG ME FOR THE LIVES OF THE SURFACE WORLD.
GENTLEMEN, PLEASE FREE OUR GUEST HERE.
*IN AVENGERS #9-10 --TOM
HE IS ABSOLUTELY NO THREAT...
NAMOR...
WHAT ROXXON DID WAS WRONG. WHAT YOU DID WAS AN ACT OF WAR. THE U.S. MILITARY WILL RETALIATE.
I'M HERE TO PLEAD WITH YOU TO STOP. AS A FRIEND.
"A FRIEND."

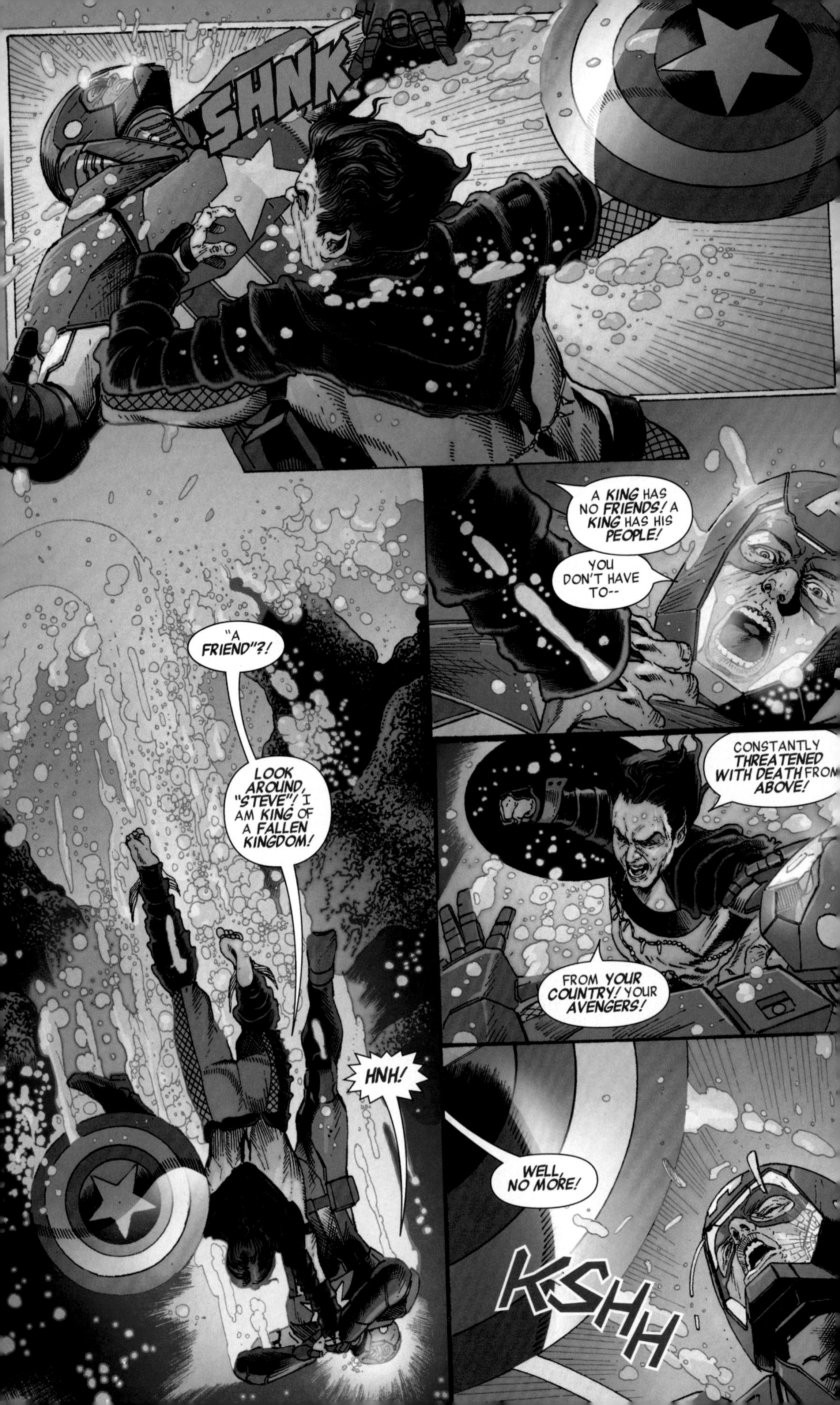
SHNK
A KING HAS NO FRIENDS! A KING HAS HIS PEOPLE!
YOU DON'T HAVE TO--
"A FRIEND"?!
LOOK AROUND, "STEVE"! I AM KING OF A FALLEN KINGDOM!
CONSTANTLY THREATENED WITH DEATH FROM ABOVE!
FROM YOUR COUNTRY! YOUR AVENGERS!
HNH!
WELL, NO MORE!
KSHH

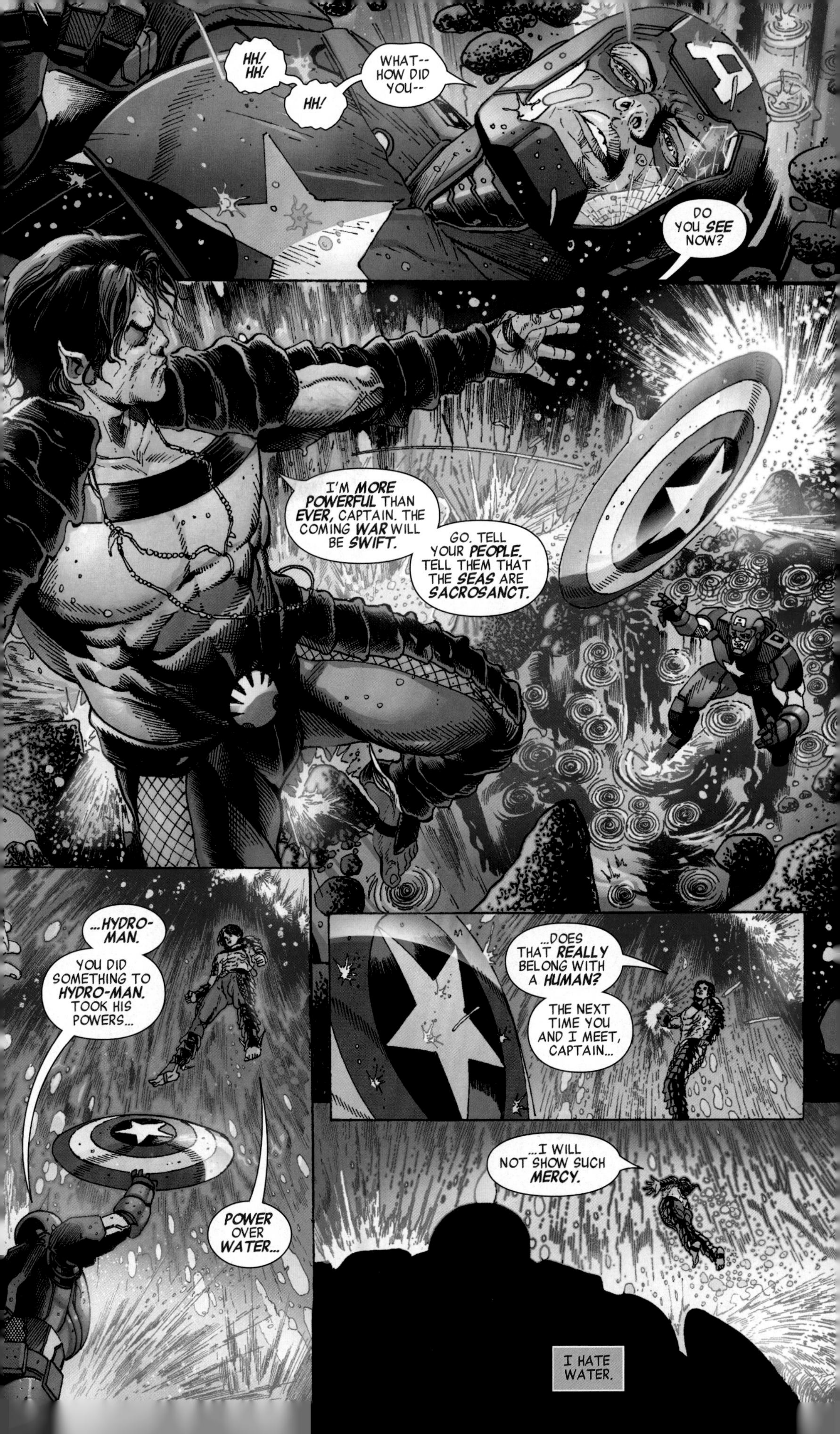
HH!
HH!
HH!
WHAT-- HOW DID YOU--
DO YOU SEE NOW?
I'M MORE POWERFUL THAN EVER, CAPTAIN. THE COMING WAR WILL BE SWIFT.
GO. TELL YOUR PEOPLE. TELL THEM THAT THE SEAS ARE SACROSANCT.
...HYDRO-MAN.
YOU DID SOMETHING TO HYDRO-MAN. TOOK HIS POWERS...
POWER OVER WATER...
...DOES THAT REALLY BELONG WITH A HUMAN?
THE NEXT TIME YOU AND I MEET, CAPTAIN...
...I WILL NOT SHOW SUCH MERCY.
I HATE WATER.

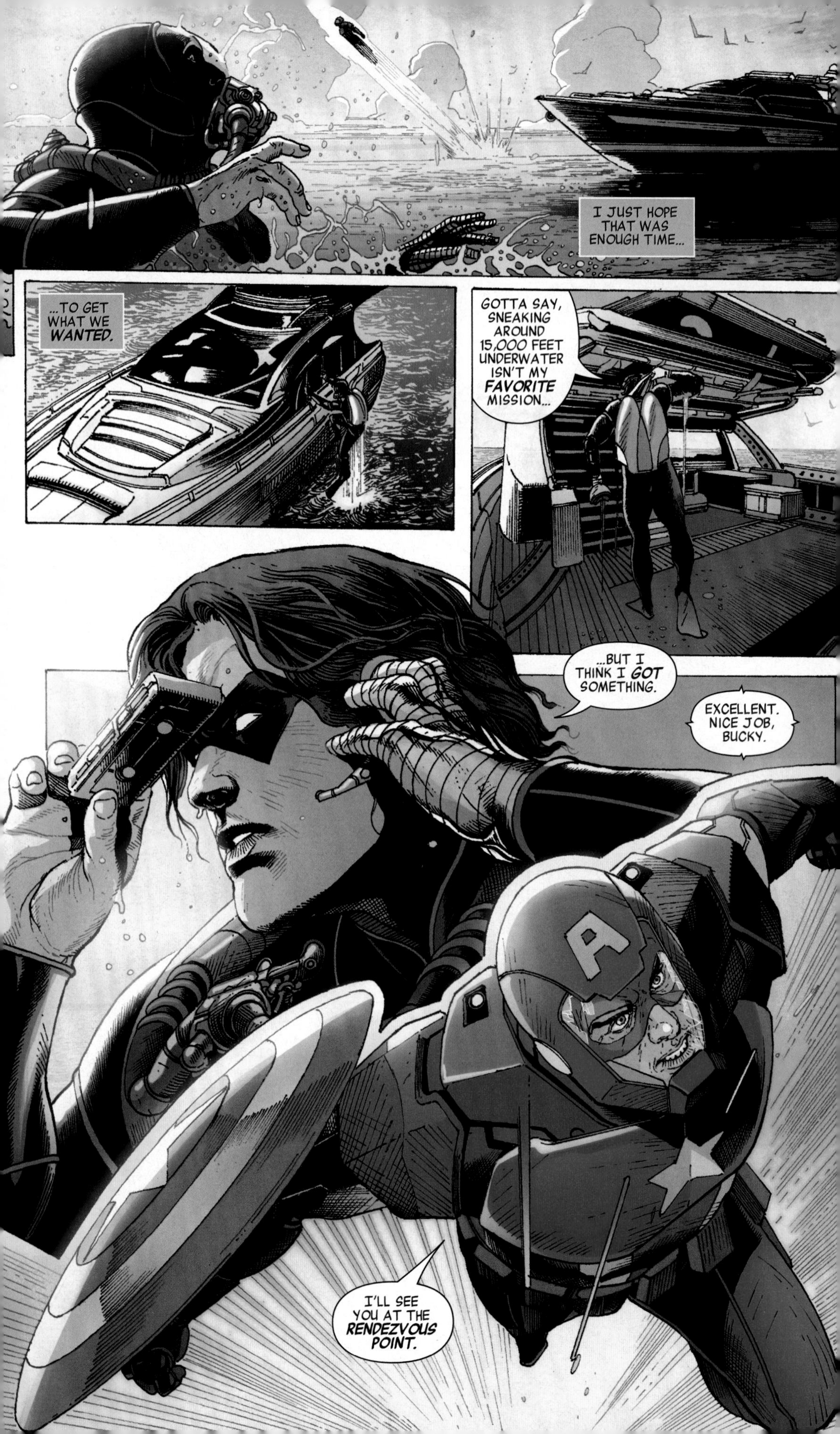
I JUST HOPE THAT WAS ENOUGH TIME...
...TO GET WHAT WE WANTED.
GOTTA SAY, SNEAKING AROUND 15,000 FEET UNDERWATER ISN'T MY FAVORITE MISSION...
...BUT I THINK I GOT SOMETHING.
EXCELLENT. NICE JOB, BUCKY.
I'LL SEE YOU AT THE RENDEZVOUS POINT.

STEVE?

HEY, NAMOR. THANKS FOR...THANKS FOR THE *SAVE* OUT THERE. I COULDN'T EVEN TELL WHICH WAY WAS UP. AND THE *WATER*, IT...

WE'VE BEEN GOING FOR SO LONG, THE *EXHAUSTION* JUST...

YOU SEEM *RATTLED.*

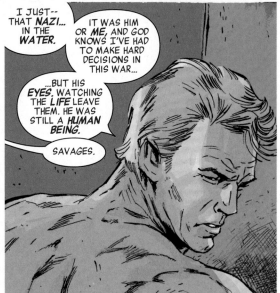

I JUST-- THAT *NAZI...* IN THE *WATER.*

IT WAS HIM OR *ME*, AND GOD KNOWS I'VE HAD TO MAKE HARD DECISIONS IN THIS WAR...

...BUT HIS *EYES.* WATCHING THE *LIFE* LEAVE THEM. HE WAS STILL A *HUMAN BEING.*

SAVAGES.

...ZIS ARE *SAVAGES.* THEY ARE THE ...EMY. IF WE HAVE ANY *CHANCE* OF *WINNING* THIS WAR...

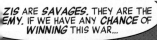

...WE NEED TO SHOW *NO MERCY.*

YOU ARE A *KIND* MAN, STEVE ROGERS, AND I SAY THIS AS A *FRIEND...*

...*WAR* HAS NO PLACE FOR *KINDNESS...*

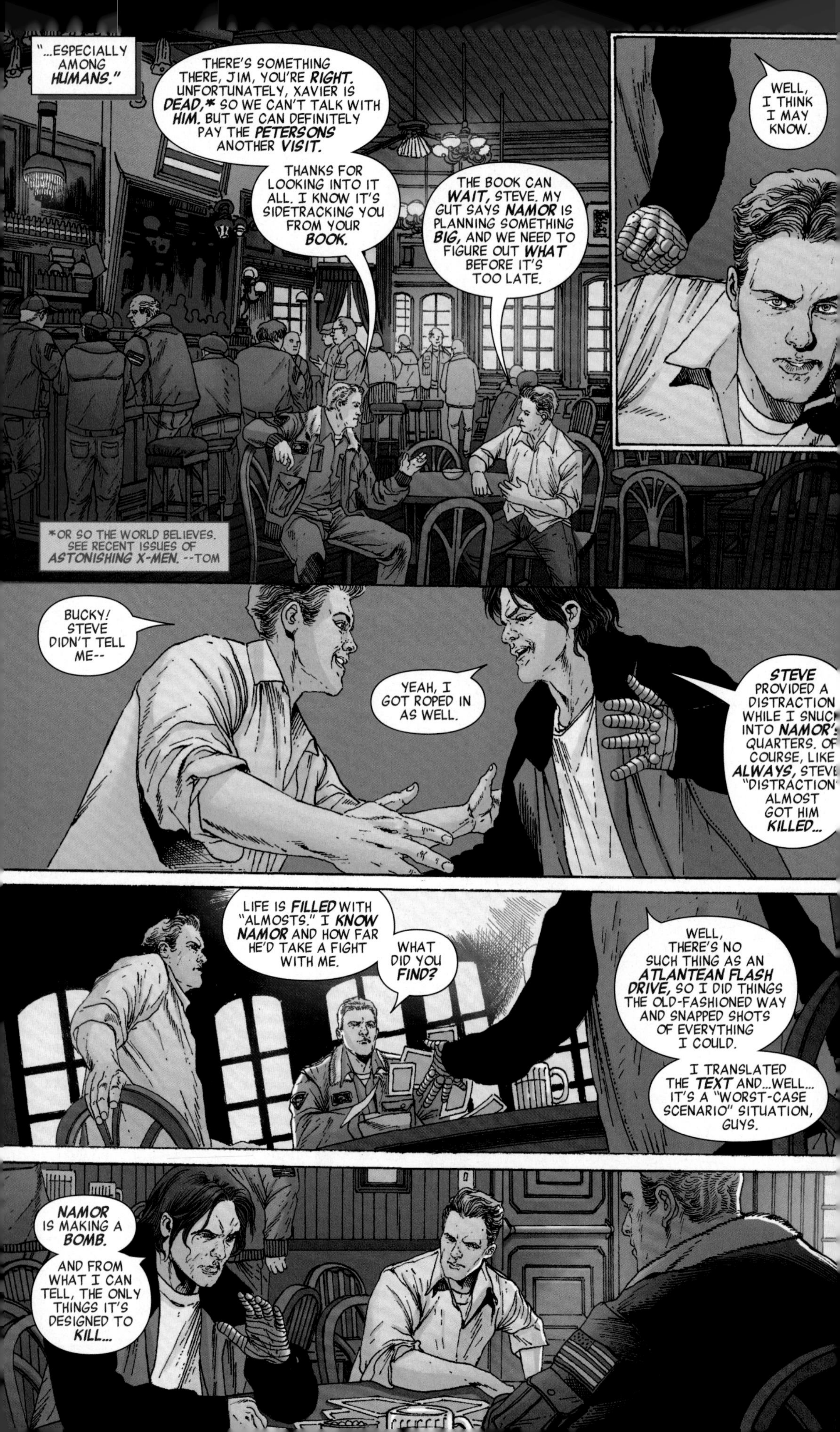

"...ESPECIALLY AMONG HUMANS."
THERE'S SOMETHING THERE, JIM, YOU'RE RIGHT. UNFORTUNATELY, XAVIER IS DEAD,* SO WE CAN'T TALK WITH HIM. BUT WE CAN DEFINITELY PAY THE PETERSONS ANOTHER VISIT.
THANKS FOR LOOKING INTO IT ALL. I KNOW IT'S SIDETRACKING YOU FROM YOUR BOOK.
THE BOOK CAN WAIT, STEVE. MY GUT SAYS NAMOR IS PLANNING SOMETHING BIG, AND WE NEED TO FIGURE OUT WHAT BEFORE IT'S TOO LATE.
*OR SO THE WORLD BELIEVES. SEE RECENT ISSUES OF ASTONISHING X-MEN. --TOM
WELL, I THINK I MAY KNOW.
BUCKY! STEVE DIDN'T TELL ME--
YEAH, I GOT ROPED IN AS WELL.
STEVE PROVIDED A DISTRACTION WHILE I SNUC INTO NAMOR' QUARTERS. OF COURSE, LIKE ALWAYS, STEVE "DISTRACTION ALMOST GOT HIM KILLED...
LIFE IS FILLED WITH "ALMOSTS." I KNOW NAMOR AND HOW FAR HE'D TAKE A FIGHT WITH ME.
WHAT DID YOU FIND?
WELL, THERE'S NO SUCH THING AS AN ATLANTEAN FLASH DRIVE, SO I DID THINGS THE OLD-FASHIONED WAY AND SNAPPED SHOTS OF EVERYTHING I COULD.
I TRANSLATED THE TEXT AND...WELL... IT'S A "WORST-CASE SCENARIO" SITUATION, GUYS.
NAMOR IS MAKING A BOMB.
AND FROM WHAT I CAN TELL, THE ONLY THINGS IT'S DESIGNED TO KILL...

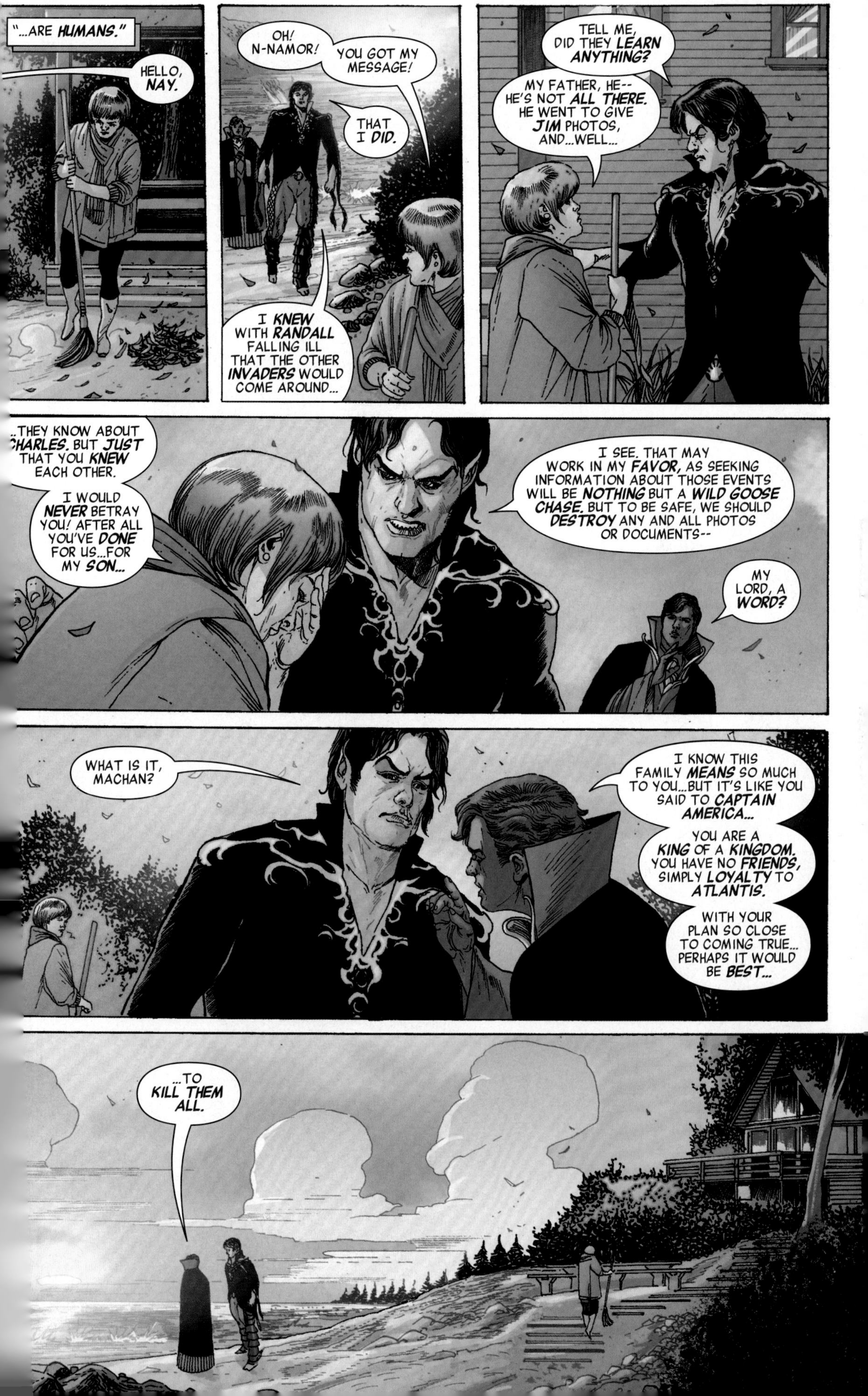
"...ARE HUMANS."
HELLO, NAY.
OH! N-NAMOR!
YOU GOT MY MESSAGE!
THAT I DID.
I KNEW WITH RANDALL FALLING ILL THAT THE OTHER INVADERS WOULD COME AROUND...
TELL ME, DID THEY LEARN ANYTHING?
MY FATHER, HE-- HE'S NOT ALL THERE. HE WENT TO GIVE JIM PHOTOS, AND...WELL...
...THEY KNOW ABOUT CHARLES. BUT JUST THAT YOU KNEW EACH OTHER.
I WOULD NEVER BETRAY YOU! AFTER ALL YOU'VE DONE FOR US...FOR MY SON...
I SEE. THAT MAY WORK IN MY FAVOR, AS SEEKING INFORMATION ABOUT THOSE EVENTS WILL BE NOTHING BUT A WILD GOOSE CHASE. BUT TO BE SAFE, WE SHOULD DESTROY ANY AND ALL PHOTOS OR DOCUMENTS--
MY LORD, A WORD?
WHAT IS IT, MACHAN?
I KNOW THIS FAMILY MEANS SO MUCH TO YOU...BUT IT'S LIKE YOU SAID TO CAPTAIN AMERICA...
YOU ARE A KING OF A KINGDOM. YOU HAVE NO FRIENDS, SIMPLY LOYALTY TO ATLANTIS.
WITH YOUR PLAN SO CLOSE TO COMING TRUE... PERHAPS IT WOULD BE BEST...
...TO KILL THEM ALL.

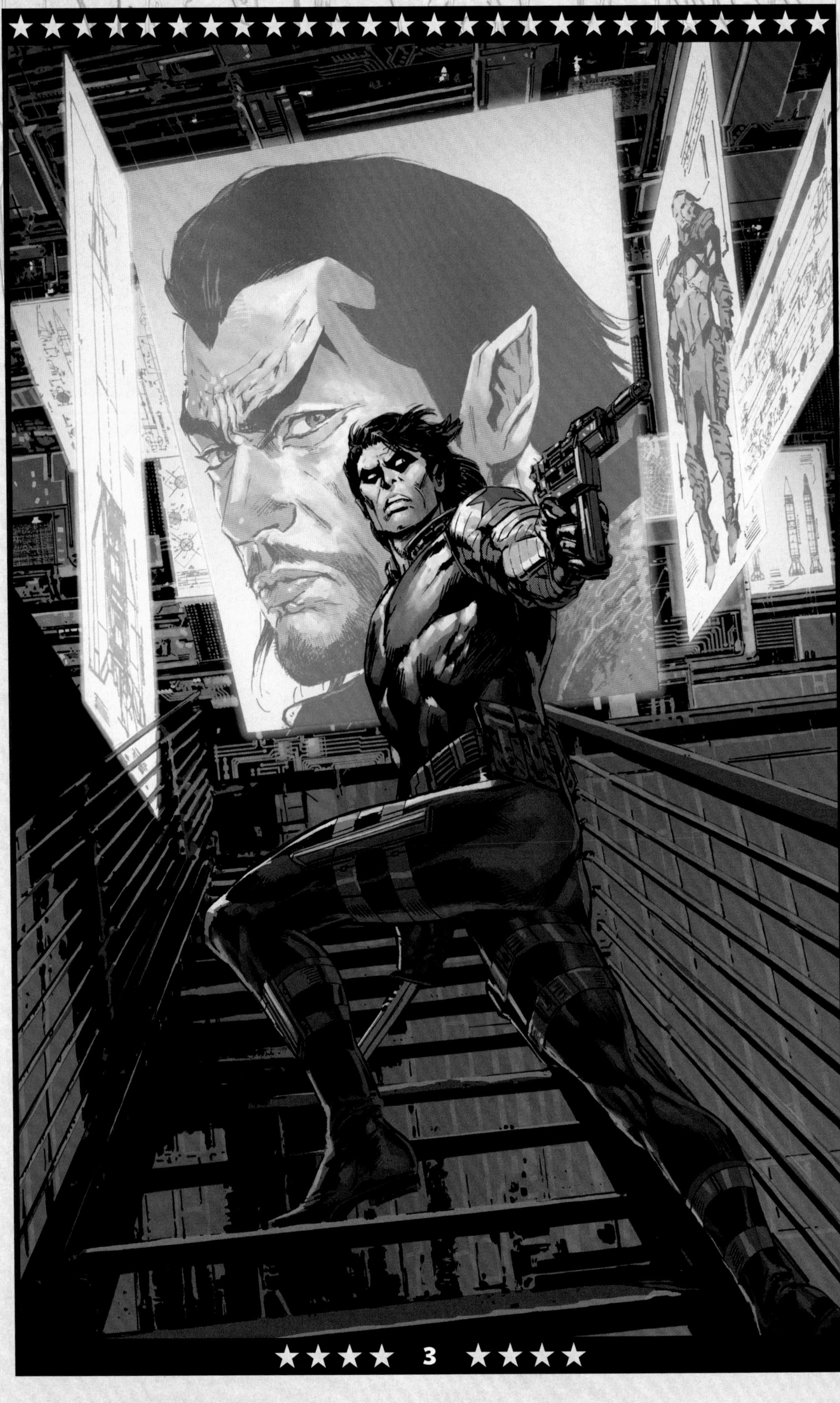
3

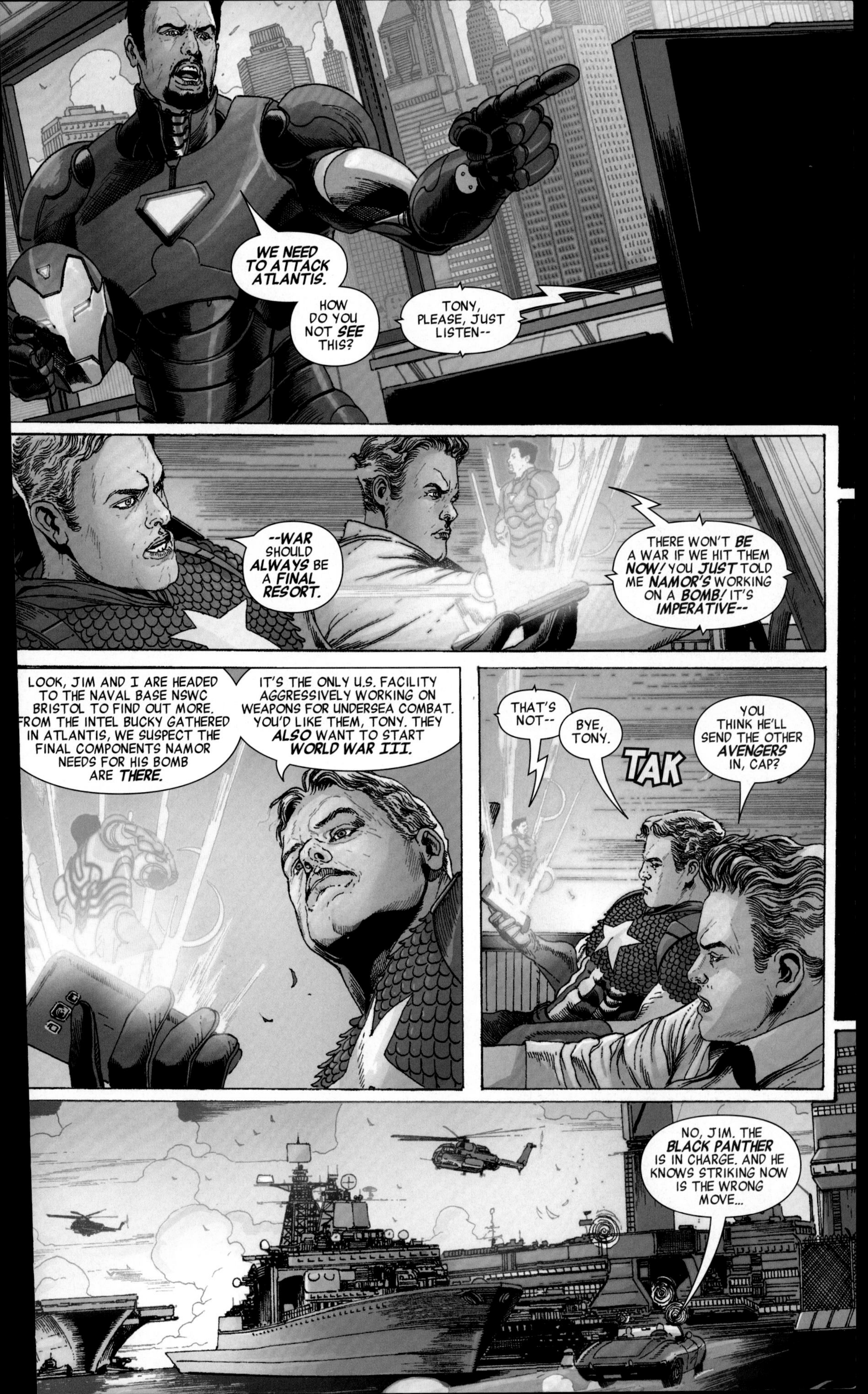

WE NEED TO ATTACK ATLANTIS.
HOW DO YOU NOT SEE THIS?
TONY, PLEASE, JUST LISTEN--
--WAR SHOULD ALWAYS BE A FINAL RESORT.
THERE WON'T BE A WAR IF WE HIT THEM NOW! YOU JUST TOLD ME NAMOR'S WORKING ON A BOMB! IT'S IMPERATIVE--
LOOK, JIM AND I ARE HEADED TO THE NAVAL BASE NSWC BRISTOL TO FIND OUT MORE. FROM THE INTEL BUCKY GATHERED IN ATLANTIS, WE SUSPECT THE FINAL COMPONENTS NAMOR NEEDS FOR HIS BOMB ARE THERE.
IT'S THE ONLY U.S. FACILITY AGGRESSIVELY WORKING ON WEAPONS FOR UNDERSEA COMBAT. YOU'D LIKE THEM, TONY. THEY ALSO WANT TO START WORLD WAR III.
THAT'S NOT--
BYE, TONY.
TAK
YOU THINK HE'LL SEND THE OTHER AVENGERS IN, CAP?
NO, JIM. THE BLACK PANTHER IS IN CHARGE. AND HE KNOWS STRIKING NOW IS THE WRONG MOVE...

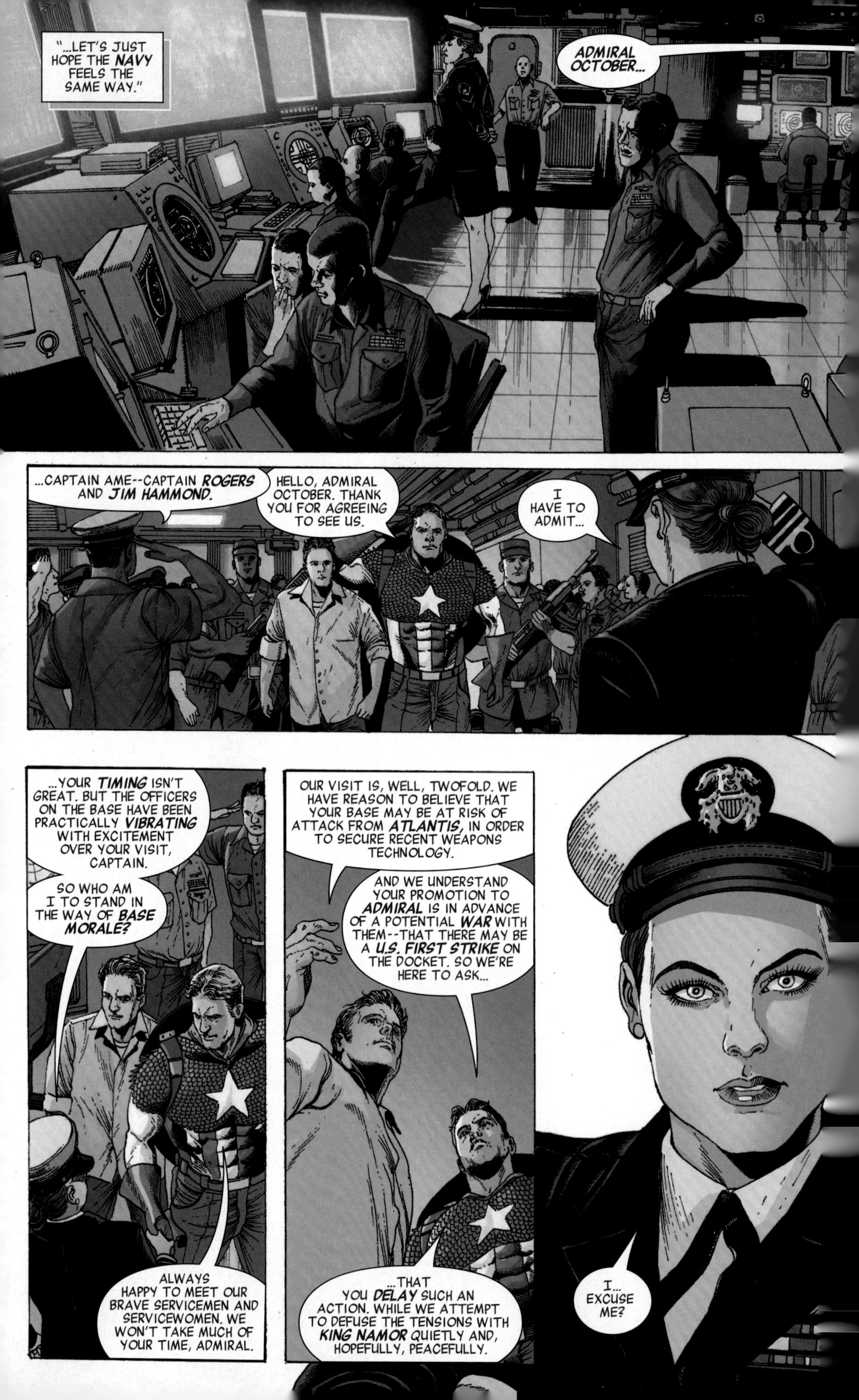
"...LET'S JUST HOPE THE NAVY FEELS THE SAME WAY."
ADMIRAL OCTOBER...
...CAPTAIN AME--CAPTAIN ROGERS AND JIM HAMMOND.
HELLO, ADMIRAL OCTOBER. THANK YOU FOR AGREEING TO SEE US.
I HAVE TO ADMIT...
...YOUR TIMING ISN'T GREAT. BUT THE OFFICERS ON THE BASE HAVE BEEN PRACTICALLY VIBRATING WITH EXCITEMENT OVER YOUR VISIT, CAPTAIN.
SO WHO AM I TO STAND IN THE WAY OF BASE MORALE?
ALWAYS HAPPY TO MEET OUR BRAVE SERVICEMEN AND SERVICEWOMEN. WE WON'T TAKE MUCH OF YOUR TIME, ADMIRAL.
OUR VISIT IS, WELL, TWOFOLD. WE HAVE REASON TO BELIEVE THAT YOUR BASE MAY BE AT RISK OF ATTACK FROM ATLANTIS, IN ORDER TO SECURE RECENT WEAPONS TECHNOLOGY.
AND WE UNDERSTAND YOUR PROMOTION TO ADMIRAL IS IN ADVANCE OF A POTENTIAL WAR WITH THEM--THAT THERE MAY BE A U.S. FIRST STRIKE ON THE DOCKET. SO WE'RE HERE TO ASK...
...THAT YOU DELAY SUCH AN ACTION. WHILE WE ATTEMPT TO DEFUSE THE TENSIONS WITH KING NAMOR QUIETLY AND, HOPEFULLY, PEACEFULLY.
I... EXCUSE ME?

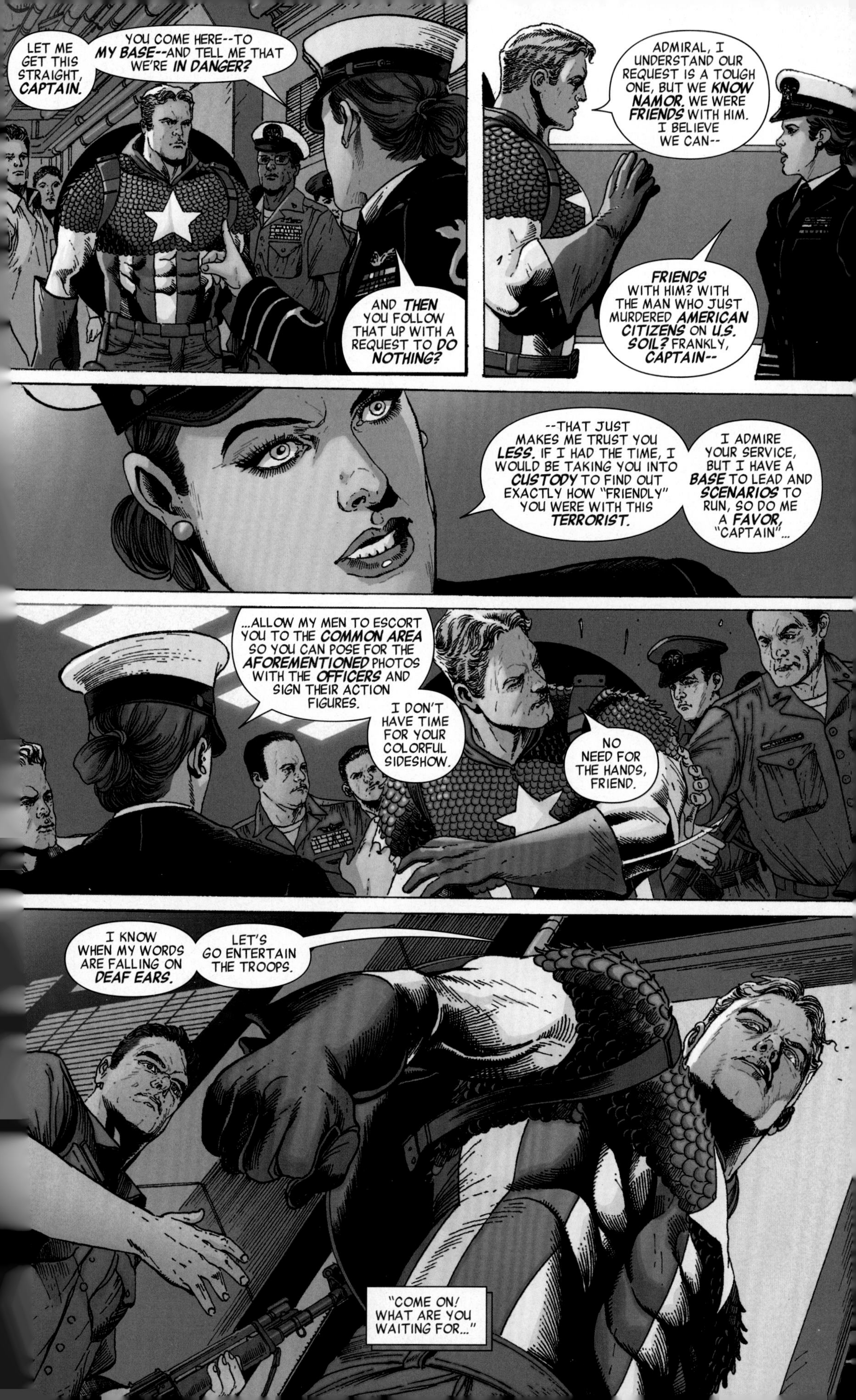
LET ME GET THIS STRAIGHT, CAPTAIN.
YOU COME HERE--TO MY BASE--AND TELL ME THAT WE'RE IN DANGER?
AND THEN YOU FOLLOW THAT UP WITH A REQUEST TO DO NOTHING?
ADMIRAL, I UNDERSTAND OUR REQUEST IS A TOUGH ONE, BUT WE KNOW NAMOR. WE WERE FRIENDS WITH HIM. I BELIEVE WE CAN--
FRIENDS WITH HIM? WITH THE MAN WHO JUST MURDERED AMERICAN CITIZENS ON U.S. SOIL? FRANKLY, CAPTAIN--
--THAT JUST MAKES ME TRUST YOU LESS. IF I HAD THE TIME, I WOULD BE TAKING YOU INTO CUSTODY TO FIND OUT EXACTLY HOW "FRIENDLY" YOU WERE WITH THIS TERRORIST.
I ADMIRE YOUR SERVICE, BUT I HAVE A BASE TO LEAD AND SCENARIOS TO RUN, SO DO ME A FAVOR, "CAPTAIN"...
...ALLOW MY MEN TO ESCORT YOU TO THE COMMON AREA SO YOU CAN POSE FOR THE AFOREMENTIONED PHOTOS WITH THE OFFICERS AND SIGN THEIR ACTION FIGURES.
I DON'T HAVE TIME FOR YOUR COLORFUL SIDESHOW.
NO NEED FOR THE HANDS, FRIEND.
I KNOW WHEN MY WORDS ARE FALLING ON DEAF EARS.
LET'S GO ENTERTAIN THE TROOPS.
"COME ON! WHAT ARE YOU WAITING FOR..."

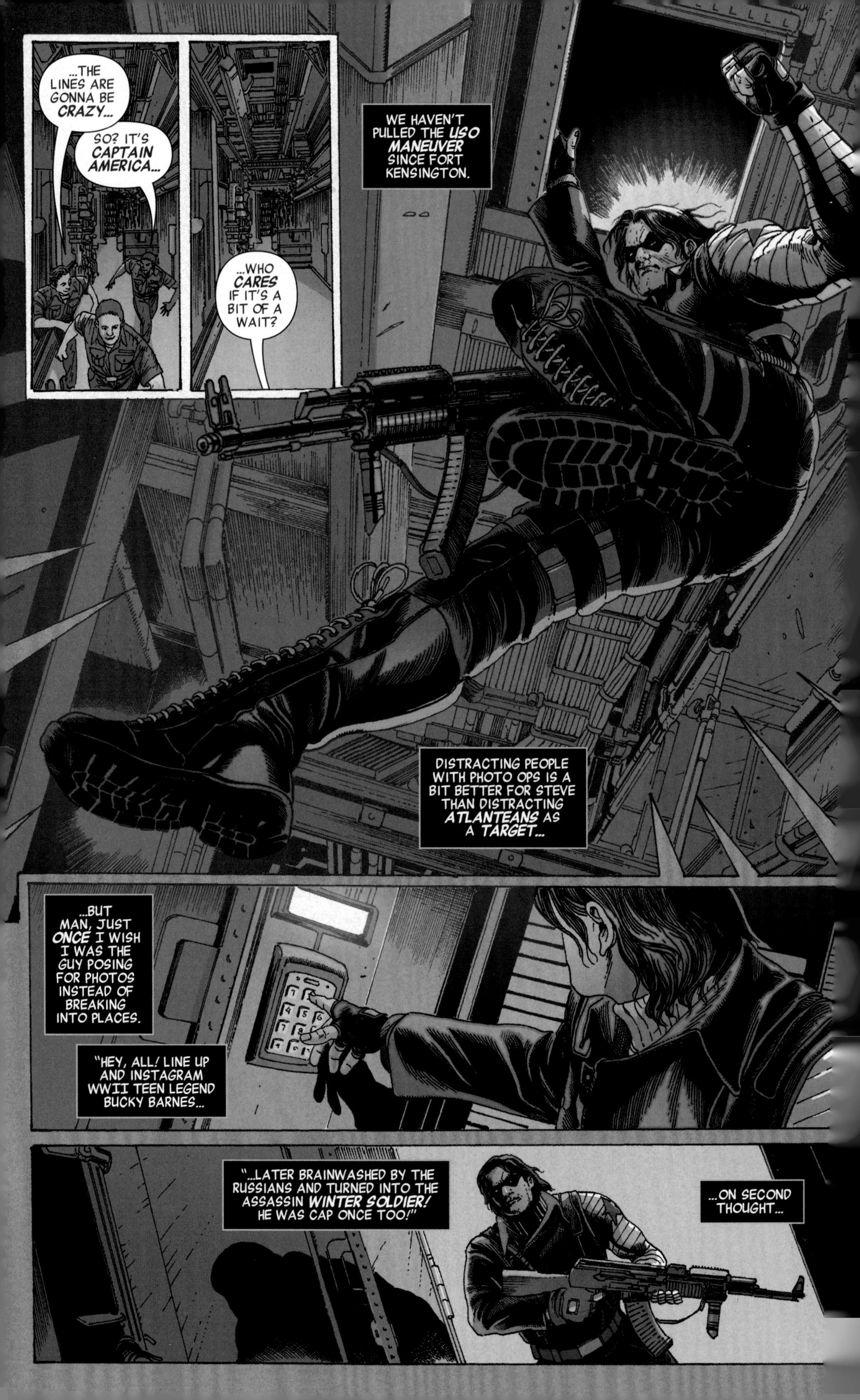
...THE LINES ARE GONNA BE CRAZY...
SO? IT'S CAPTAIN AMERICA...
...WHO CARES IF IT'S A BIT OF A WAIT?
WE HAVEN'T PULLED THE USO MANEUVER SINCE FORT KENSINGTON.
DISTRACTING PEOPLE WITH PHOTO OPS IS A BIT BETTER FOR STEVE THAN DISTRACTING ATLANTEANS AS A TARGET...
...BUT MAN, JUST ONCE I WISH I WAS THE GUY POSING FOR PHOTOS INSTEAD OF BREAKING INTO PLACES.
"HEY, ALL! LINE UP AND INSTAGRAM WWII TEEN LEGEND BUCKY BARNES...
"...LATER BRAINWASHED BY THE RUSSIANS AND TURNED INTO THE ASSASSIN WINTER SOLDIER! HE WAS CAP ONCE TOO!"
...ON SECOND THOUGHT...

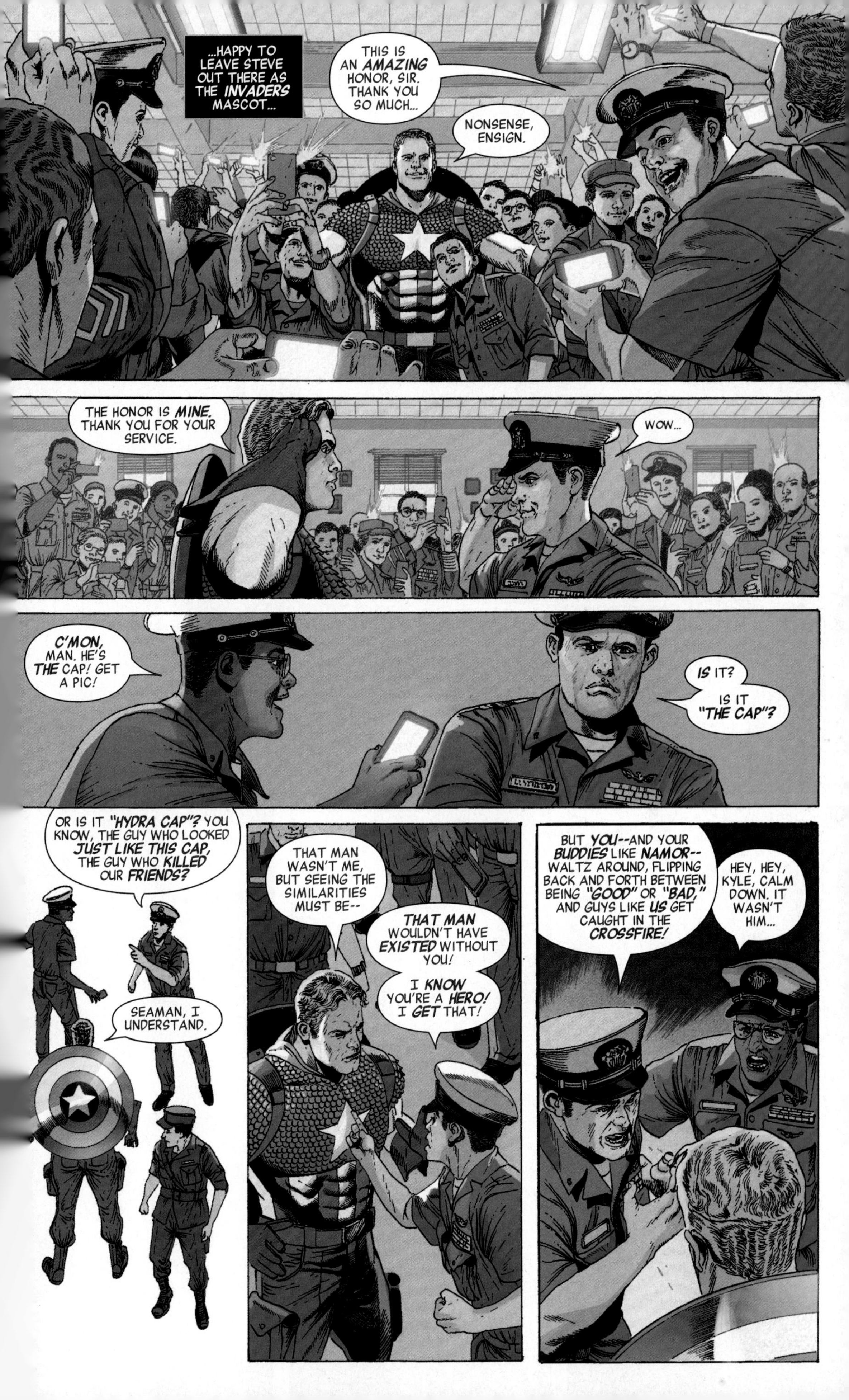
...HAPPY TO LEAVE STEVE OUT THERE AS THE INVADERS MASCOT...
THIS IS AN AMAZING HONOR, SIR. THANK YOU SO MUCH...
NONSENSE, ENSIGN.
THE HONOR IS MINE. THANK YOU FOR YOUR SERVICE.
WOW...
C'MON, MAN. HE'S THE CAP! GET A PIC!
IS IT?
IS IT "THE CAP"?
OR IS IT "HYDRA CAP"? YOU KNOW, THE GUY WHO LOOKED JUST LIKE THIS CAP, THE GUY WHO KILLED OUR FRIENDS?
SEAMAN, I UNDERSTAND.
THAT MAN WASN'T ME, BUT SEEING THE SIMILARITIES MUST BE--
THAT MAN WOULDN'T HAVE EXISTED WITHOUT YOU!
I KNOW YOU'RE A HERO! I GET THAT!
BUT YOU--AND YOUR BUDDIES LIKE NAMOR--WALTZ AROUND, FLIPPING BACK AND FORTH BETWEEN BEING "GOOD" OR "BAD," AND GUYS LIKE US GET CAUGHT IN THE CROSSFIRE!
HEY, HEY, KYLE, CALM DOWN. IT WASN'T HIM...

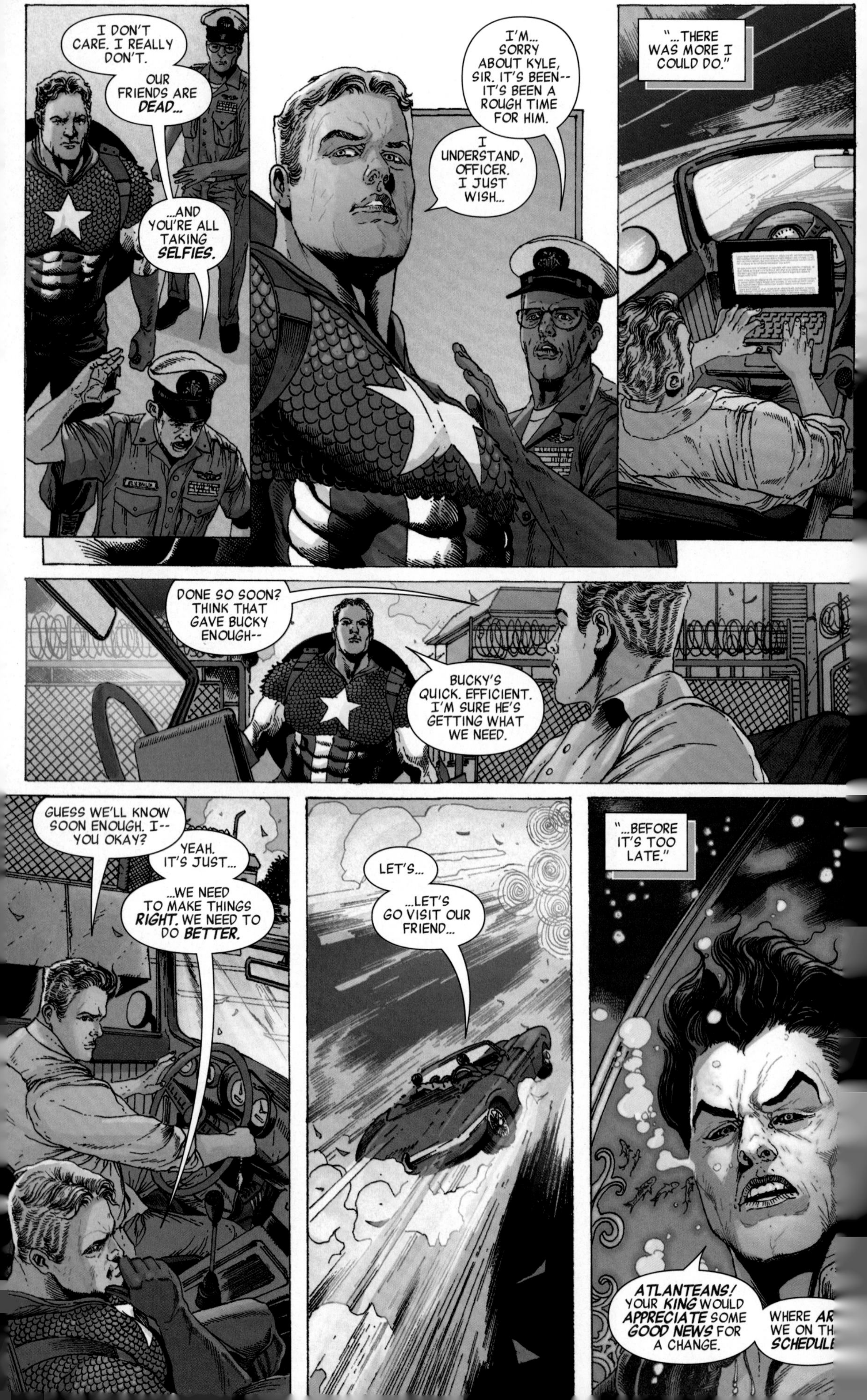
I DON'T CARE. I REALLY DON'T.
OUR FRIENDS ARE DEAD...
...AND YOU'RE ALL TAKING SELFIES.
I'M... SORRY ABOUT KYLE, SIR. IT'S BEEN-- IT'S BEEN A ROUGH TIME FOR HIM.
I UNDERSTAND, OFFICER. I JUST WISH...
"...THERE WAS MORE I COULD DO."
DONE SO SOON? THINK THAT GAVE BUCKY ENOUGH--
BUCKY'S QUICK. EFFICIENT. I'M SURE HE'S GETTING WHAT WE NEED.
GUESS WE'LL KNOW SOON ENOUGH. I-- YOU OKAY?
YEAH. IT'S JUST...
...WE NEED TO MAKE THINGS RIGHT. WE NEED TO DO BETTER.
LET'S...
...LET'S GO VISIT OUR FRIEND...
"...BEFORE IT'S TOO LATE."
ATLANTEANS! YOUR KING WOULD APPRECIATE SOME GOOD NEWS FOR A CHANGE.
WHERE AR WE ON TH SCHEDUL

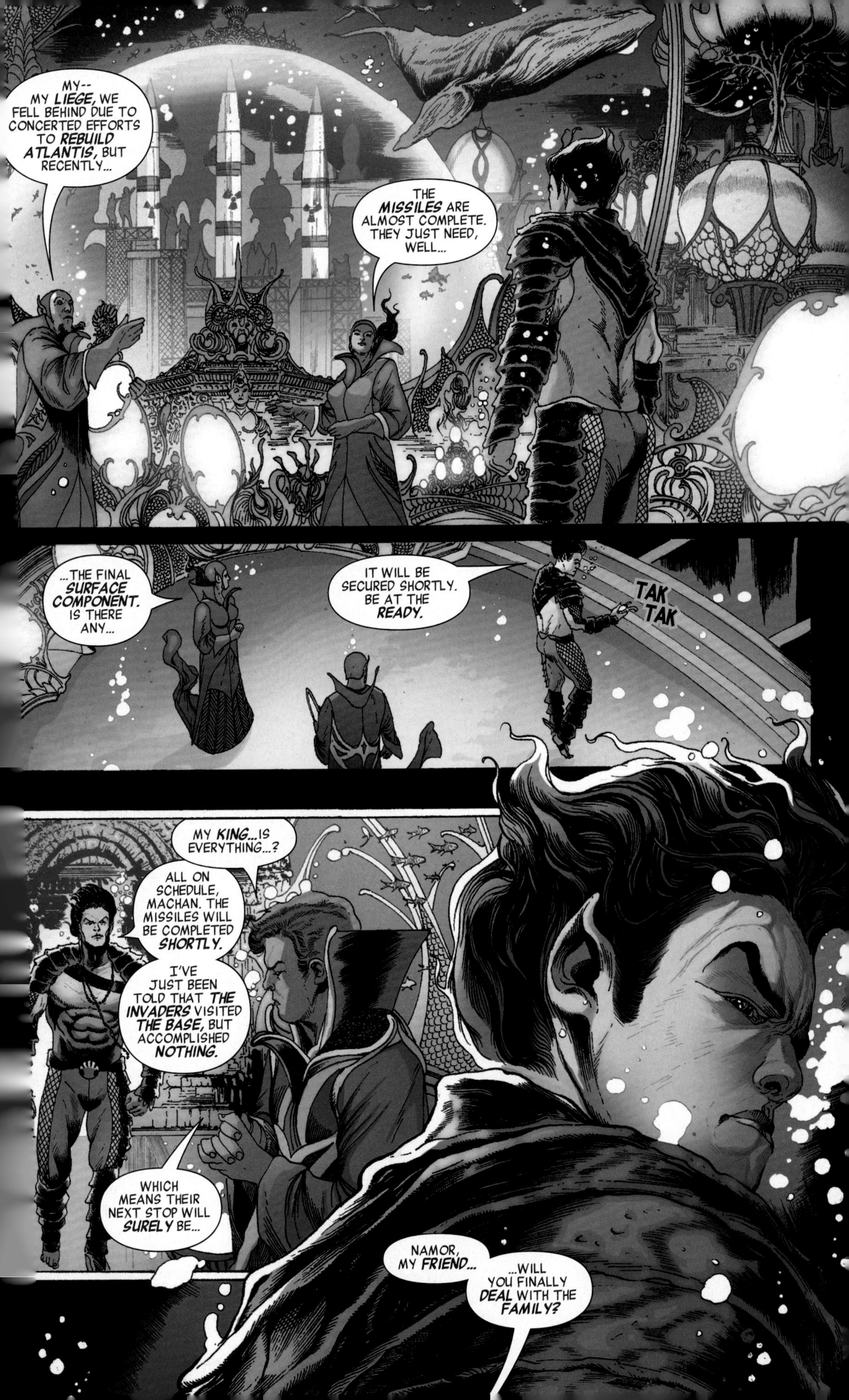
MY-- MY LIEGE, WE FELL BEHIND DUE TO CONCERTED EFFORTS TO REBUILD ATLANTIS, BUT RECENTLY...
THE MISSILES ARE ALMOST COMPLETE. THEY JUST NEED, WELL...
...THE FINAL SURFACE COMPONENT. IS THERE ANY...
IT WILL BE SECURED SHORTLY. BE AT THE READY.
TAK TAK
MY KING...IS EVERYTHING...?
ALL ON SCHEDULE, MACHAN. THE MISSILES WILL BE COMPLETED SHORTLY.
I'VE JUST BEEN TOLD THAT THE INVADERS VISITED THE BASE, BUT ACCOMPLISHED NOTHING.
WHICH MEANS THEIR NEXT STOP WILL SURELY BE...
NAMOR, MY FRIEND...
...WILL YOU FINALLY DEAL WITH THE FAMILY?

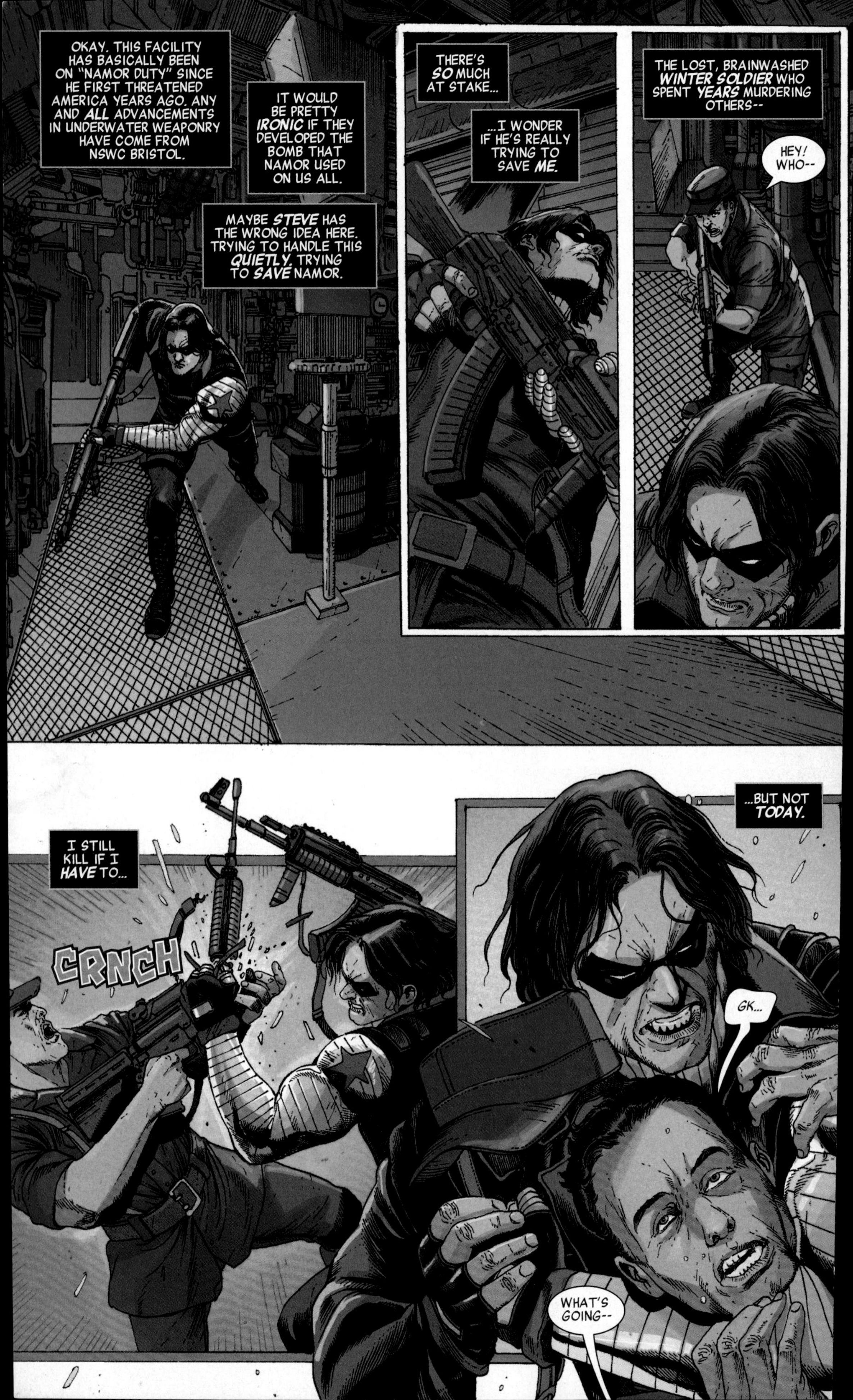
OKAY. THIS FACILITY HAS BASICALLY BEEN ON "NAMOR DUTY" SINCE HE FIRST THREATENED AMERICA YEARS AGO. ANY AND ALL ADVANCEMENTS IN UNDERWATER WEAPONRY HAVE COME FROM NSWC BRISTOL.
IT WOULD BE PRETTY IRONIC IF THEY DEVELOPED THE BOMB THAT NAMOR USED ON US ALL.
MAYBE STEVE HAS THE WRONG IDEA HERE. TRYING TO HANDLE THIS QUIETLY. TRYING TO SAVE NAMOR.
THERE'S SO MUCH AT STAKE...
...I WONDER IF HE'S REALLY TRYING TO SAVE ME.
THE LOST, BRAINWASHED WINTER SOLDIER WHO SPENT YEARS MURDERING OTHERS--
HEY! WHO--
I STILL KILL IF I HAVE TO...
CRNCH
...BUT NOT TODAY.
GK...
WHAT'S GOING--

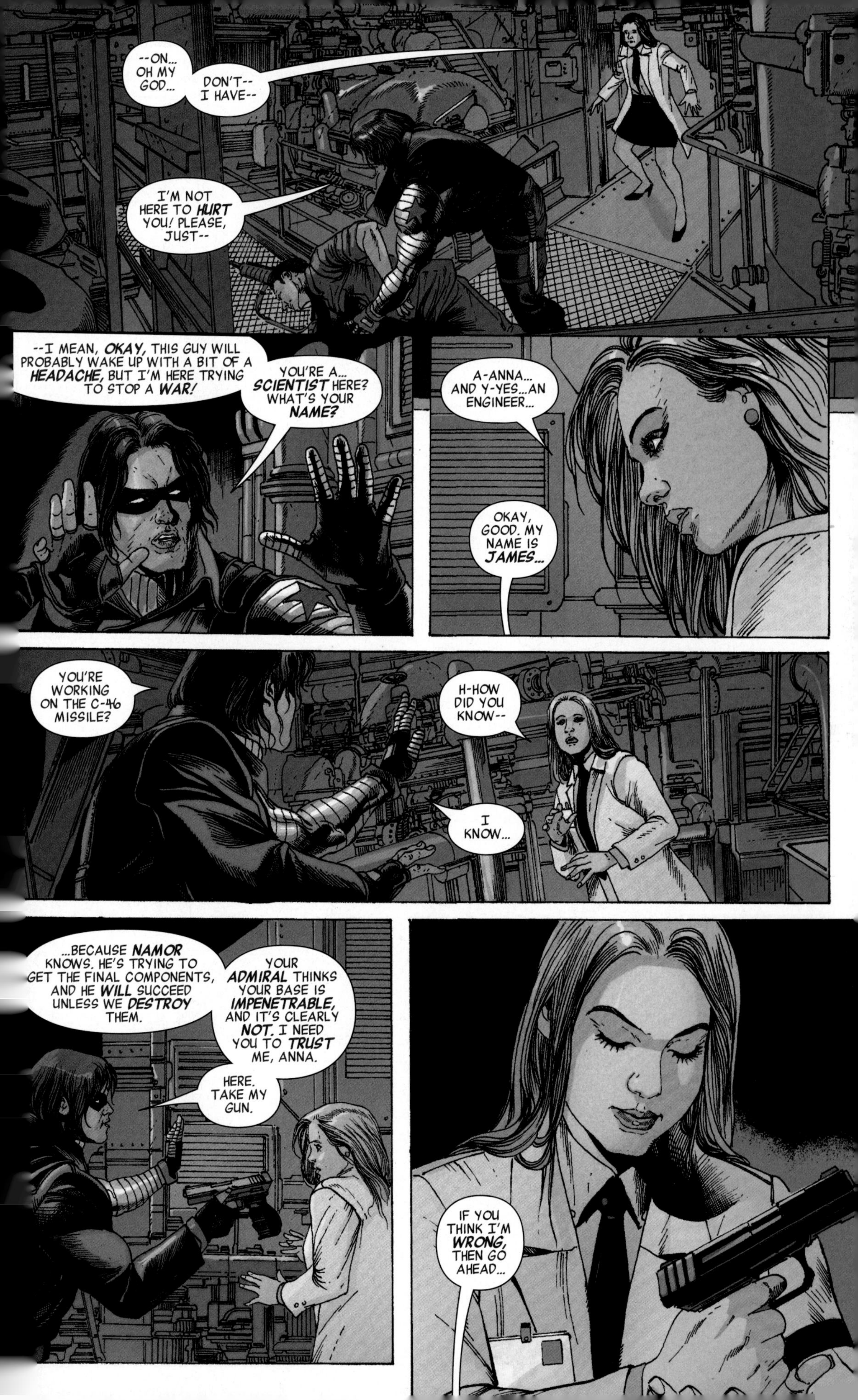
--ON... OH MY GOD...
DON'T-- I HAVE--
I'M NOT HERE TO HURT YOU! PLEASE, JUST--
--I MEAN, OKAY, THIS GUY WILL PROBABLY WAKE UP WITH A BIT OF A HEADACHE, BUT I'M HERE TRYING TO STOP A WAR!
YOU'RE A... SCIENTIST HERE? WHAT'S YOUR NAME?
A-ANNA... AND Y-YES...AN ENGINEER...
OKAY, GOOD. MY NAME IS JAMES...
YOU'RE WORKING ON THE C-46 MISSILE?
H-HOW DID YOU KNOW--
I KNOW...
...BECAUSE NAMOR KNOWS. HE'S TRYING TO GET THE FINAL COMPONENTS, AND HE WILL SUCCEED UNLESS WE DESTROY THEM.
YOUR ADMIRAL THINKS YOUR BASE IS IMPENETRABLE, AND IT'S CLEARLY NOT. I NEED YOU TO TRUST ME, ANNA.
HERE. TAKE MY GUN.
IF YOU THINK I'M WRONG, THEN GO AHEAD...

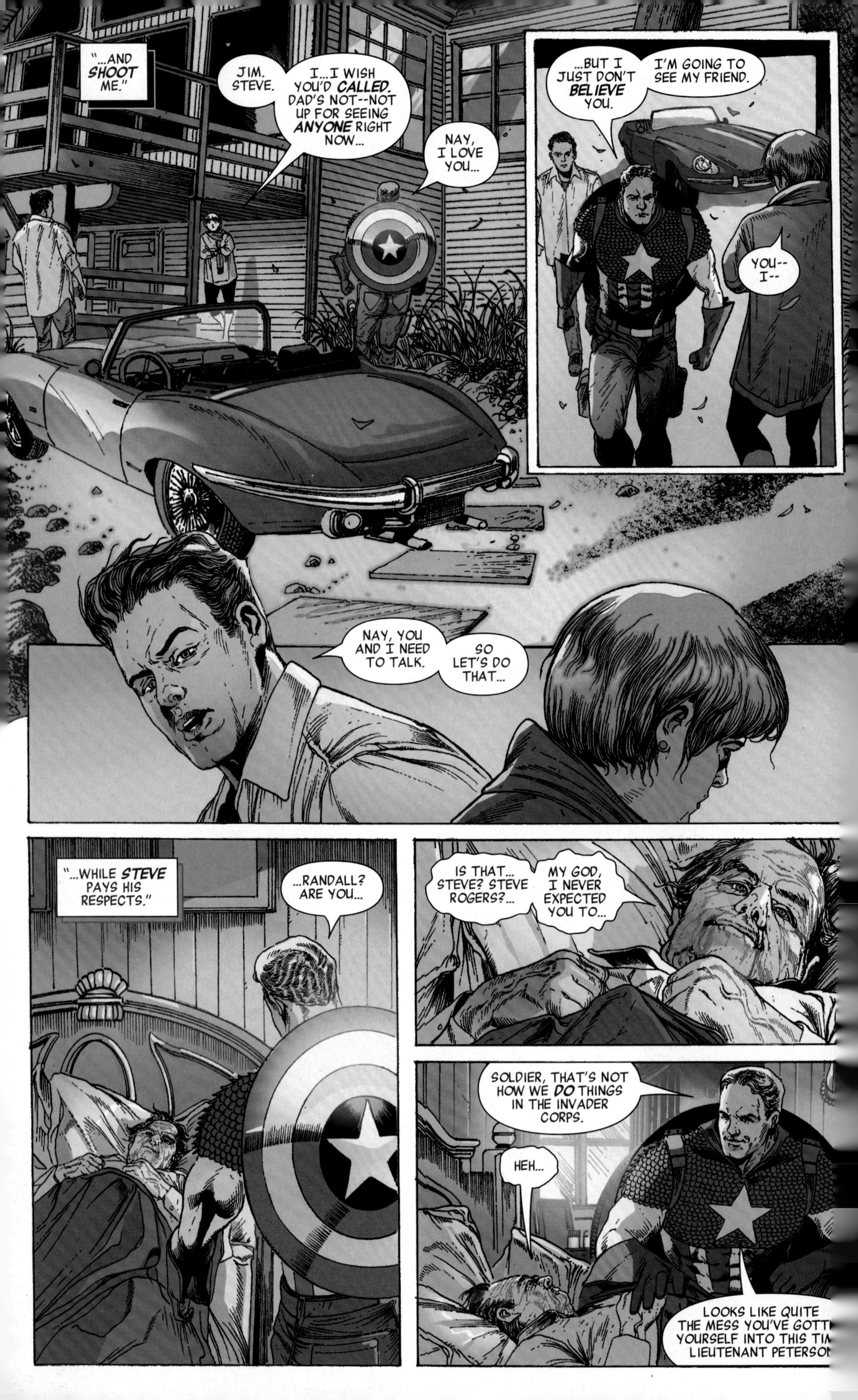
"...AND SHOOT ME."
JIM. STEVE.
I...I WISH YOU'D CALLED. DAD'S NOT--NOT UP FOR SEEING ANYONE RIGHT NOW...
NAY, I LOVE YOU...
...BUT I JUST DON'T BELIEVE YOU.
I'M GOING TO SEE MY FRIEND.
YOU-- I--
NAY, YOU AND I NEED TO TALK.
SO LET'S DO THAT...
"...WHILE STEVE PAYS HIS RESPECTS."
...RANDALL? ARE YOU...
IS THAT... STEVE? STEVE ROGERS?...
MY GOD, I NEVER EXPECTED YOU TO...
SOLDIER, THAT'S NOT HOW WE DO THINGS IN THE INVADER CORPS.
HEH...

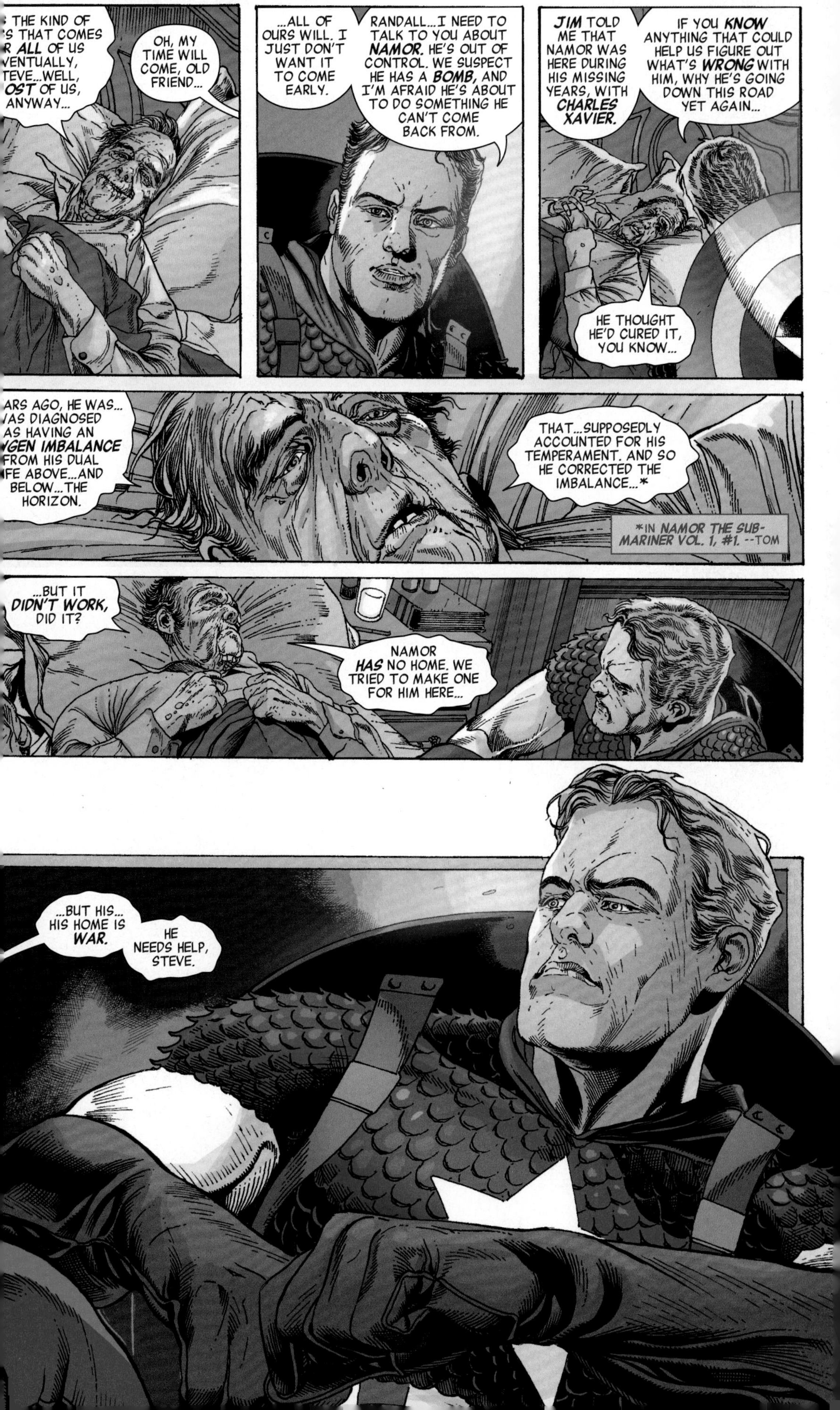

...S THE KIND OF ...S THAT COMES ...R ALL OF US ...VENTUALLY, ...TEVE...WELL, ...OST OF US, ANYWAY...
OH, MY TIME WILL COME, OLD FRIEND...
...ALL OF OURS WILL. I JUST DON'T WANT IT TO COME EARLY.
RANDALL...I NEED TO TALK TO YOU ABOUT NAMOR. HE'S OUT OF CONTROL. WE SUSPECT HE HAS A BOMB, AND I'M AFRAID HE'S ABOUT TO DO SOMETHING HE CAN'T COME BACK FROM.
JIM TOLD ME THAT NAMOR WAS HERE DURING HIS MISSING YEARS, WITH CHARLES XAVIER.
IF YOU KNOW ANYTHING THAT COULD HELP US FIGURE OUT WHAT'S WRONG WITH HIM, WHY HE'S GOING DOWN THIS ROAD YET AGAIN...
HE THOUGHT HE'D CURED IT, YOU KNOW...
...ARS AGO, HE WAS... ...VAS DIAGNOSED AS HAVING AN ...YGEN IMBALANCE FROM HIS DUAL ...FE ABOVE...AND BELOW...THE HORIZON.
THAT...SUPPOSEDLY ACCOUNTED FOR HIS TEMPERAMENT. AND SO HE CORRECTED THE IMBALANCE...*
*IN NAMOR THE SUB-MARINER VOL. 1, #1. --TOM
...BUT IT DIDN'T WORK, DID IT?
NAMOR HAS NO HOME. WE TRIED TO MAKE ONE FOR HIM HERE...
...BUT HIS... HIS HOME IS WAR.
HE NEEDS HELP, STEVE.

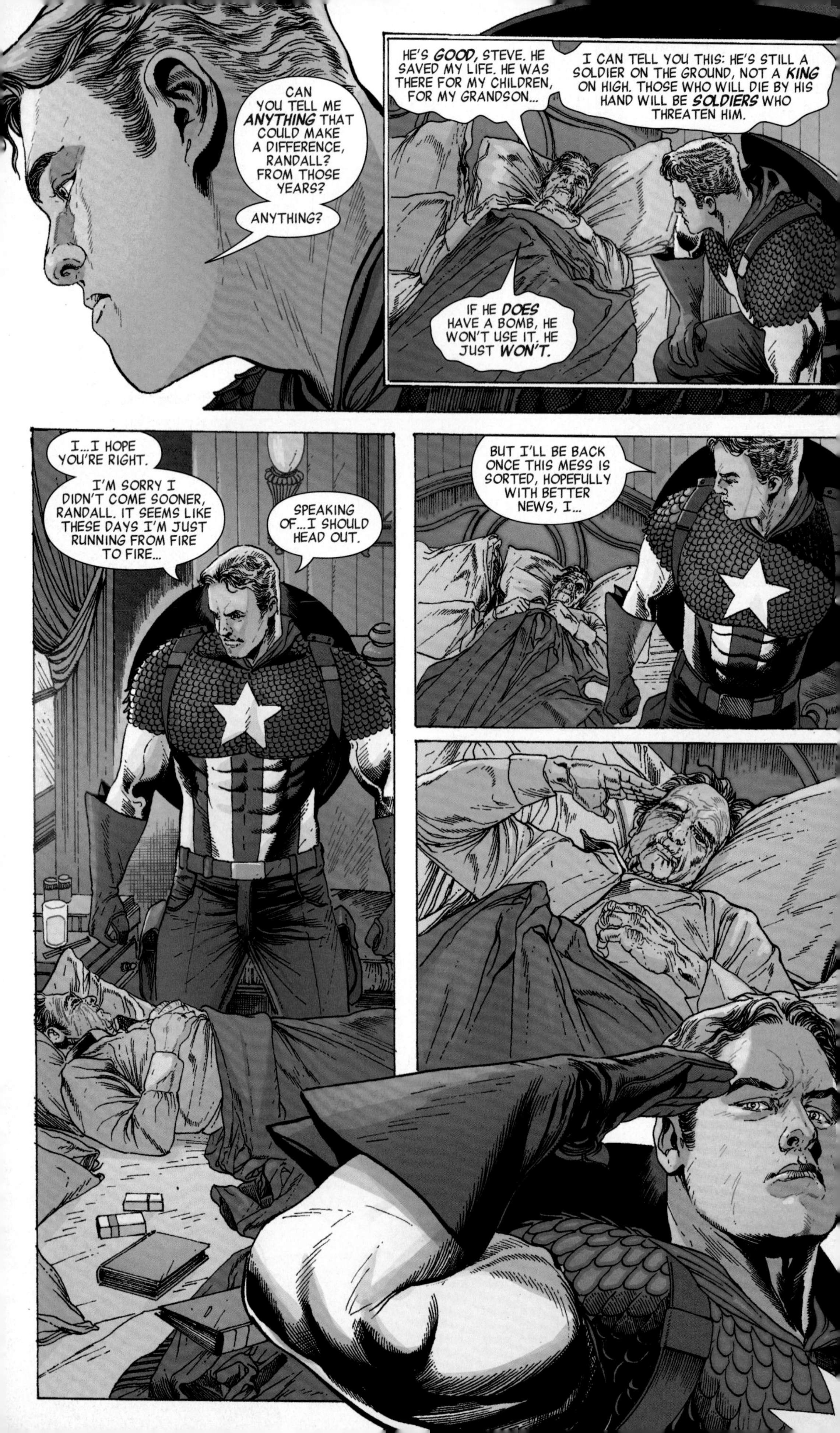
CAN YOU TELL ME ANYTHING THAT COULD MAKE A DIFFERENCE, RANDALL? FROM THOSE YEARS?
ANYTHING?
HE'S GOOD, STEVE. HE SAVED MY LIFE. HE WAS THERE FOR MY CHILDREN, FOR MY GRANDSON...
I CAN TELL YOU THIS: HE'S STILL A SOLDIER ON THE GROUND, NOT A KING ON HIGH. THOSE WHO WILL DIE BY HIS HAND WILL BE SOLDIERS WHO THREATEN HIM.
IF HE DOES HAVE A BOMB, HE WON'T USE IT. HE JUST WON'T.
I...I HOPE YOU'RE RIGHT.
I'M SORRY I DIDN'T COME SOONER, RANDALL. IT SEEMS LIKE THESE DAYS I'M JUST RUNNING FROM FIRE TO FIRE...
SPEAKING OF...I SHOULD HEAD OUT.
BUT I'LL BE BACK ONCE THIS MESS IS SORTED, HOPEFULLY WITH BETTER NEWS, I...

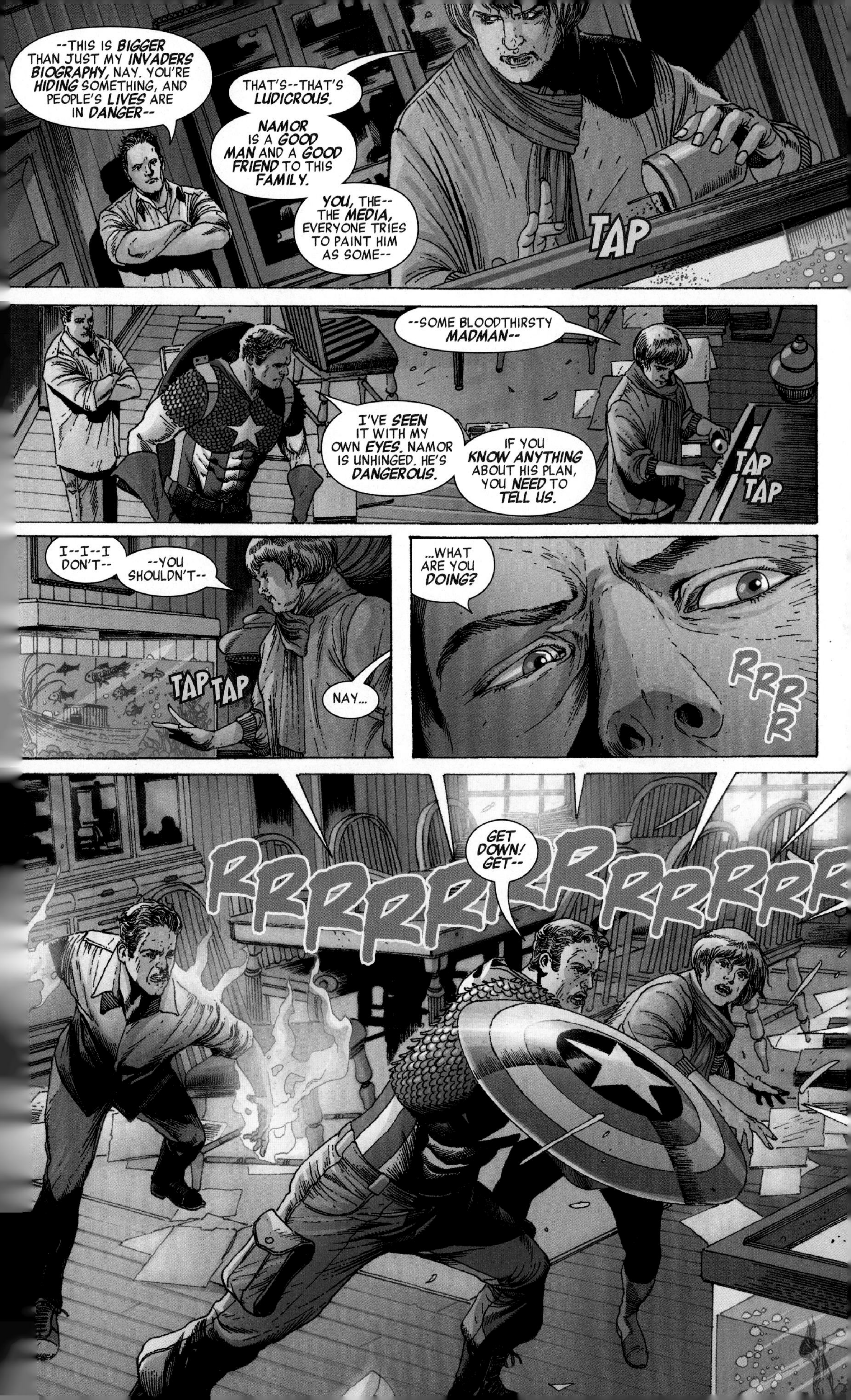
--THIS IS BIGGER THAN JUST MY INVADERS BIOGRAPHY, NAY. YOU'RE HIDING SOMETHING, AND PEOPLE'S LIVES ARE IN DANGER--
THAT'S--THAT'S LUDICROUS.
NAMOR IS A GOOD MAN AND A GOOD FRIEND TO THIS FAMILY.
YOU, THE-- THE MEDIA, EVERYONE TRIES TO PAINT HIM AS SOME--
TAP
--SOME BLOODTHIRSTY MADMAN--
I'VE SEEN IT WITH MY OWN EYES. NAMOR IS UNHINGED. HE'S DANGEROUS.
IF YOU KNOW ANYTHING ABOUT HIS PLAN, YOU NEED TO TELL US.
TAP TAP
I--I--I DON'T--
--YOU SHOULDN'T--
TAP TAP
NAY...
...WHAT ARE YOU DOING?
RRRR
GET DOWN! GET--
RRRRRRRRRRRRRR

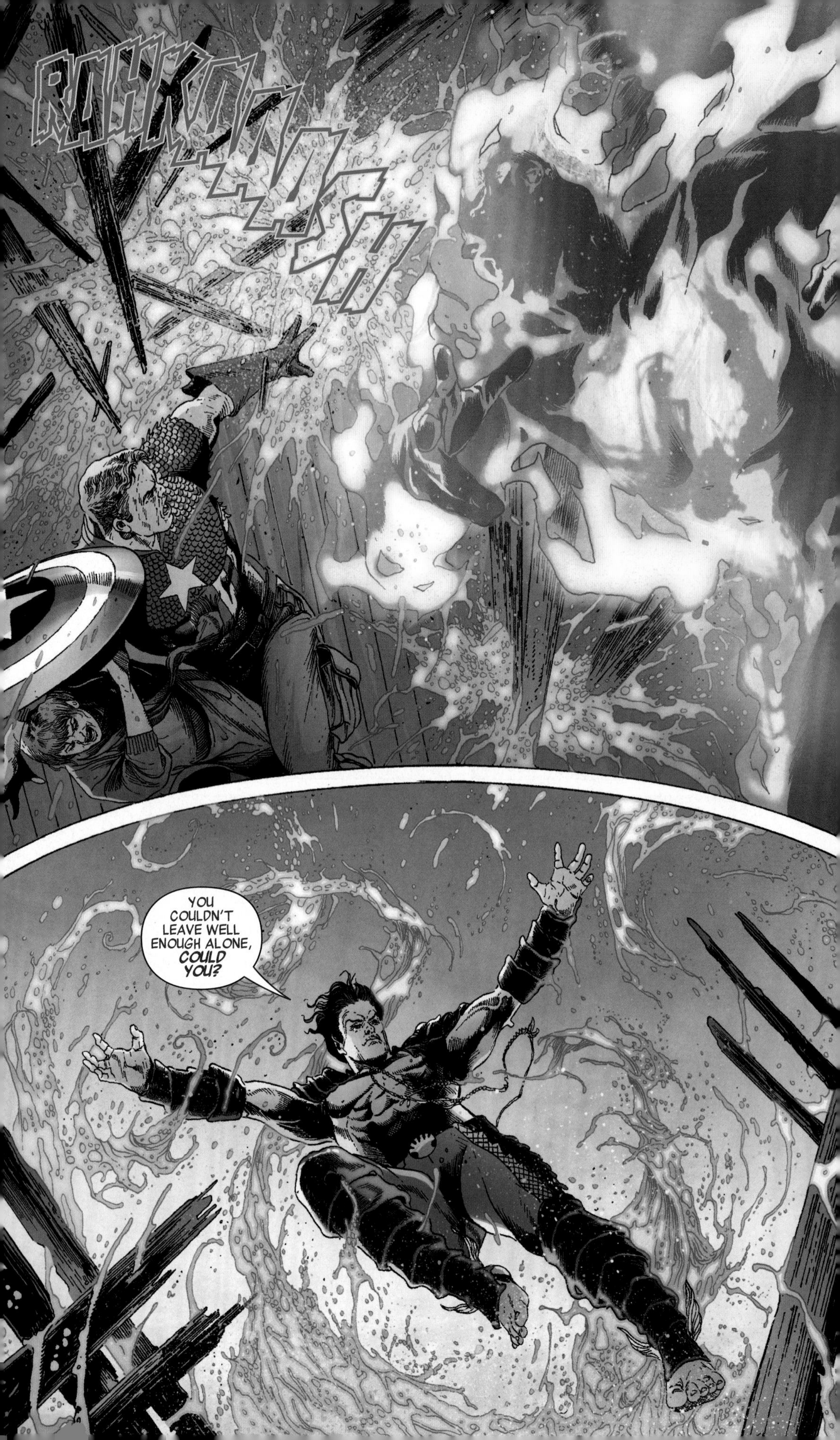
YOU COULDN'T LEAVE WELL ENOUGH ALONE, COULD YOU?

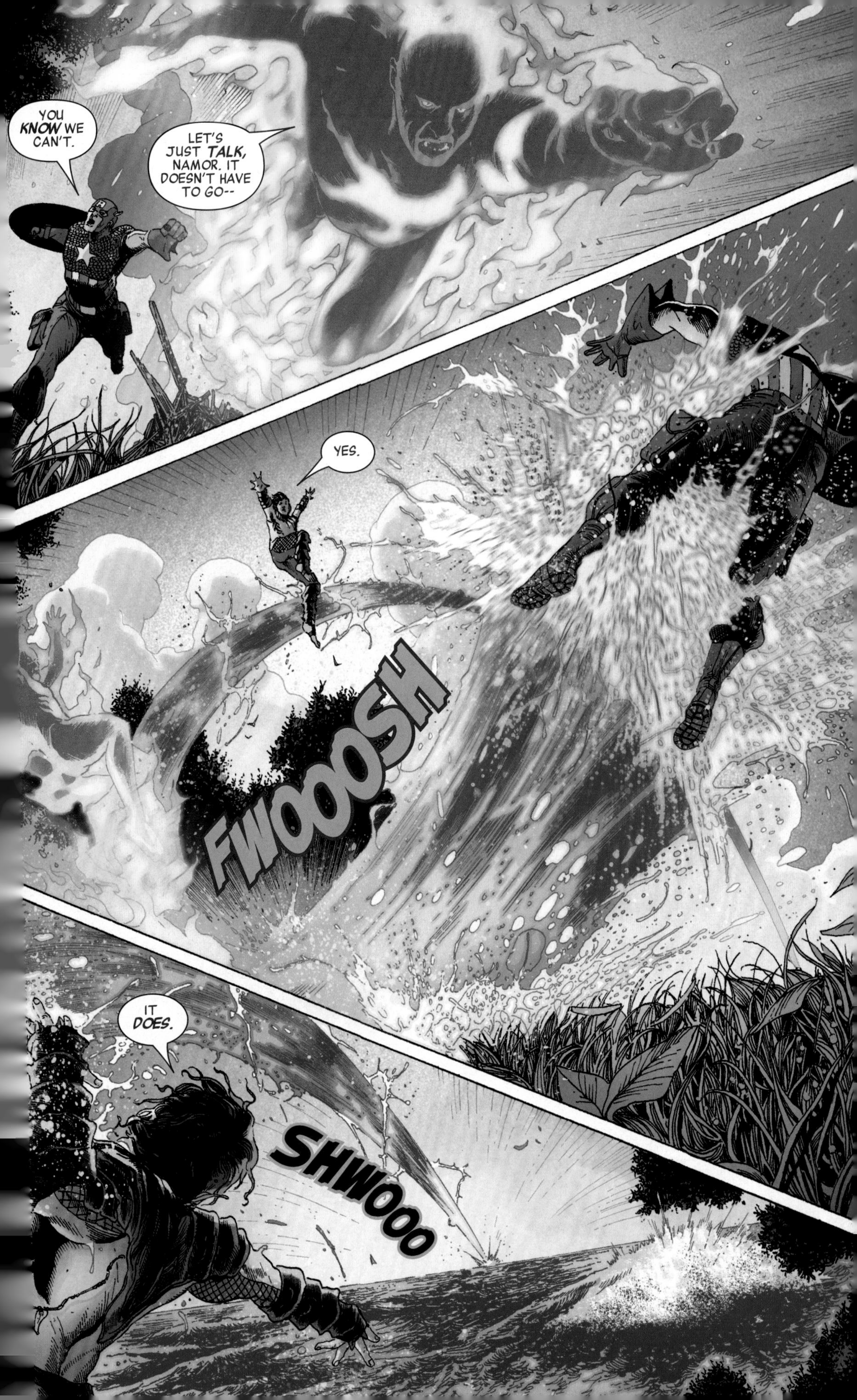
LET'S JUST TALK, NAMOR. IT DOESN'T HAVE TO GO--
YOU KNOW WE CAN'T.
YES.
FWOOOSH
IT DOES.
SHWOOO

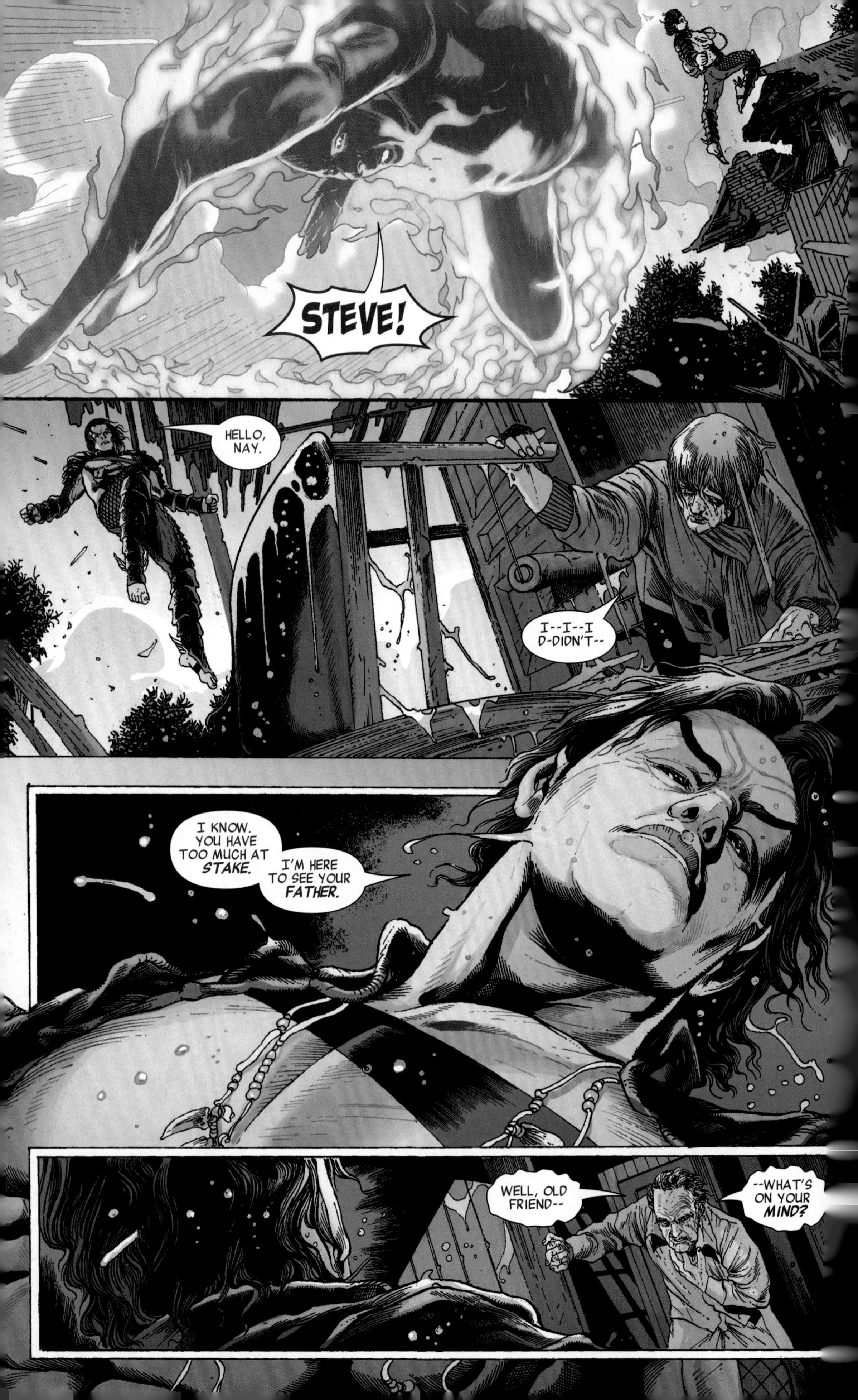
STEVE!
HELLO, NAY.
I--I--I D-DIDN'T--
I KNOW. YOU HAVE TOO MUCH AT STAKE.
I'M HERE TO SEE YOUR FATHER.
WELL, OLD FRIEND--
--WHAT'S ON YOUR MIND?

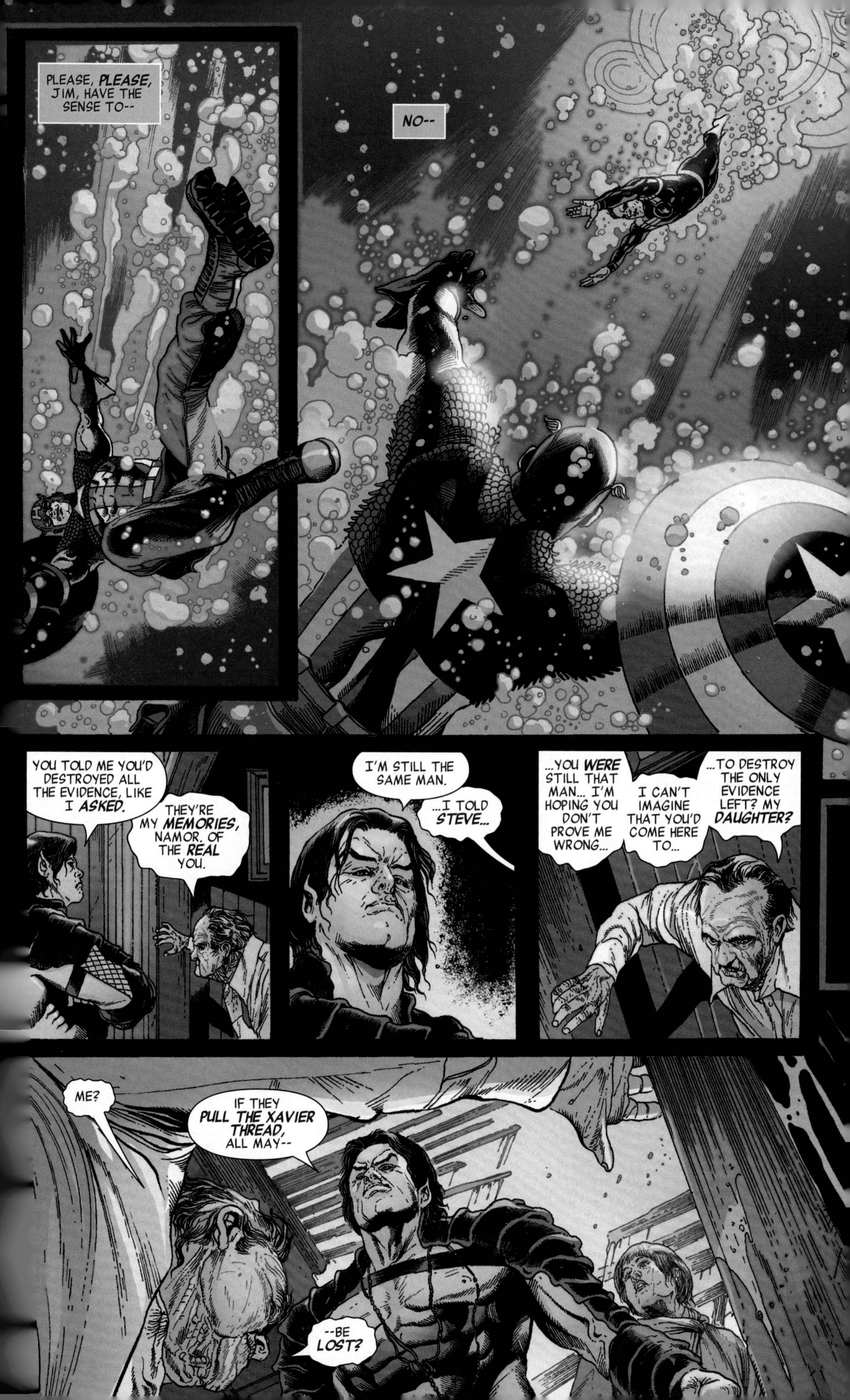

PLEASE, PLEASE, JIM, HAVE THE SENSE TO--
NO--
YOU TOLD ME YOU'D DESTROYED ALL THE EVIDENCE, LIKE I ASKED.
THEY'RE MY MEMORIES, NAMOR. OF THE REAL YOU.
I'M STILL THE SAME MAN.
...I TOLD STEVE...
...YOU WERE STILL THAT MAN... I'M HOPING YOU DON'T PROVE ME WRONG...
I CAN'T IMAGINE THAT YOU'D COME HERE TO...
...TO DESTROY THE ONLY EVIDENCE LEFT? MY DAUGHTER?
ME?
IF THEY PULL THE XAVIER THREAD, ALL MAY--
--BE LOST?

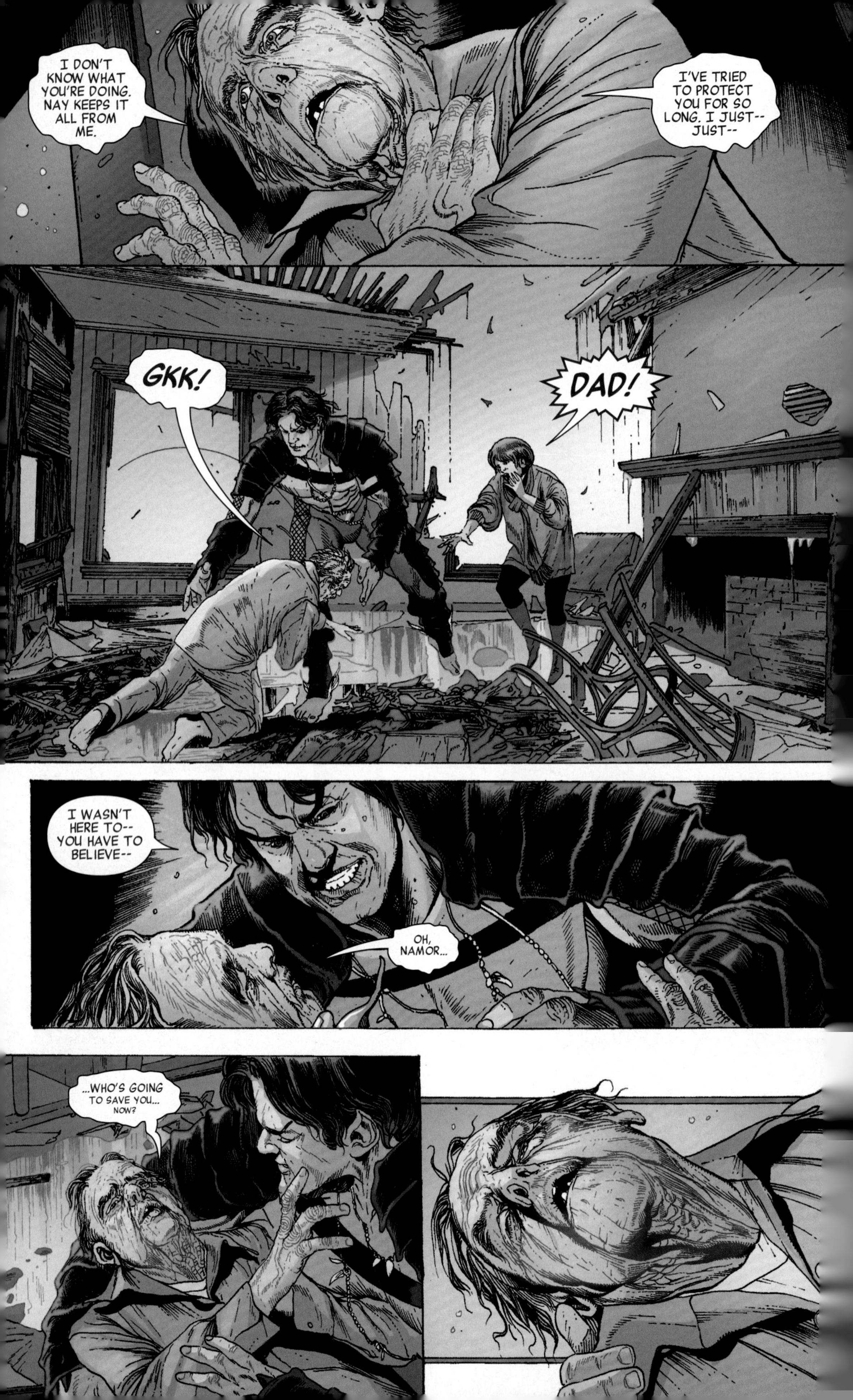
I DON'T KNOW WHAT YOU'RE DOING. NAY KEEPS IT ALL FROM ME.
I'VE TRIED TO PROTECT YOU FOR SO LONG. I JUST-- JUST--
GKK!
DAD!
I WASN'T HERE TO-- YOU HAVE TO BELIEVE--
OH, NAMOR...
...WHO'S GOING TO SAVE YOU... NOW?

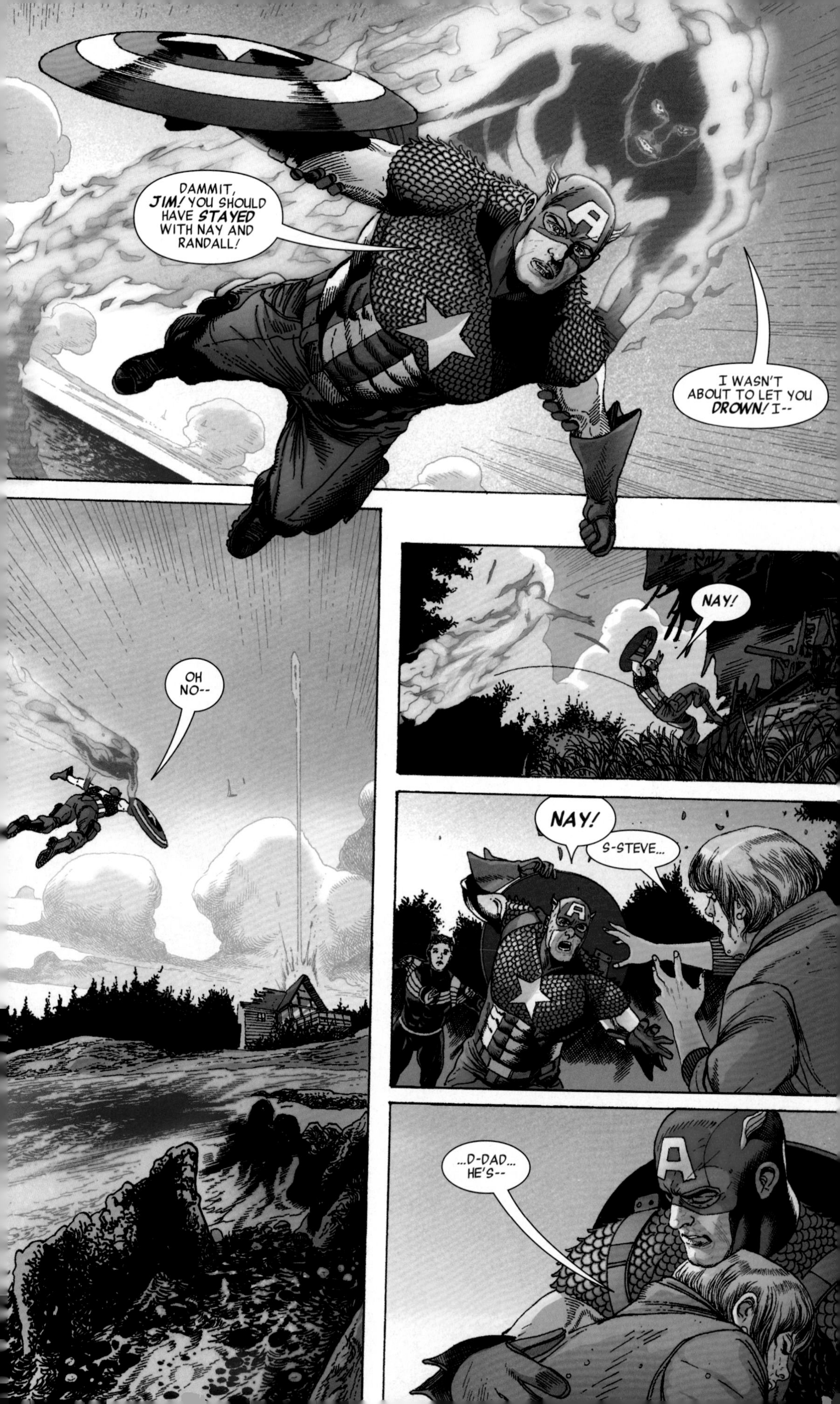
DAMMIT, JIM! YOU SHOULD HAVE STAYED WITH NAY AND RANDALL!
I WASN'T ABOUT TO LET YOU DROWN! I--
OH NO--
NAY!
NAY!
S-STEVE...
...D-DAD... HE'S--

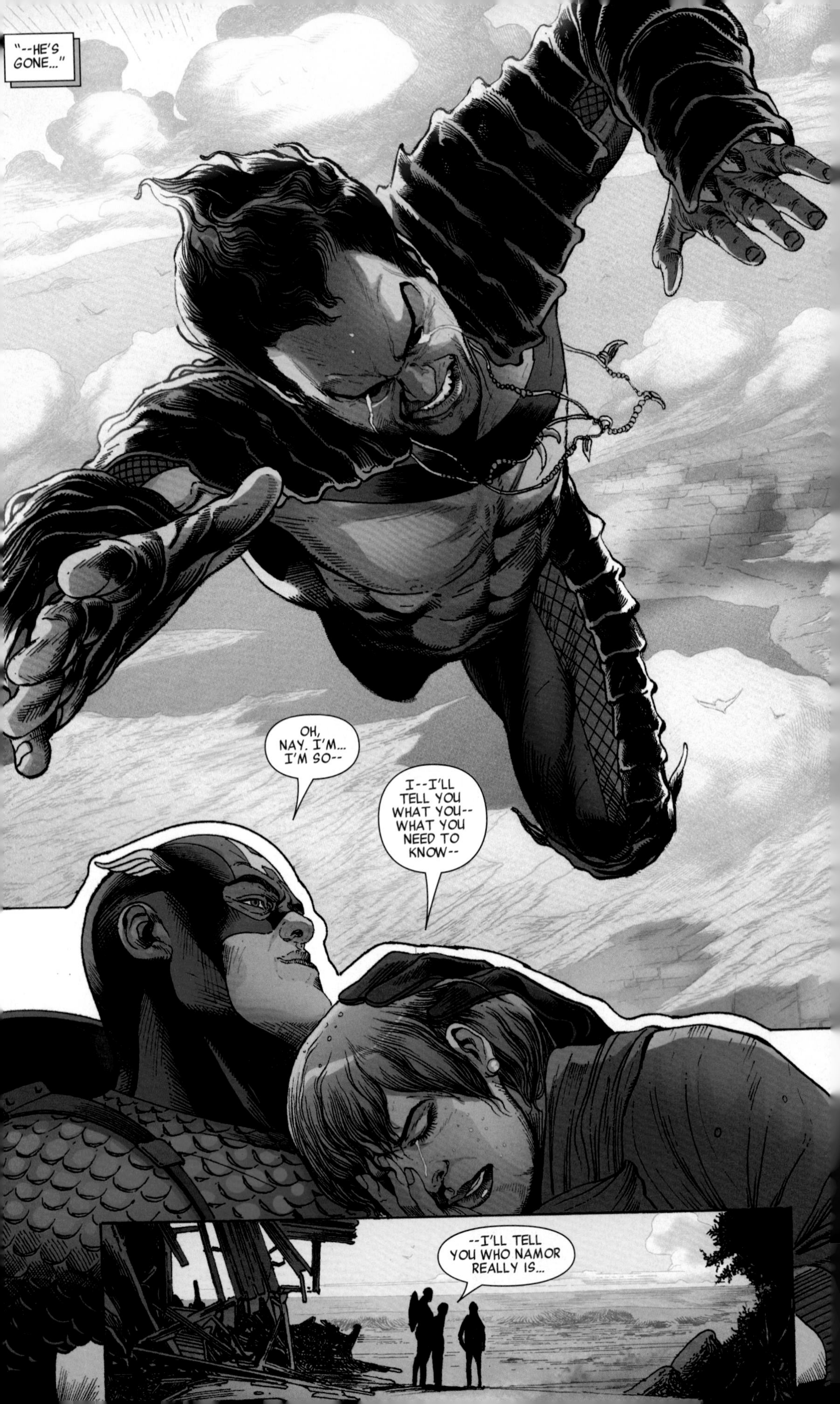
"--HE'S GONE..."
OH, NAY. I'M... I'M SO--
I--I'LL TELL YOU WHAT YOU--WHAT YOU NEED TO KNOW--
--I'LL TELL YOU WHO NAMOR REALLY IS...

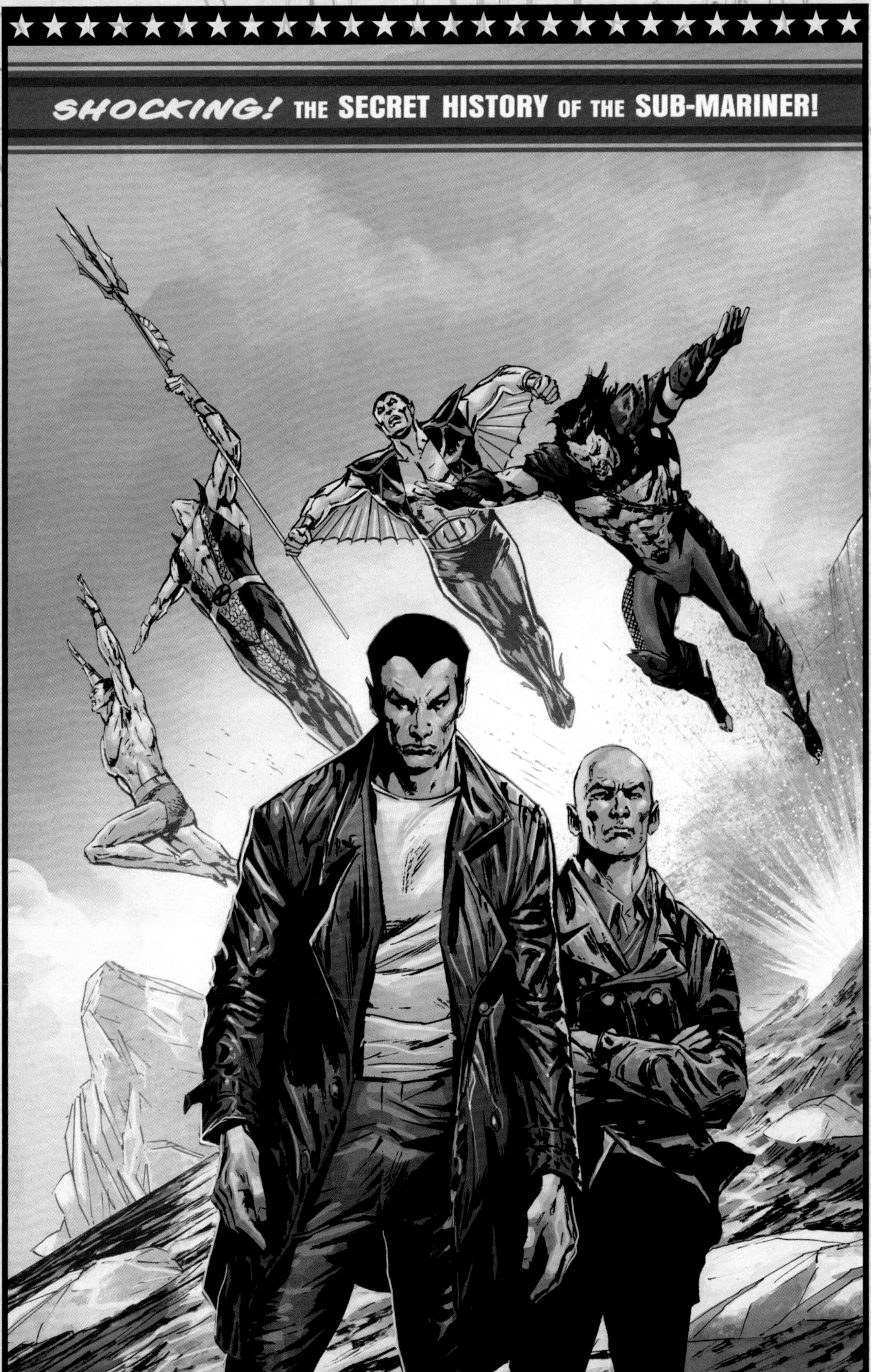
SHOCKING! THE SECRET HISTORY OF THE SUB-MARINER!

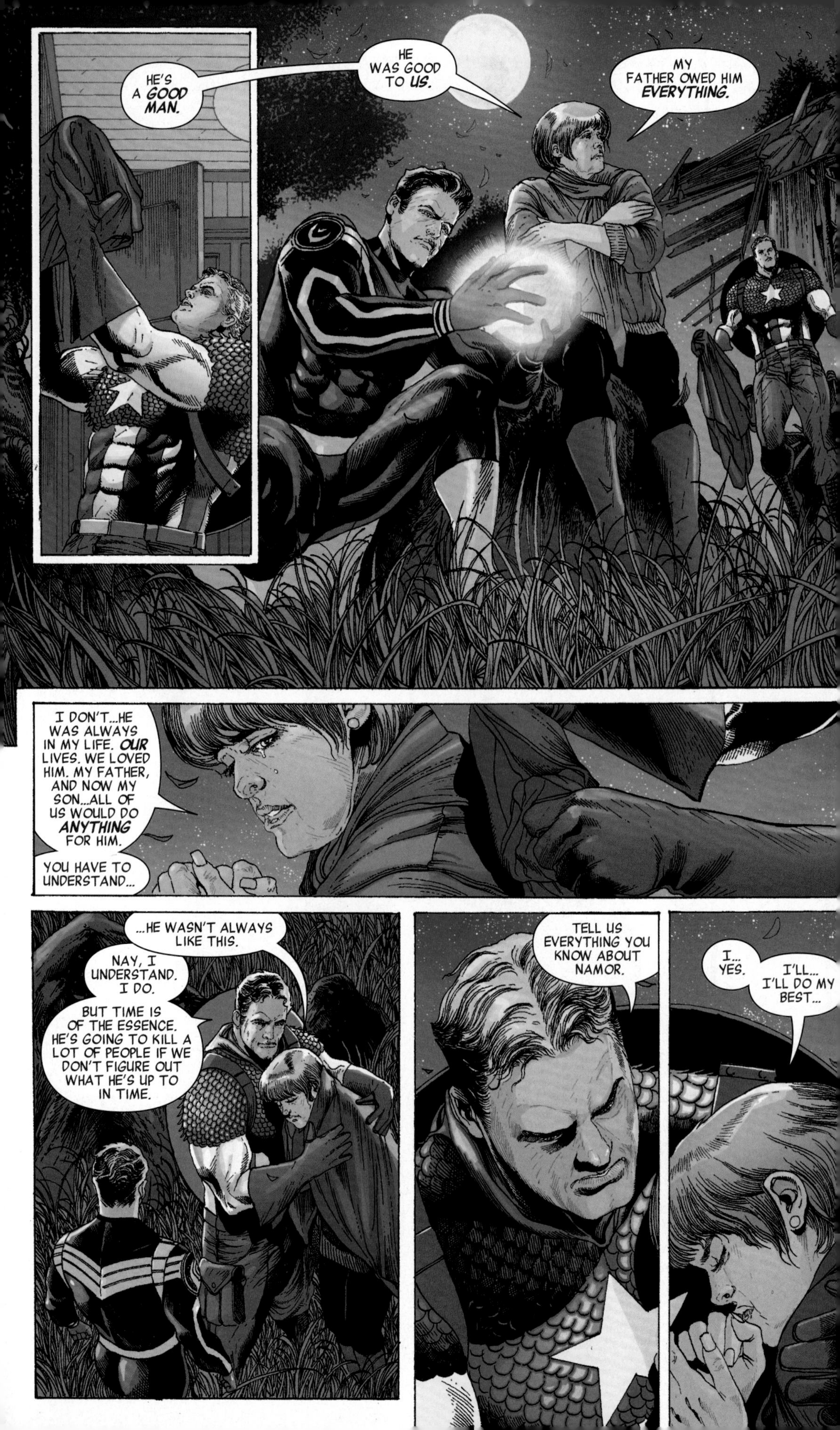
HE'S A GOOD MAN.
HE WAS GOOD TO US.
MY FATHER OWED HIM EVERYTHING.
I DON'T...HE WAS ALWAYS IN MY LIFE. OUR LIVES. WE LOVED HIM. MY FATHER, AND NOW MY SON...ALL OF US WOULD DO ANYTHING FOR HIM.
YOU HAVE TO UNDERSTAND...
...HE WASN'T ALWAYS LIKE THIS.
NAY, I UNDERSTAND. I DO.
BUT TIME IS OF THE ESSENCE. HE'S GOING TO KILL A LOT OF PEOPLE IF WE DON'T FIGURE OUT WHAT HE'S UP TO IN TIME.
TELL US EVERYTHING YOU KNOW ABOUT NAMOR.
I... YES.
I'LL... I'LL DO MY BEST...

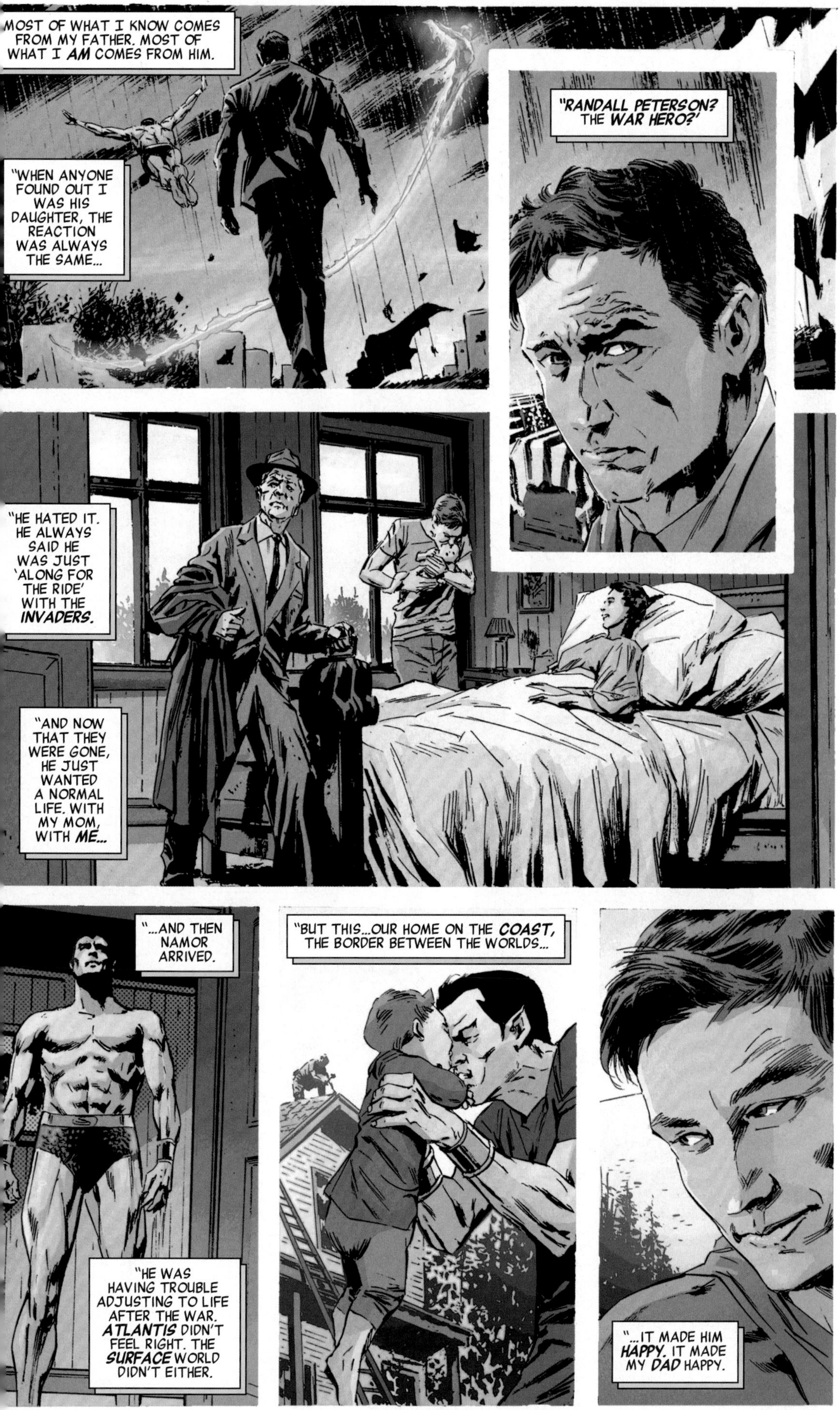
MOST OF WHAT I KNOW COMES FROM MY FATHER. MOST OF WHAT I AM COMES FROM HIM.
"WHEN ANYONE FOUND OUT I WAS HIS DAUGHTER, THE REACTION WAS ALWAYS THE SAME...
"RANDALL PETERSON? THE WAR HERO?'
"HE HATED IT. HE ALWAYS SAID HE WAS JUST 'ALONG FOR THE RIDE' WITH THE INVADERS.
"AND NOW THAT THEY WERE GONE, HE JUST WANTED A NORMAL LIFE. WITH MY MOM, WITH ME...
"...AND THEN NAMOR ARRIVED.
"HE WAS HAVING TROUBLE ADJUSTING TO LIFE AFTER THE WAR. ATLANTIS DIDN'T FEEL RIGHT. THE SURFACE WORLD DIDN'T EITHER.
"BUT THIS...OUR HOME ON THE COAST, THE BORDER BETWEEN THE WORLDS...
"...IT MADE HIM HAPPY. IT MADE MY DAD HAPPY.

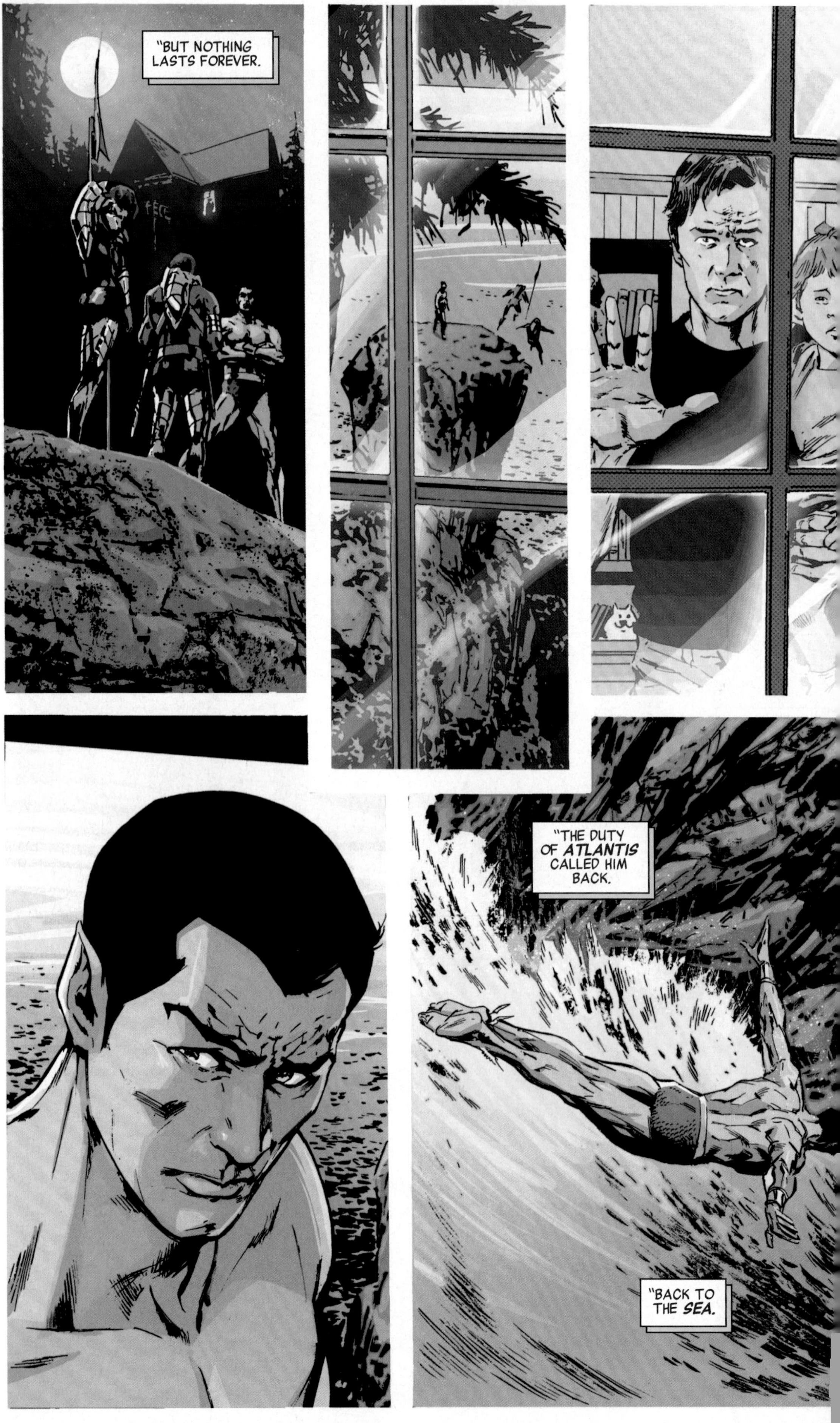
"BUT NOTHING LASTS FOREVER.
"THE DUTY OF ATLANTIS CALLED HIM BACK.
"BACK TO THE SEA.

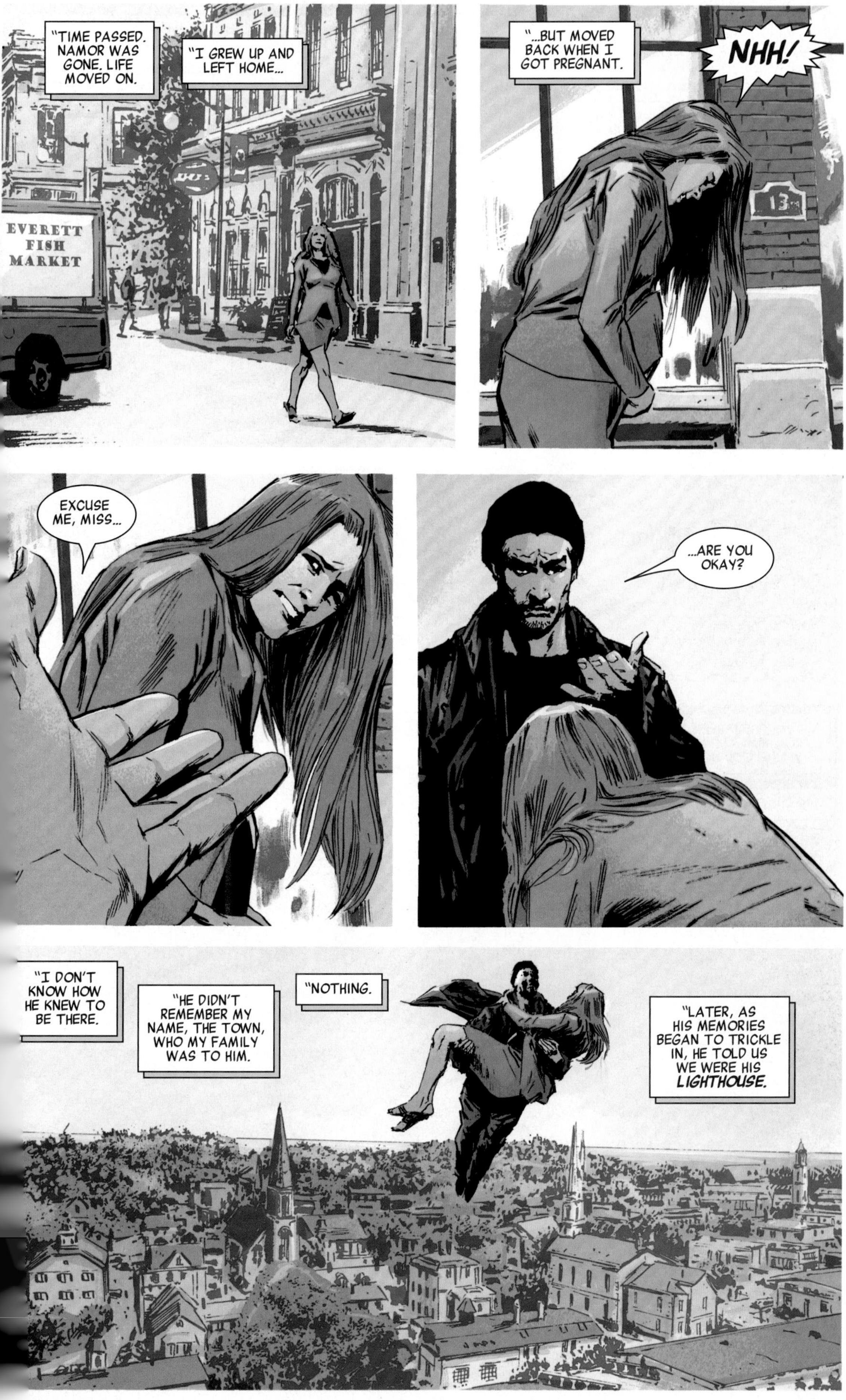
"TIME PASSED. NAMOR WAS GONE. LIFE MOVED ON.
"I GREW UP AND LEFT HOME...
EVERETT FISH MARKET
"...BUT MOVED BACK WHEN I GOT PREGNANT.
NHH!
EXCUSE ME, MISS...
...ARE YOU OKAY?
"I DON'T KNOW HOW HE KNEW TO BE THERE.
"HE DIDN'T REMEMBER MY NAME, THE TOWN, WHO MY FAMILY WAS TO HIM.
"NOTHING.
"LATER, AS HIS MEMORIES BEGAN TO TRICKLE IN, HE TOLD US WE WERE HIS LIGHTHOUSE.

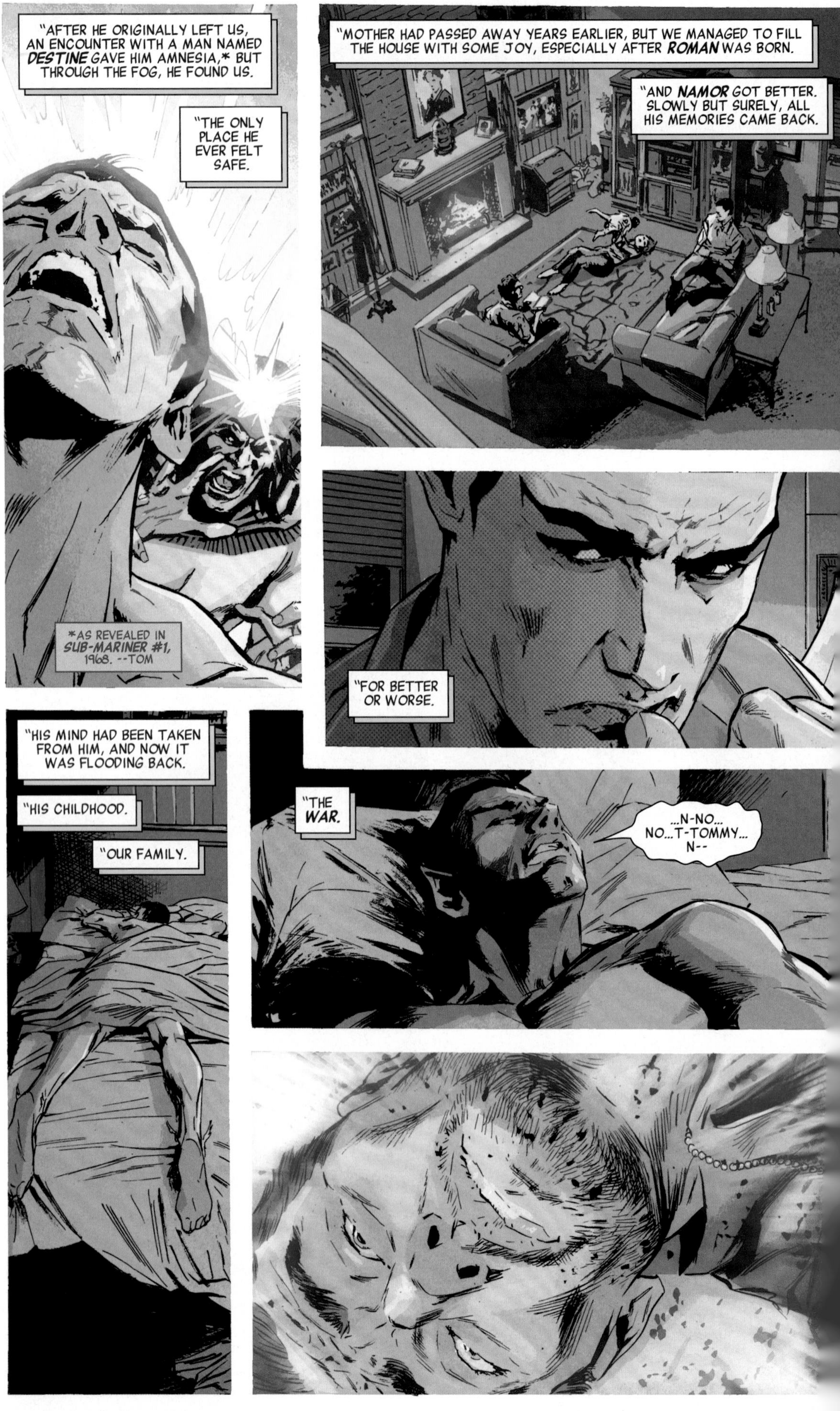
"AFTER HE ORIGINALLY LEFT US, AN ENCOUNTER WITH A MAN NAMED DESTINE GAVE HIM AMNESIA,* BUT THROUGH THE FOG, HE FOUND US.
"THE ONLY PLACE HE EVER FELT SAFE.
*AS REVEALED IN SUB-MARINER #1, 1968. --TOM
"MOTHER HAD PASSED AWAY YEARS EARLIER, BUT WE MANAGED TO FILL THE HOUSE WITH SOME JOY, ESPECIALLY AFTER ROMAN WAS BORN.
"AND NAMOR GOT BETTER. SLOWLY BUT SURELY, ALL HIS MEMORIES CAME BACK.
"FOR BETTER OR WORSE.
"HIS MIND HAD BEEN TAKEN FROM HIM, AND NOW IT WAS FLOODING BACK.
"HIS CHILDHOOD.
"OUR FAMILY.
"THE WAR.
...N-NO... NO...T-TOMMY... N--

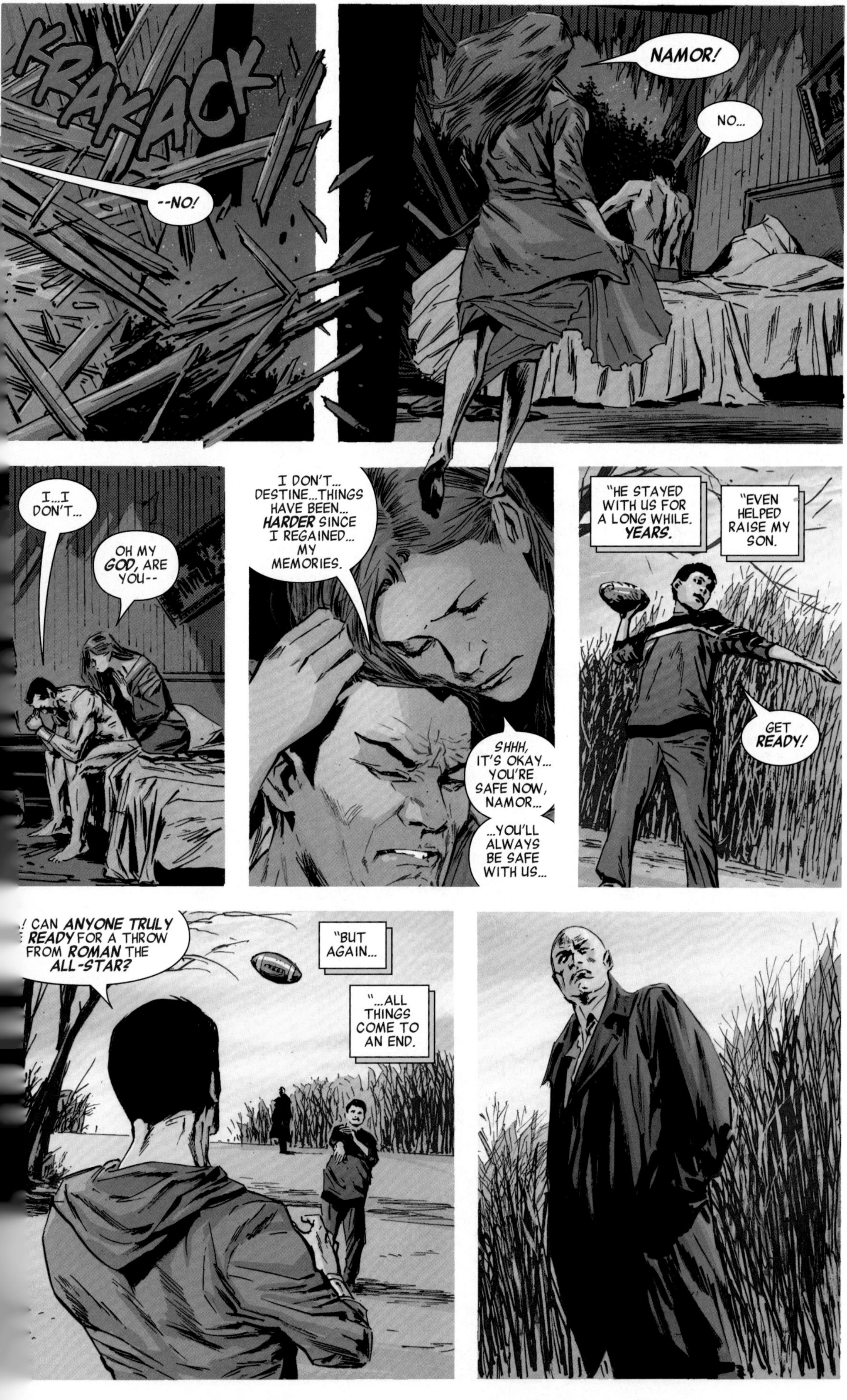
KRAKACK
--NO!
NAMOR!
NO...
I...I DON'T...
OH MY GOD, ARE YOU--
I DON'T... DESTINE...THINGS HAVE BEEN... HARDER SINCE I REGAINED... MY MEMORIES.
SHHH, IT'S OKAY... YOU'RE SAFE NOW, NAMOR...
...YOU'LL ALWAYS BE SAFE WITH US...
"HE STAYED WITH US FOR A LONG WHILE. YEARS.
"EVEN HELPED RAISE MY SON.
GET READY!
CAN ANYONE TRULY READY FOR A THROW FROM ROMAN THE ALL-STAR?
"BUT AGAIN...
"...ALL THINGS COME TO AN END.

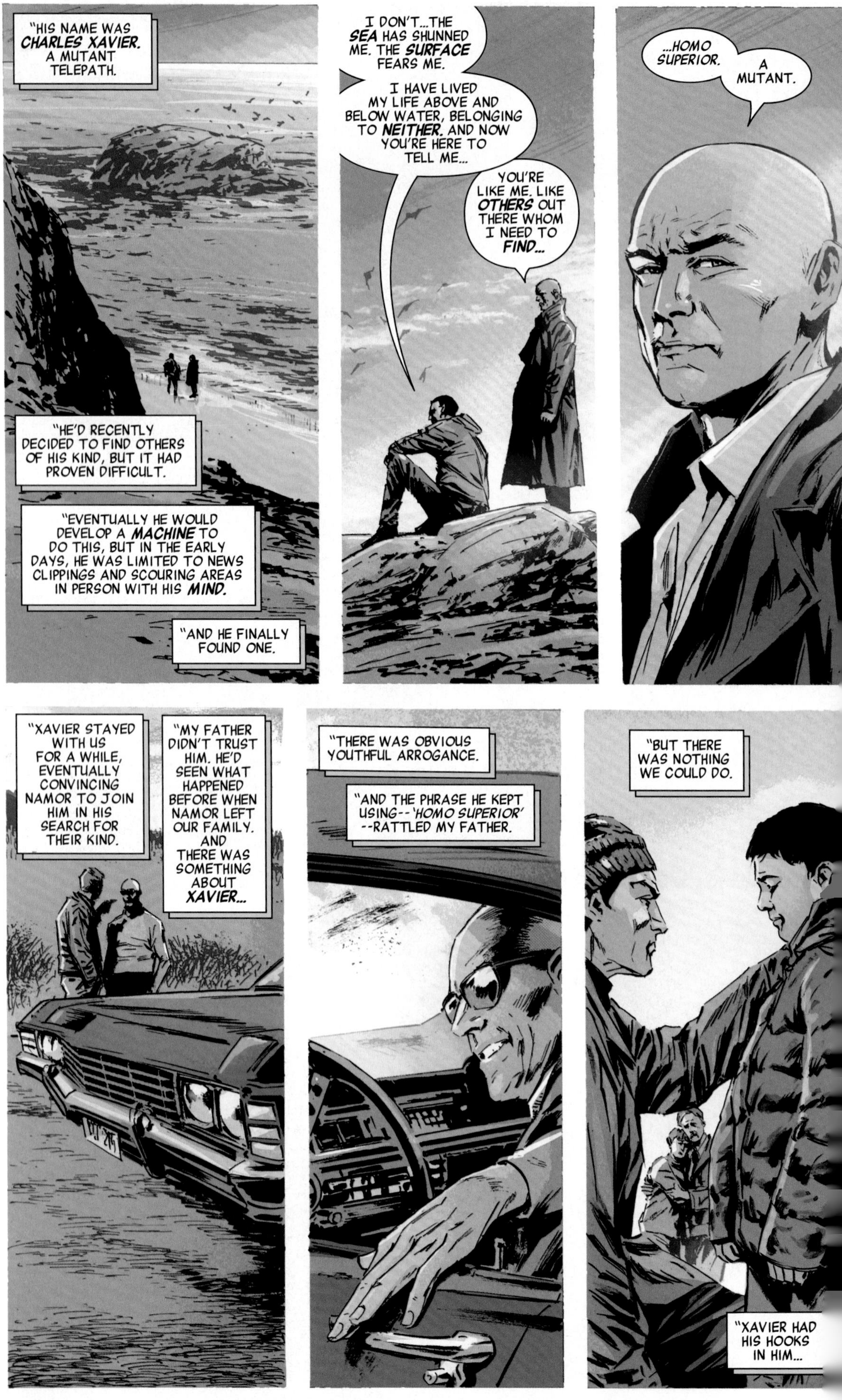
"HIS NAME WAS CHARLES XAVIER. A MUTANT TELEPATH.
"HE'D RECENTLY DECIDED TO FIND OTHERS OF HIS KIND, BUT IT HAD PROVEN DIFFICULT.
"EVENTUALLY HE WOULD DEVELOP A MACHINE TO DO THIS, BUT IN THE EARLY DAYS, HE WAS LIMITED TO NEWS CLIPPINGS AND SCOURING AREAS IN PERSON WITH HIS MIND.
"AND HE FINALLY FOUND ONE.
I DON'T...THE SEA HAS SHUNNED ME. THE SURFACE FEARS ME.
I HAVE LIVED MY LIFE ABOVE AND BELOW WATER, BELONGING TO NEITHER. AND NOW YOU'RE HERE TO TELL ME...
YOU'RE LIKE ME. LIKE OTHERS OUT THERE WHOM I NEED TO FIND...
...HOMO SUPERIOR.
A MUTANT.
"XAVIER STAYED WITH US FOR A WHILE, EVENTUALLY CONVINCING NAMOR TO JOIN HIM IN HIS SEARCH FOR THEIR KIND.
"MY FATHER DIDN'T TRUST HIM. HE'D SEEN WHAT HAPPENED BEFORE WHEN NAMOR LEFT OUR FAMILY. AND THERE WAS SOMETHING ABOUT XAVIER...
"THERE WAS OBVIOUS YOUTHFUL ARROGANCE.
"AND THE PHRASE HE KEPT USING--'HOMO SUPERIOR' --RATTLED MY FATHER.
"BUT THERE WAS NOTHING WE COULD DO.
"XAVIER HAD HIS HOOKS IN HIM...

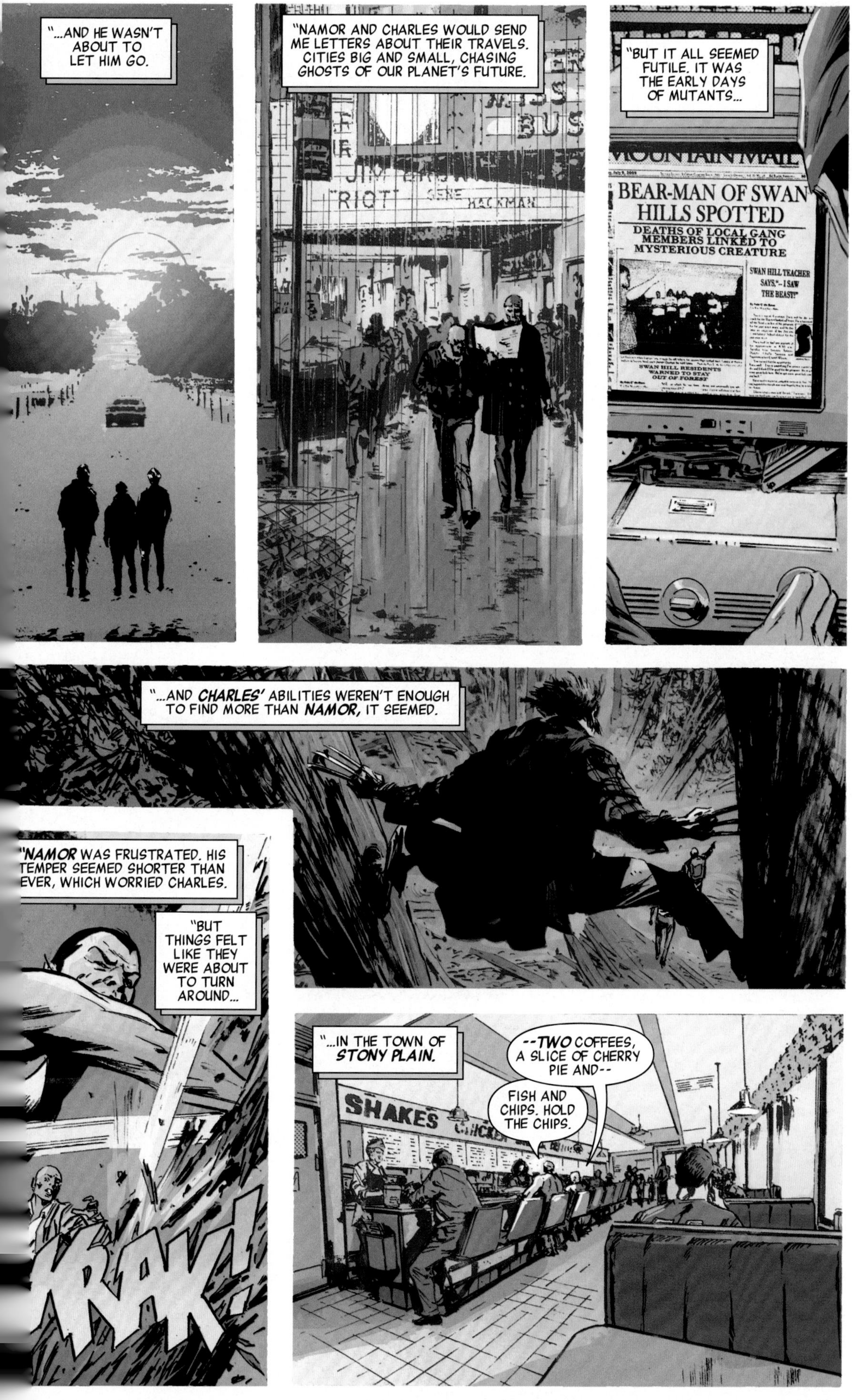
"...AND HE WASN'T ABOUT TO LET HIM GO.
"NAMOR AND CHARLES WOULD SEND ME LETTERS ABOUT THEIR TRAVELS. CITIES BIG AND SMALL, CHASING GHOSTS OF OUR PLANET'S FUTURE.
"RIOT"
GENE HACKMAN
"BUT IT ALL SEEMED FUTILE. IT WAS THE EARLY DAYS OF MUTANTS...
MOUNTAIN MAIL
BEAR-MAN OF SWAN HILLS SPOTTED
DEATHS OF LOCAL GANG MEMBERS LINKED TO MYSTERIOUS CREATURE
SWAN HILL TEACHER SAYS,"--I SAW THE BEAST!"
SWAN HILL RESIDENTS WARNED TO STAY OUT OF FOREST
"...AND CHARLES' ABILITIES WEREN'T ENOUGH TO FIND MORE THAN NAMOR, IT SEEMED.
"NAMOR WAS FRUSTRATED. HIS TEMPER SEEMED SHORTER THAN EVER, WHICH WORRIED CHARLES.
"BUT THINGS FELT LIKE THEY WERE ABOUT TO TURN AROUND...
RAK!
"...IN THE TOWN OF STONY PLAIN.
SHAKES
--TWO COFFEES, A SLICE OF CHERRY PIE AND--
FISH AND CHIPS. HOLD THE CHIPS.

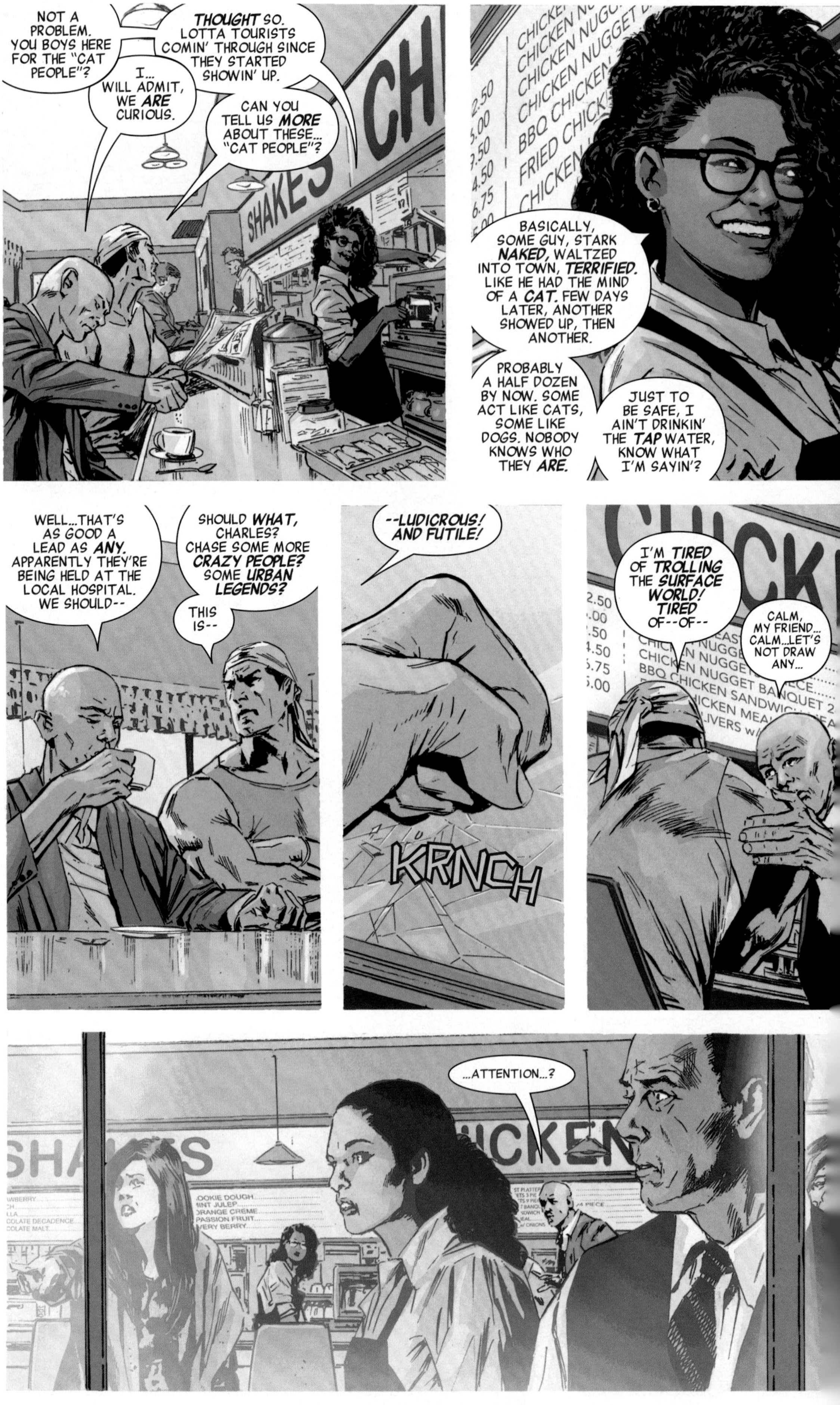

NOT A PROBLEM. YOU BOYS HERE FOR THE "CAT PEOPLE"?
I... WILL ADMIT, WE ARE CURIOUS.
THOUGHT SO. LOTTA TOURISTS COMIN' THROUGH SINCE THEY STARTED SHOWIN' UP.
CAN YOU TELL US MORE ABOUT THESE... "CAT PEOPLE"?
SHAKES
CH
BASICALLY, SOME GUY, STARK NAKED, WALTZED INTO TOWN, TERRIFIED. LIKE HE HAD THE MIND OF A CAT. FEW DAYS LATER, ANOTHER SHOWED UP, THEN ANOTHER.
PROBABLY A HALF DOZEN BY NOW. SOME ACT LIKE CATS, SOME LIKE DOGS. NOBODY KNOWS WHO THEY ARE.
JUST TO BE SAFE, I AIN'T DRINKIN' THE TAP WATER, KNOW WHAT I'M SAYIN'?
WELL...THAT'S AS GOOD A LEAD AS ANY. APPARENTLY THEY'RE BEING HELD AT THE LOCAL HOSPITAL. WE SHOULD--
SHOULD WHAT, CHARLES? CHASE SOME MORE CRAZY PEOPLE? SOME URBAN LEGENDS?
THIS IS--
--LUDICROUS! AND FUTILE!
KRNCH
I'M TIRED OF TROLLING THE SURFACE WORLD! TIRED OF--OF--
CALM, MY FRIEND... CALM...LET'S NOT DRAW ANY...
...ATTENTION...?

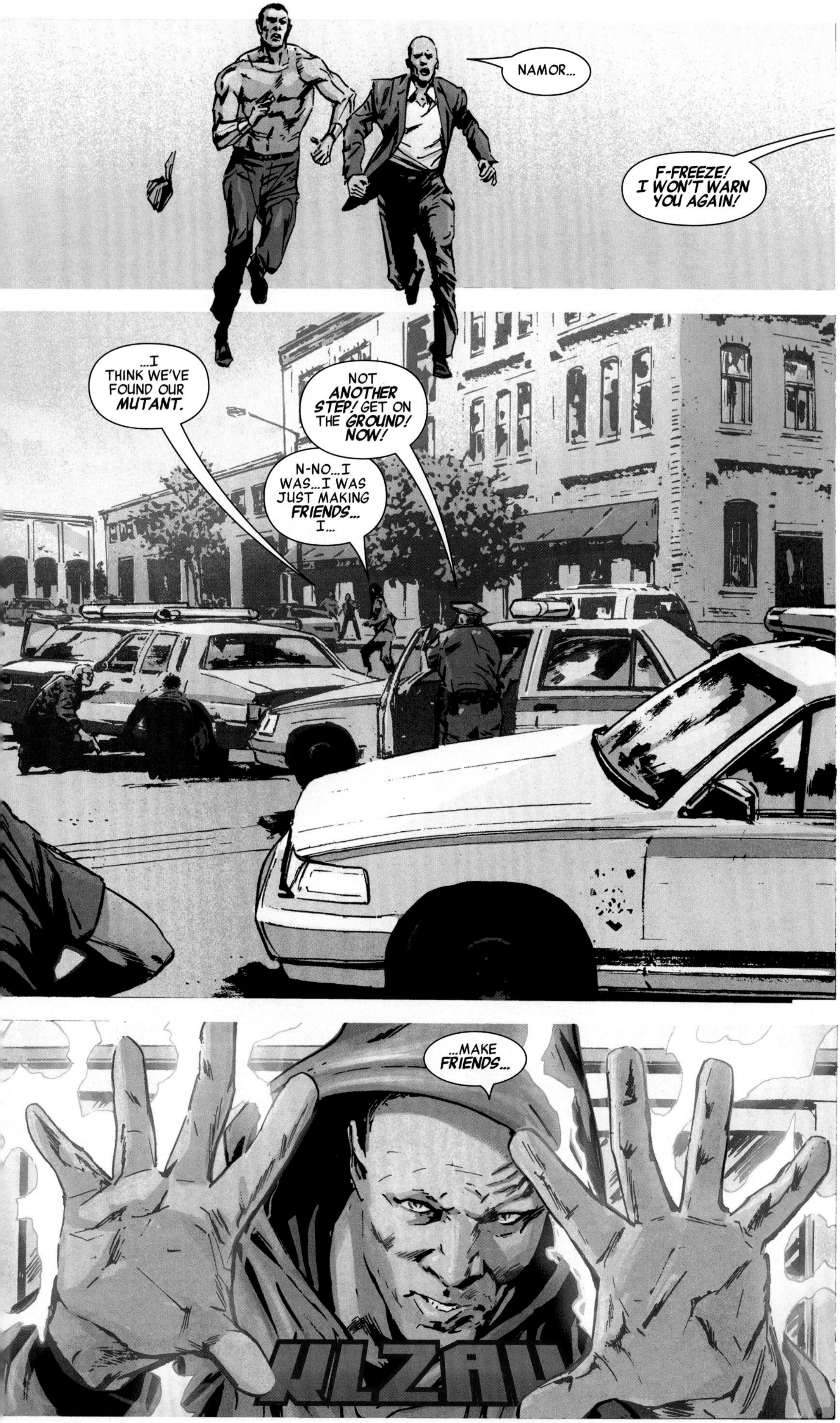
NAMOR...
F-FREEZE! I WON'T WARN YOU AGAIN!
...I THINK WE'VE FOUND OUR MUTANT.
NOT ANOTHER STEP! GET ON THE GROUND! NOW!
N-NO...I WAS...I WAS JUST MAKING FRIENDS... I...
...MAKE FRIENDS...

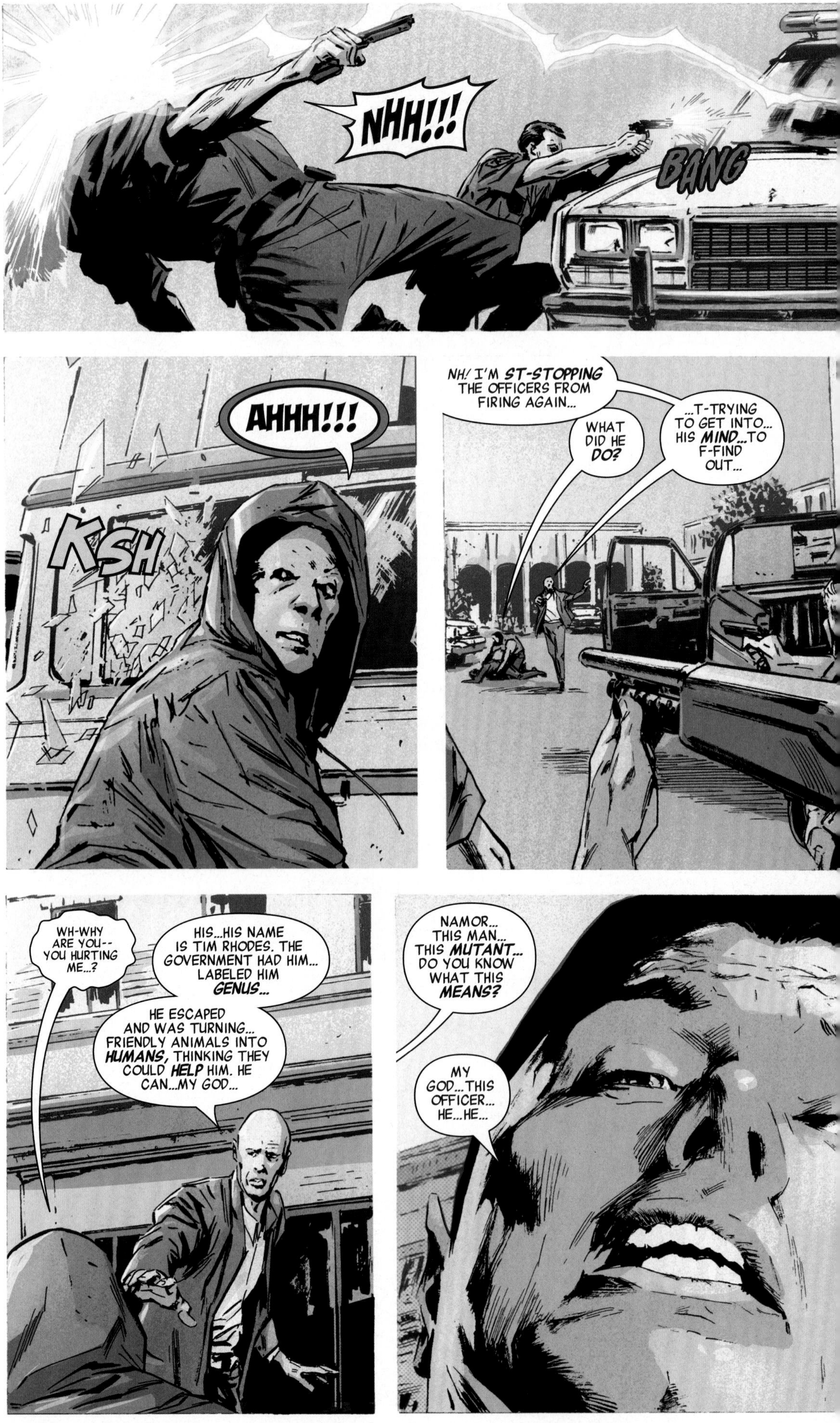
NHH!!!
BANG
AHHH!!!
KSH
NH! I'M ST-STOPPING THE OFFICERS FROM FIRING AGAIN...
WHAT DID HE DO?
...T-TRYING TO GET INTO... HIS MIND...TO F-FIND OUT...
WH-WHY ARE YOU-- YOU HURTING ME...?
HIS...HIS NAME IS TIM RHODES. THE GOVERNMENT HAD HIM... LABELED HIM GENUS...
HE ESCAPED AND WAS TURNING... FRIENDLY ANIMALS INTO HUMANS, THINKING THEY COULD HELP HIM. HE CAN...MY GOD...
NAMOR... THIS MAN... THIS MUTANT... DO YOU KNOW WHAT THIS MEANS?
MY GOD...THIS OFFICER... HE...HE...

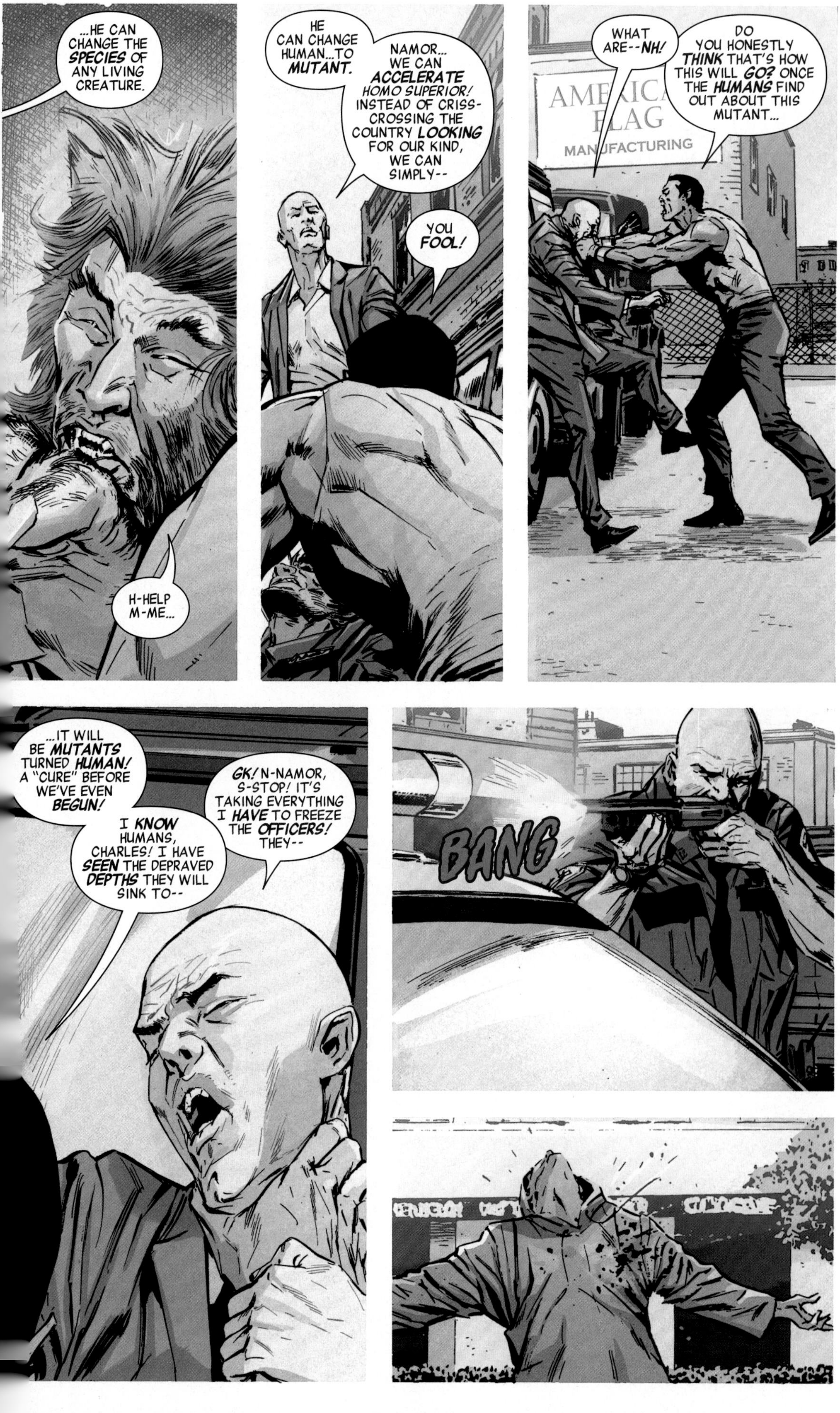
...HE CAN CHANGE THE SPECIES OF ANY LIVING CREATURE.
H-HELP M-ME...
HE CAN CHANGE HUMAN...TO MUTANT.
NAMOR... WE CAN ACCELERATE HOMO SUPERIOR! INSTEAD OF CRISS-CROSSING THE COUNTRY LOOKING FOR OUR KIND, WE CAN SIMPLY--
YOU FOOL!
WHAT ARE--NH!
DO YOU HONESTLY THINK THAT'S HOW THIS WILL GO? ONCE THE HUMANS FIND OUT ABOUT THIS MUTANT...
...IT WILL BE MUTANTS TURNED HUMAN! A "CURE" BEFORE WE'VE EVEN BEGUN!
I KNOW HUMANS, CHARLES! I HAVE SEEN THE DEPRAVED DEPTHS THEY WILL SINK TO--
GK! N-NAMOR, S-STOP! IT'S TAKING EVERYTHING I HAVE TO FREEZE THE OFFICERS! THEY--
BANG

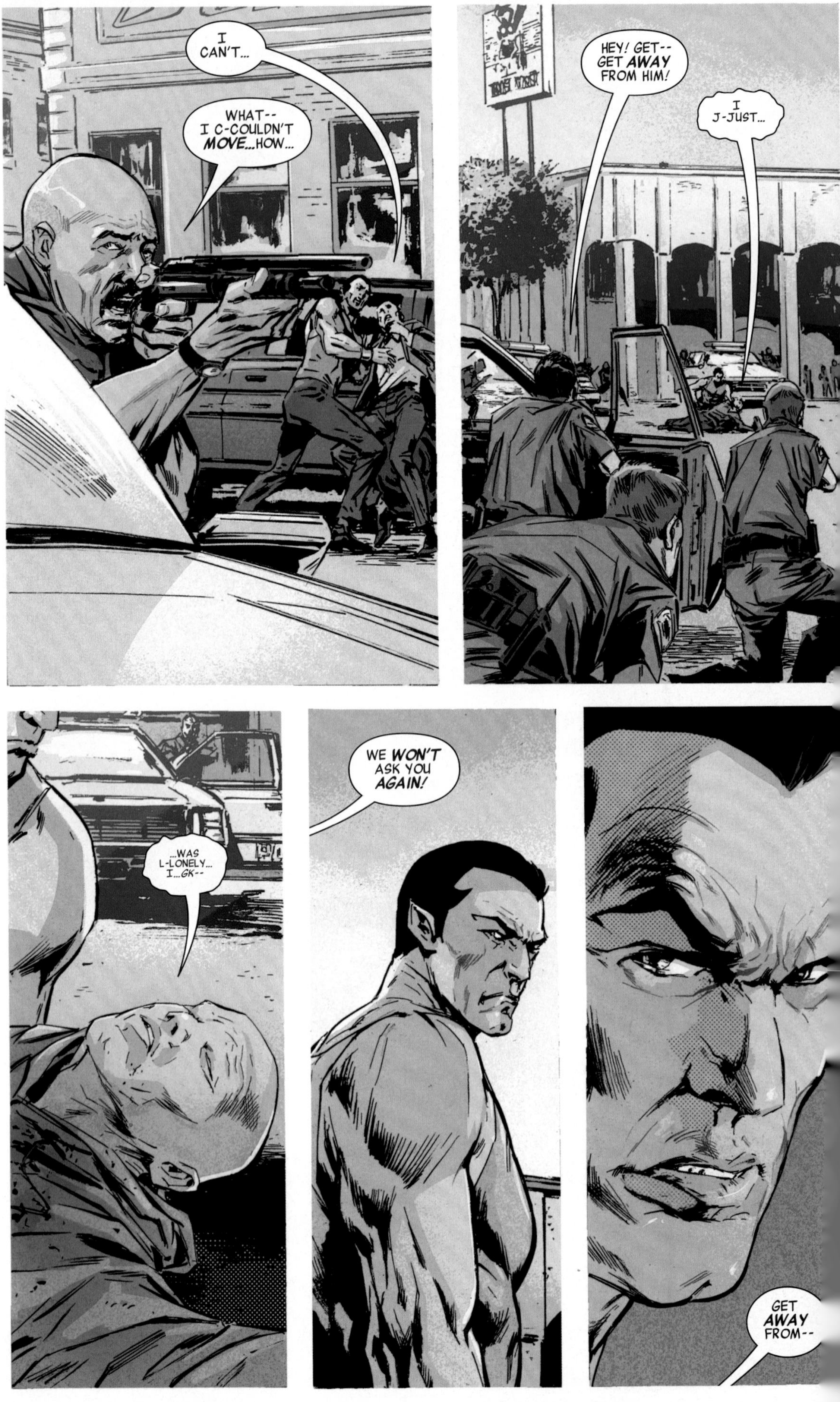
I CAN'T...
WHAT-- I C-COULDN'T MOVE...HOW...
HEY! GET-- GET AWAY FROM HIM!
I J-JUST...
...WAS L-LONELY... I...GK--
WE WON'T ASK YOU AGAIN!
GET AWAY FROM--

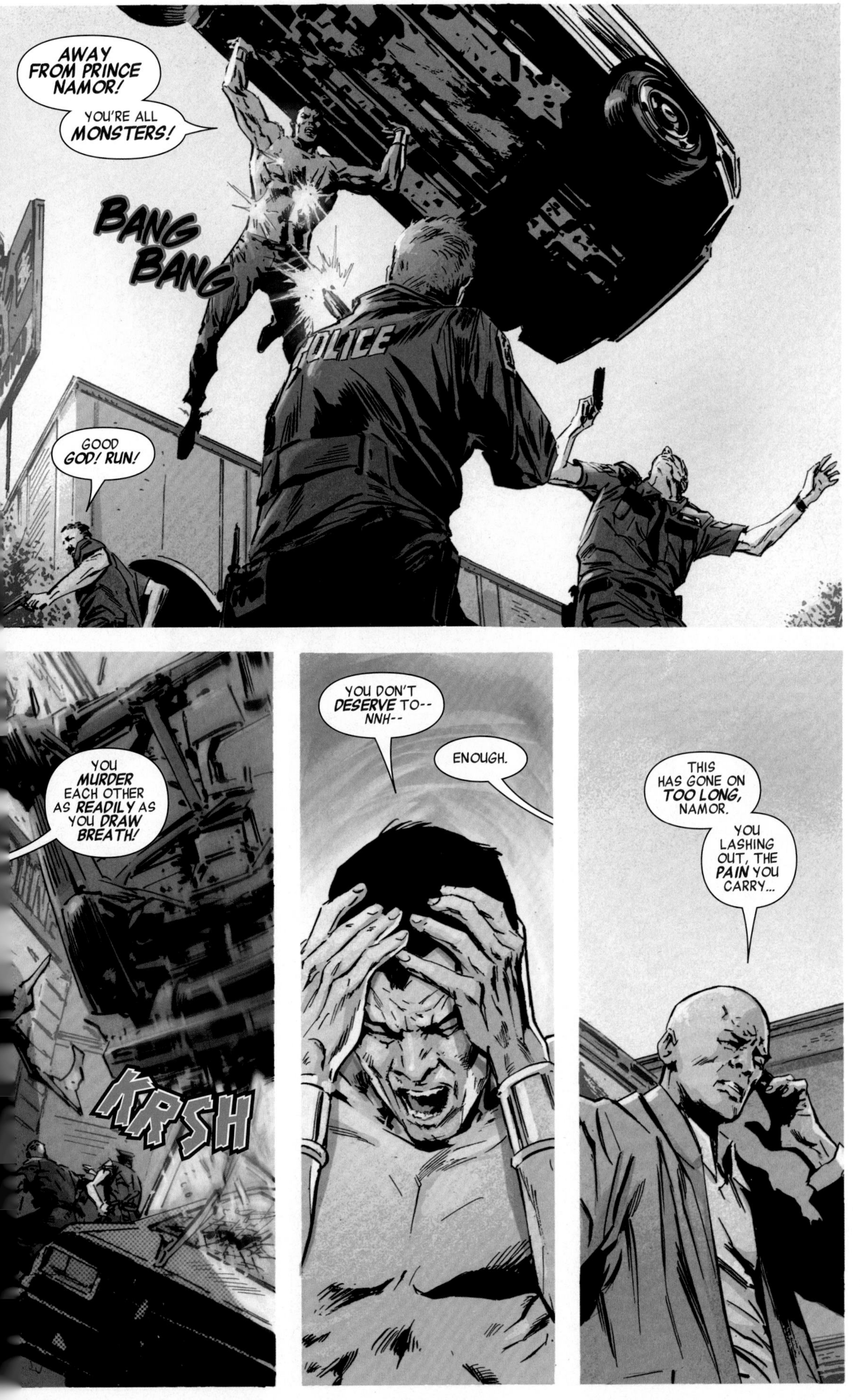
AWAY FROM PRINCE NAMOR!
YOU'RE ALL MONSTERS!
BANG BANG
POLICE
GOOD GOD! RUN!
YOU MURDER EACH OTHER AS READILY AS YOU DRAW BREATH!
KRSH
YOU DON'T DESERVE TO-- NNH--
ENOUGH.
THIS HAS GONE ON TOO LONG, NAMOR.
YOU LASHING OUT, THE PAIN YOU CARRY...

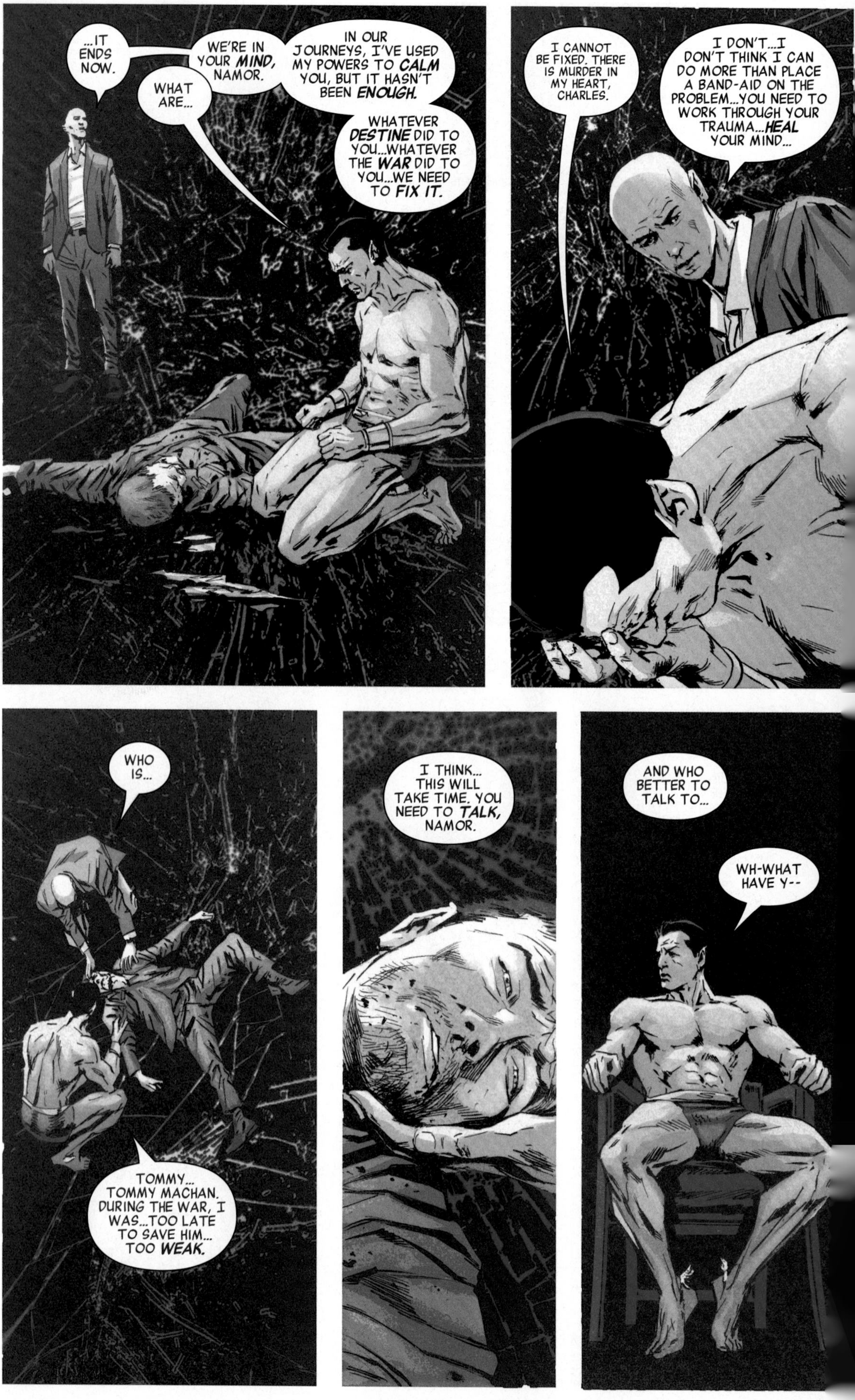
...IT ENDS NOW.
WE'RE IN YOUR **MIND,** NAMOR.
WHAT ARE...
IN OUR JOURNEYS, I'VE USED MY POWERS TO **CALM** YOU, BUT IT HASN'T BEEN **ENOUGH.**
WHATEVER **DESTINE** DID TO YOU...WHATEVER THE **WAR** DID TO YOU...WE NEED TO **FIX IT.**
I CANNOT BE FIXED. THERE IS MURDER IN MY HEART, CHARLES.
I DON'T...I DON'T THINK I CAN DO MORE THAN PLACE A BAND-AID ON THE PROBLEM...YOU NEED TO WORK THROUGH YOUR TRAUMA...**HEAL** YOUR MIND...
WHO IS...
TOMMY... TOMMY MACHAN. DURING THE WAR, I WAS...TOO LATE TO SAVE HIM... TOO **WEAK.**
I THINK... THIS WILL TAKE TIME. YOU NEED TO **TALK,** NAMOR.
AND WHO BETTER TO TALK TO...
WH-WHAT HAVE Y--

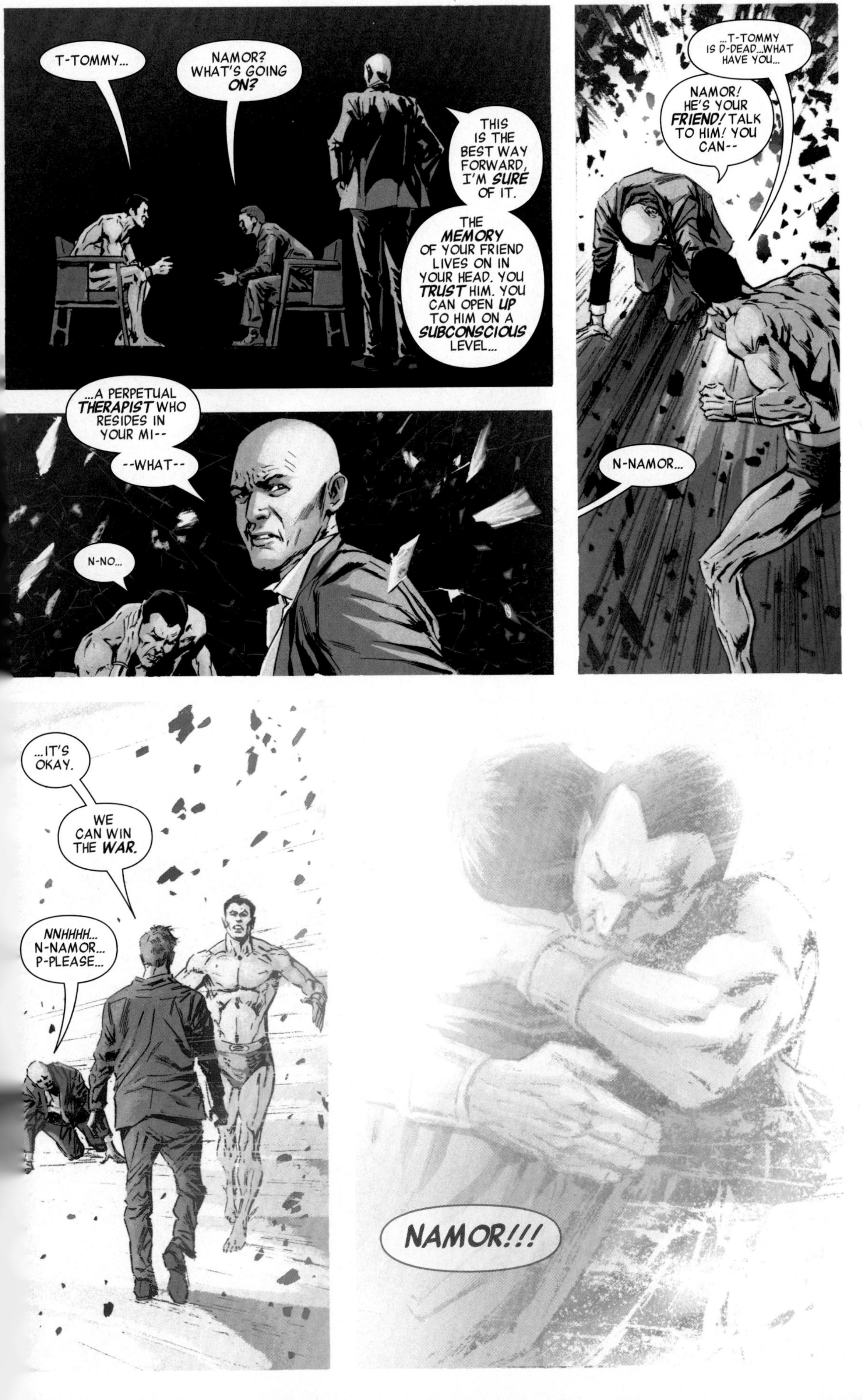
T-TOMMY...
NAMOR? WHAT'S GOING ON?
THIS IS THE BEST WAY FORWARD, I'M SURE OF IT.
THE MEMORY OF YOUR FRIEND LIVES ON IN YOUR HEAD. YOU TRUST HIM. YOU CAN OPEN UP TO HIM ON A SUBCONSCIOUS LEVEL...
...A PERPETUAL THERAPIST WHO RESIDES IN YOUR MI--
--WHAT--
N-NO...
...T-TOMMY IS D-DEAD...WHAT HAVE YOU...
NAMOR! HE'S YOUR FRIEND! TALK TO HIM! YOU CAN--
N-NAMOR...
...IT'S OKAY.
WE CAN WIN THE WAR.
NNHHHH... N-NAMOR... P-PLEASE...
NAMOR!!!

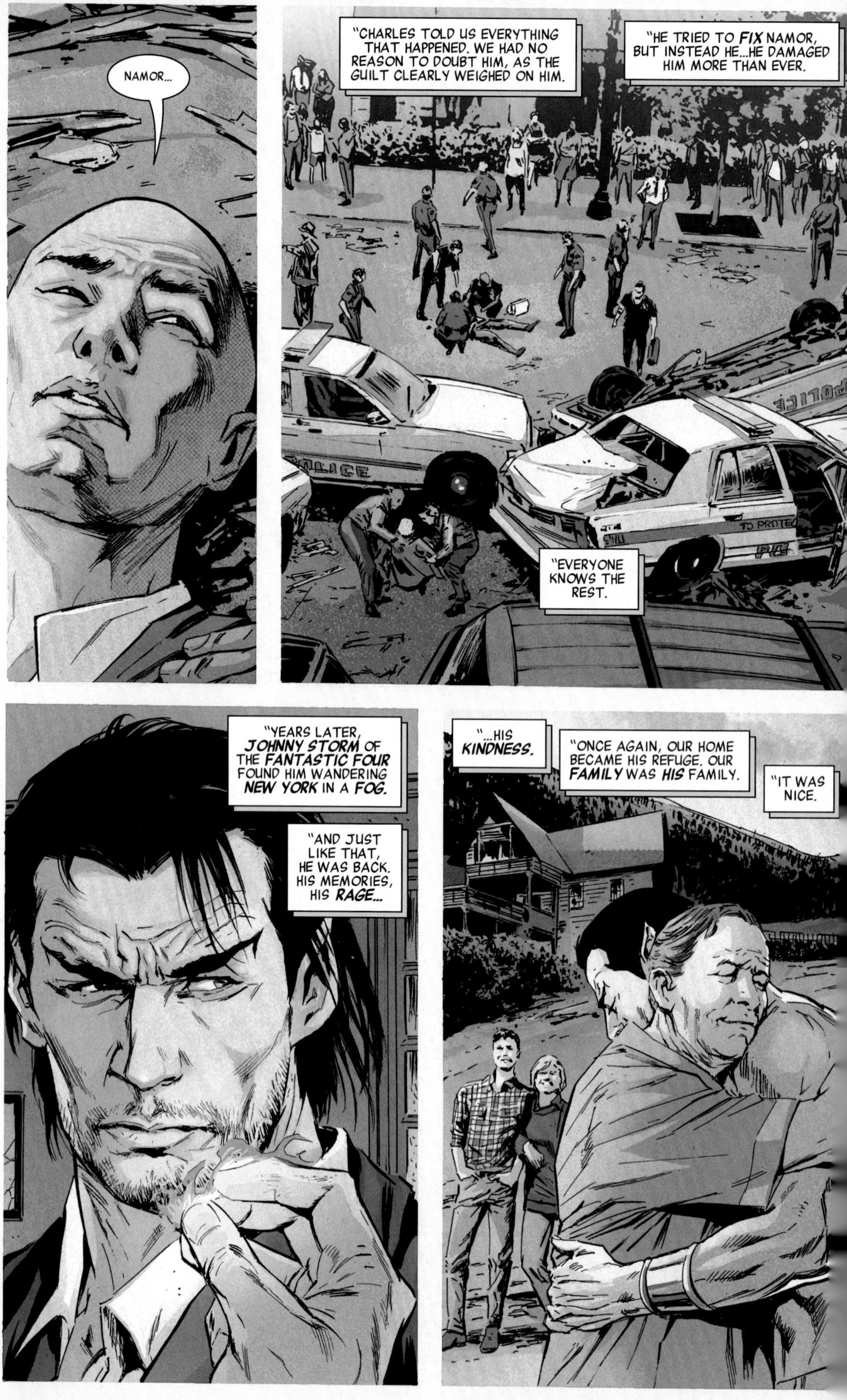
NAMOR...
"CHARLES TOLD US EVERYTHING THAT HAPPENED. WE HAD NO REASON TO DOUBT HIM, AS THE GUILT CLEARLY WEIGHED ON HIM.
"HE TRIED TO FIX NAMOR, BUT INSTEAD HE...HE DAMAGED HIM MORE THAN EVER.
"EVERYONE KNOWS THE REST.
"YEARS LATER, JOHNNY STORM OF THE FANTASTIC FOUR FOUND HIM WANDERING NEW YORK IN A FOG.
"AND JUST LIKE THAT, HE WAS BACK. HIS MEMORIES, HIS RAGE...
"...HIS KINDNESS.
"ONCE AGAIN, OUR HOME BECAME HIS REFUGE. OUR FAMILY WAS HIS FAMILY.
"IT WAS NICE.

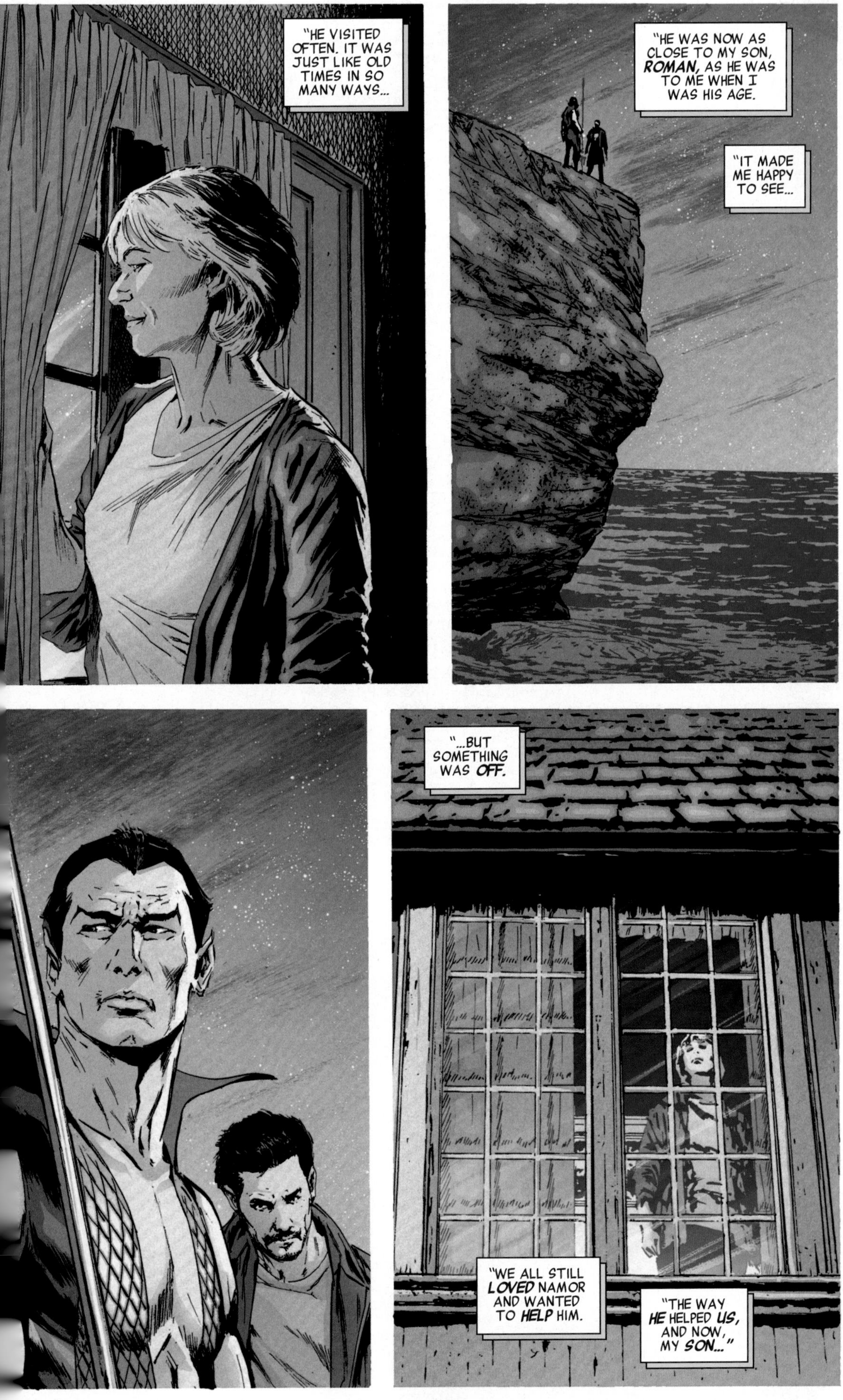
"HE VISITED OFTEN. IT WAS JUST LIKE OLD TIMES IN SO MANY WAYS...
"HE WAS NOW AS CLOSE TO MY SON, ROMAN, AS HE WAS TO ME WHEN I WAS HIS AGE.
"IT MADE ME HAPPY TO SEE...
"...BUT SOMETHING WAS OFF.
"WE ALL STILL LOVED NAMOR AND WANTED TO HELP HIM.
"THE WAY HE HELPED US, AND NOW, MY SON..."

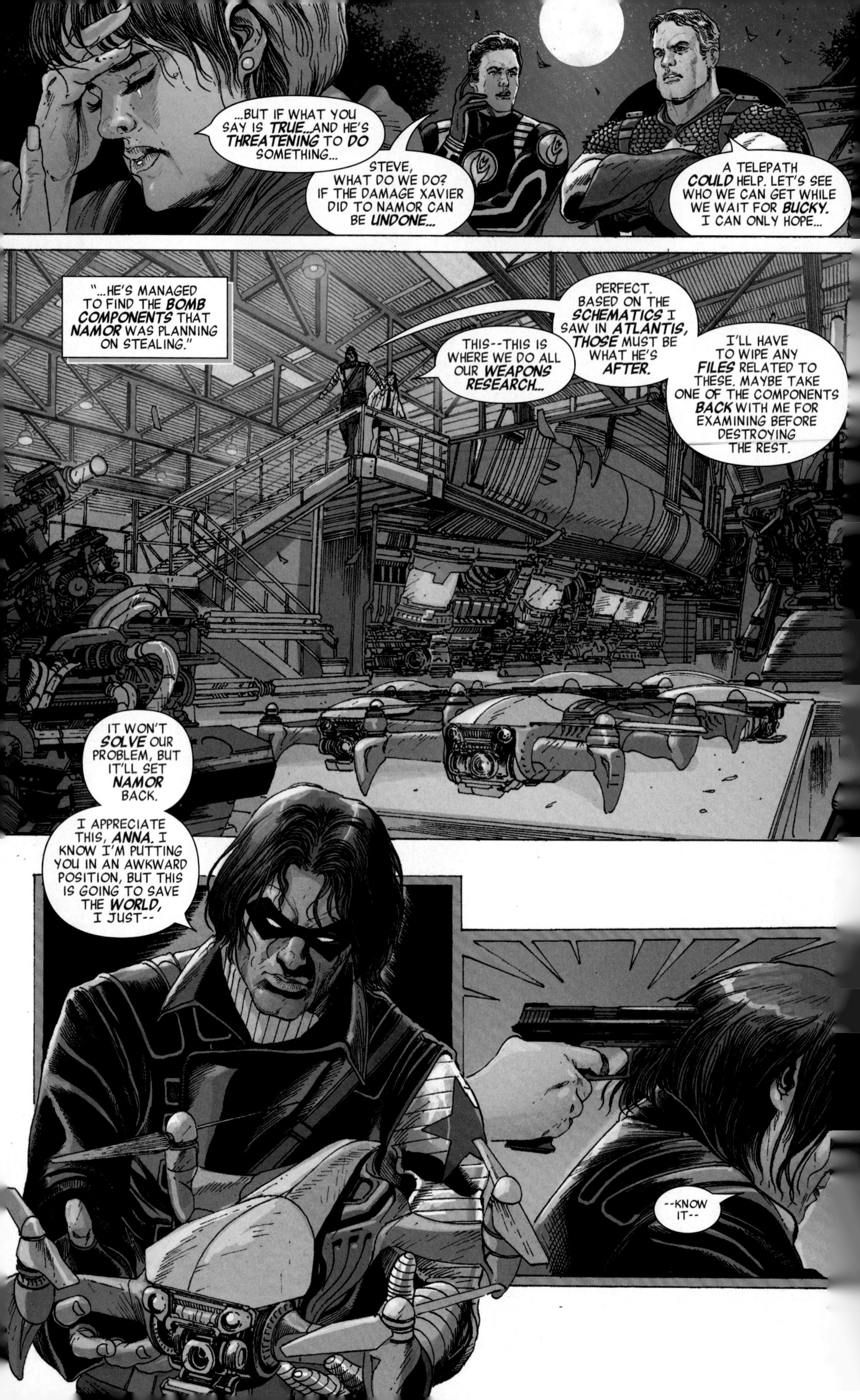
...BUT IF WHAT YOU SAY IS TRUE...AND HE'S THREATENING TO DO SOMETHING...
STEVE, WHAT DO WE DO? IF THE DAMAGE XAVIER DID TO NAMOR CAN BE UNDONE...
A TELEPATH COULD HELP. LET'S SEE WHO WE CAN GET WHILE WE WAIT FOR BUCKY. I CAN ONLY HOPE...
"...HE'S MANAGED TO FIND THE BOMB COMPONENTS THAT NAMOR WAS PLANNING ON STEALING."
THIS--THIS IS WHERE WE DO ALL OUR WEAPONS RESEARCH...
PERFECT. BASED ON THE SCHEMATICS I SAW IN ATLANTIS, THOSE MUST BE WHAT HE'S AFTER.
I'LL HAVE TO WIPE ANY FILES RELATED TO THESE. MAYBE TAKE ONE OF THE COMPONENTS BACK WITH ME FOR EXAMINING BEFORE DESTROYING THE REST.
IT WON'T SOLVE OUR PROBLEM, BUT IT'LL SET NAMOR BACK.
I APPRECIATE THIS, ANNA. I KNOW I'M PUTTING YOU IN AN AWKWARD POSITION, BUT THIS IS GOING TO SAVE THE WORLD, I JUST--
--KNOW IT--

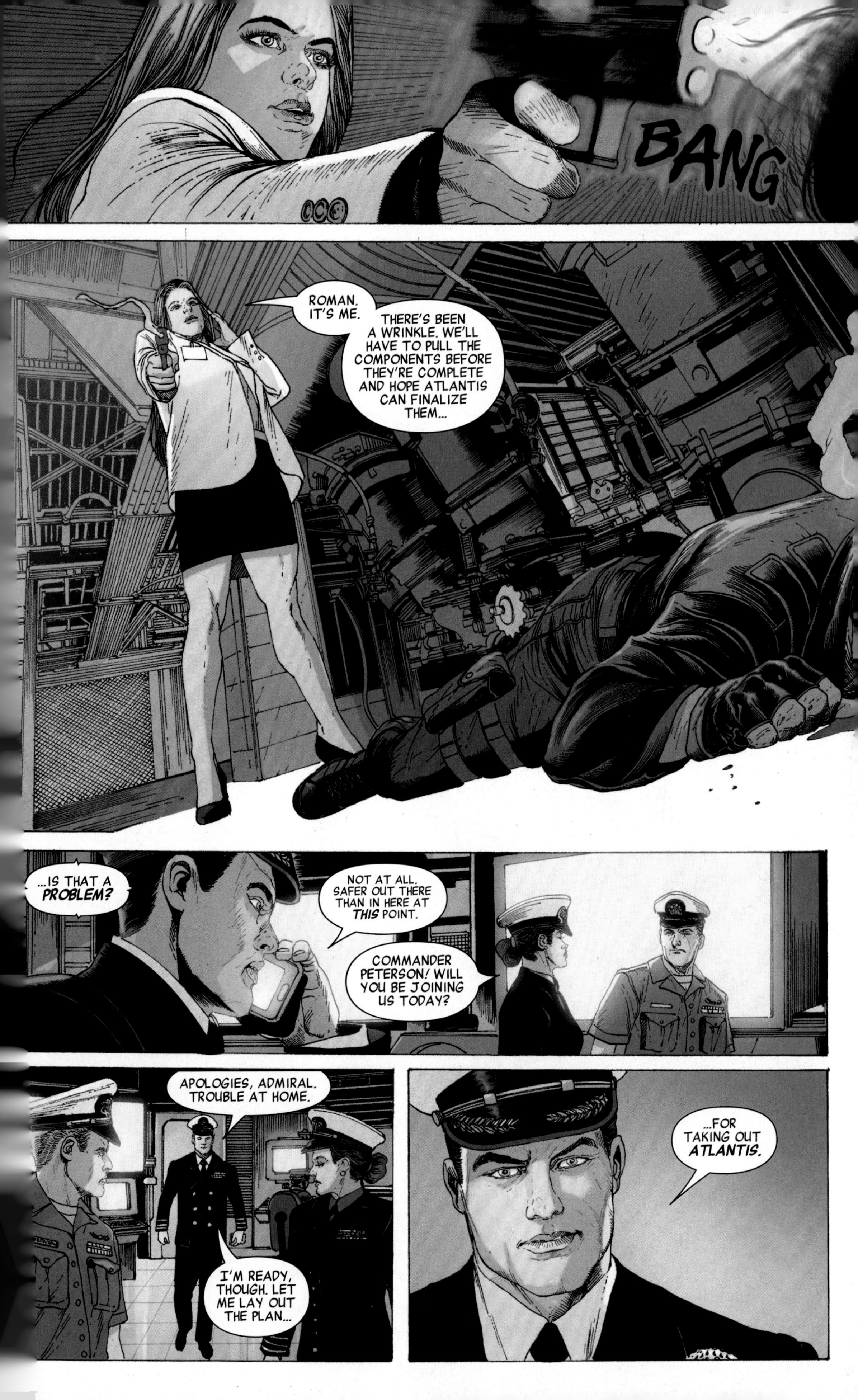
BANG
ROMAN. IT'S ME.
THERE'S BEEN A WRINKLE. WE'LL HAVE TO PULL THE COMPONENTS BEFORE THEY'RE COMPLETE AND HOPE ATLANTIS CAN FINALIZE THEM...
...IS THAT A PROBLEM?
NOT AT ALL. SAFER OUT THERE THAN IN HERE AT THIS POINT.
COMMANDER PETERSON! WILL YOU BE JOINING US TODAY?
APOLOGIES, ADMIRAL. TROUBLE AT HOME.
I'M READY, THOUGH. LET ME LAY OUT THE PLAN...
...FOR TAKING OUT ATLANTIS.

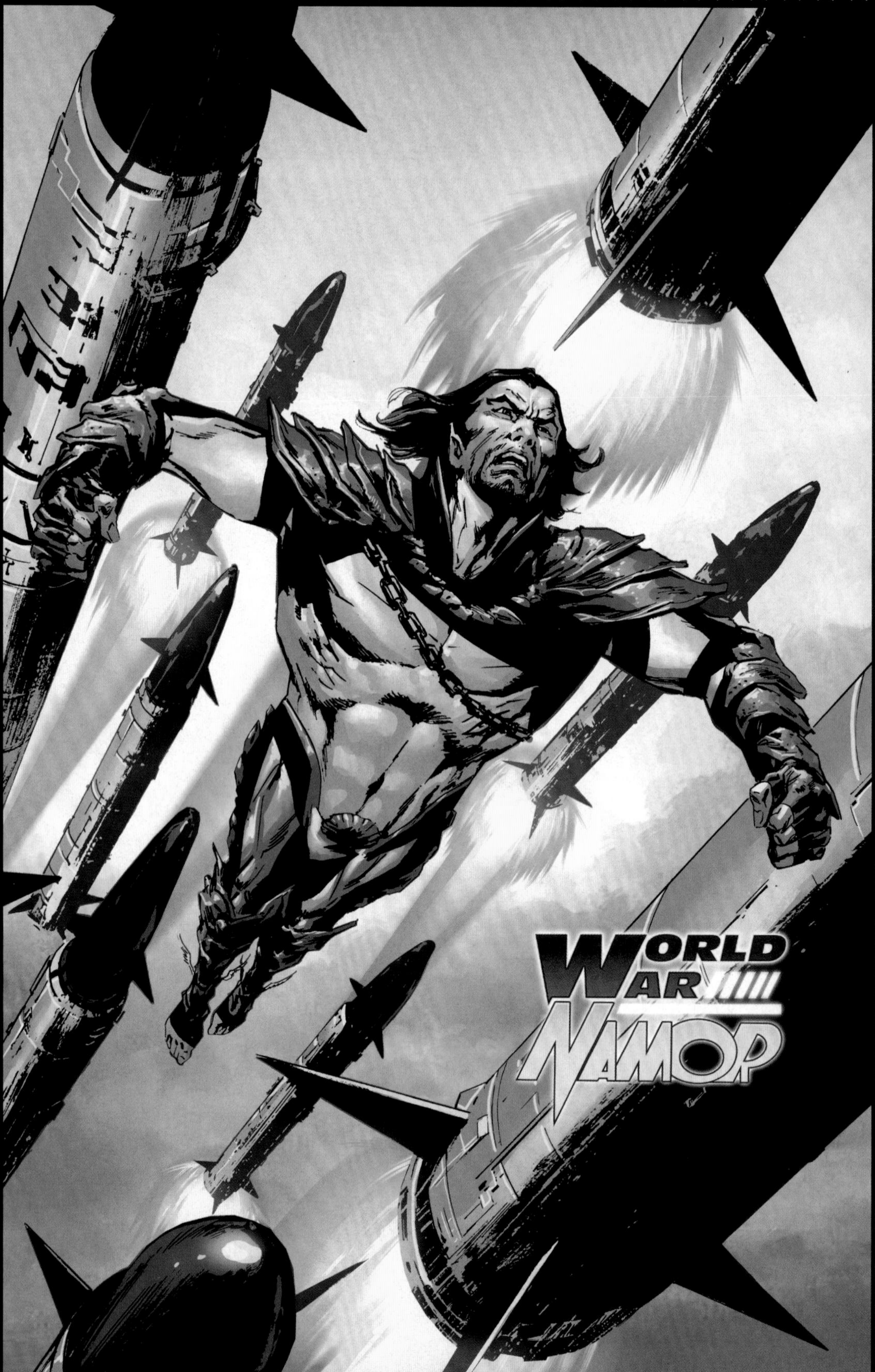
WORLD WAR
NAMOR

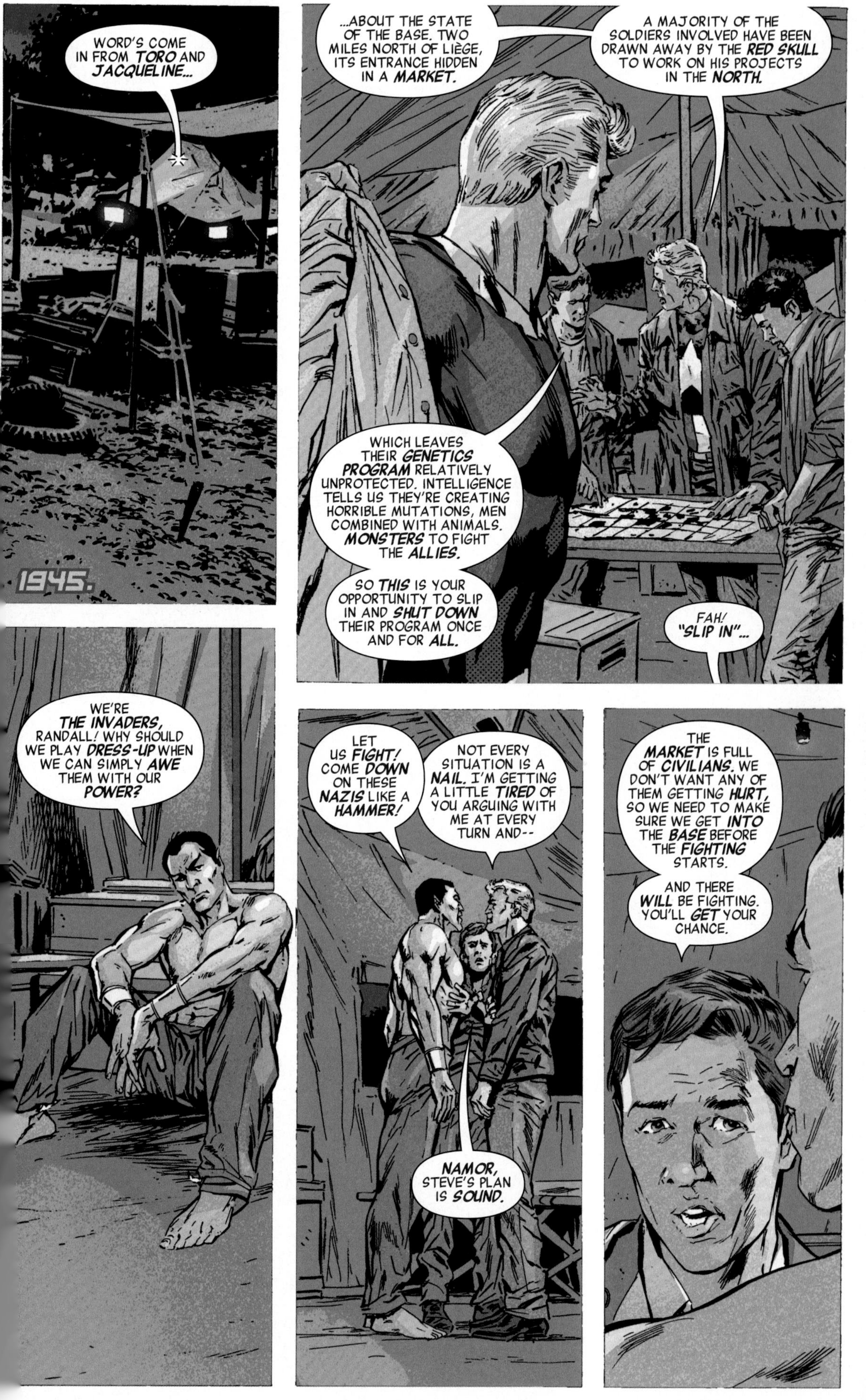
WORD'S COME IN FROM TORO AND JACQUELINE...
1945.
...ABOUT THE STATE OF THE BASE. TWO MILES NORTH OF LIÈGE, ITS ENTRANCE HIDDEN IN A MARKET.
A MAJORITY OF THE SOLDIERS INVOLVED HAVE BEEN DRAWN AWAY BY THE RED SKULL TO WORK ON HIS PROJECTS IN THE NORTH.
WHICH LEAVES THEIR GENETICS PROGRAM RELATIVELY UNPROTECTED. INTELLIGENCE TELLS US THEY'RE CREATING HORRIBLE MUTATIONS, MEN COMBINED WITH ANIMALS. MONSTERS TO FIGHT THE ALLIES.
SO THIS IS YOUR OPPORTUNITY TO SLIP IN AND SHUT DOWN THEIR PROGRAM ONCE AND FOR ALL.
FAH! "SLIP IN"...
WE'RE THE INVADERS, RANDALL! WHY SHOULD WE PLAY DRESS-UP WHEN WE CAN SIMPLY AWE THEM WITH OUR POWER?
LET US FIGHT! COME DOWN ON THESE NAZIS LIKE A HAMMER!
NOT EVERY SITUATION IS A NAIL. I'M GETTING A LITTLE TIRED OF YOU ARGUING WITH ME AT EVERY TURN AND--
NAMOR, STEVE'S PLAN IS SOUND.
THE MARKET IS FULL OF CIVILIANS. WE DON'T WANT ANY OF THEM GETTING HURT, SO WE NEED TO MAKE SURE WE GET INTO THE BASE BEFORE THE FIGHTING STARTS.
AND THERE WILL BE FIGHTING. YOU'LL GET YOUR CHANCE.

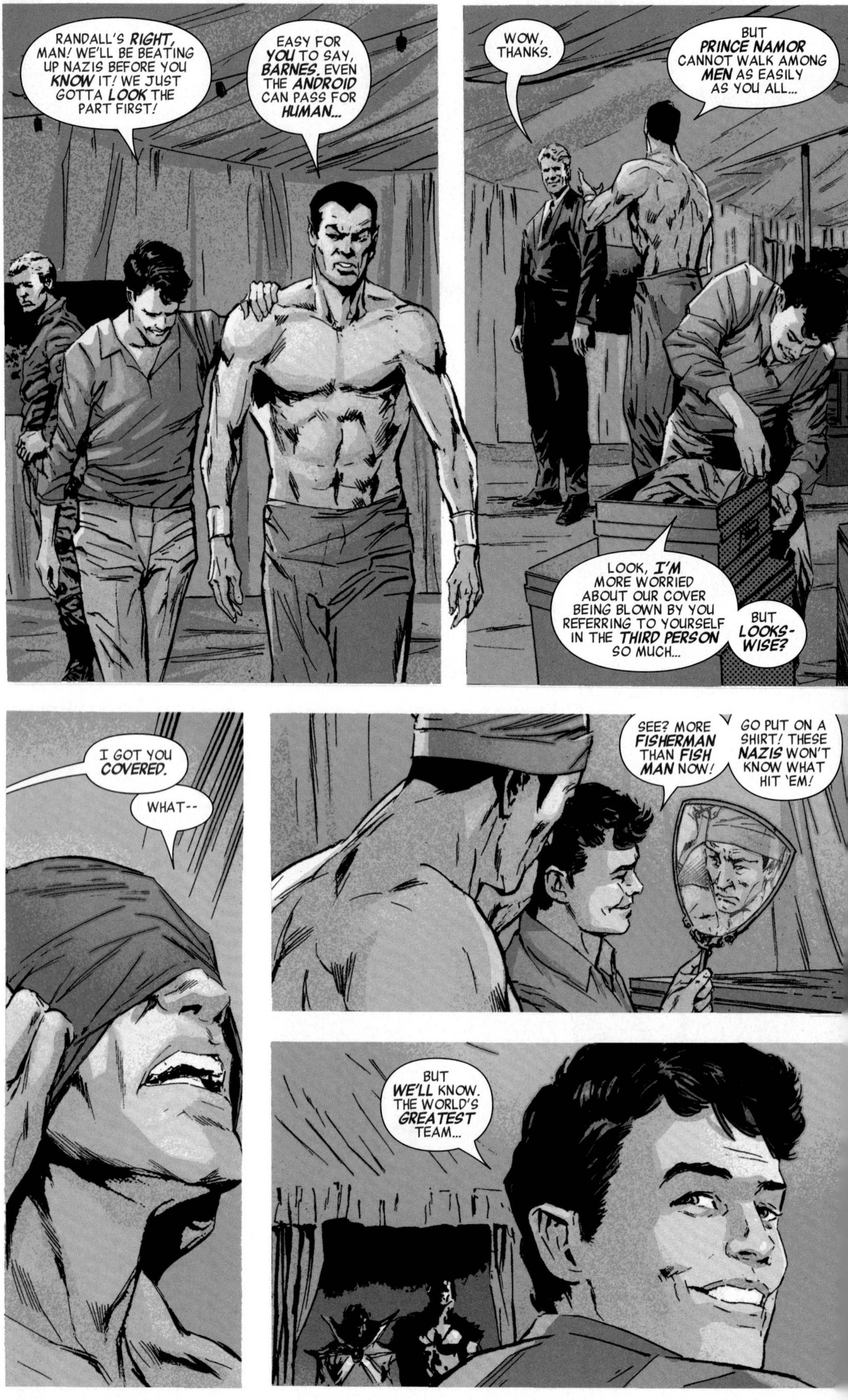
RANDALL'S RIGHT, MAN! WE'LL BE BEATING UP NAZIS BEFORE YOU KNOW IT! WE JUST GOTTA LOOK THE PART FIRST!
EASY FOR YOU TO SAY, BARNES. EVEN THE ANDROID CAN PASS FOR HUMAN...
WOW, THANKS.
BUT PRINCE NAMOR CANNOT WALK AMONG MEN AS EASILY AS YOU ALL...
LOOK, I'M MORE WORRIED ABOUT OUR COVER BEING BLOWN BY YOU REFERRING TO YOURSELF IN THE THIRD PERSON SO MUCH...
BUT LOOKS-WISE?
I GOT YOU COVERED.
WHAT--
SEE? MORE FISHERMAN THAN FISH MAN NOW!
GO PUT ON A SHIRT! THESE NAZIS WON'T KNOW WHAT HIT 'EM!
BUT WE'LL KNOW. THE WORLD'S GREATEST TEAM...

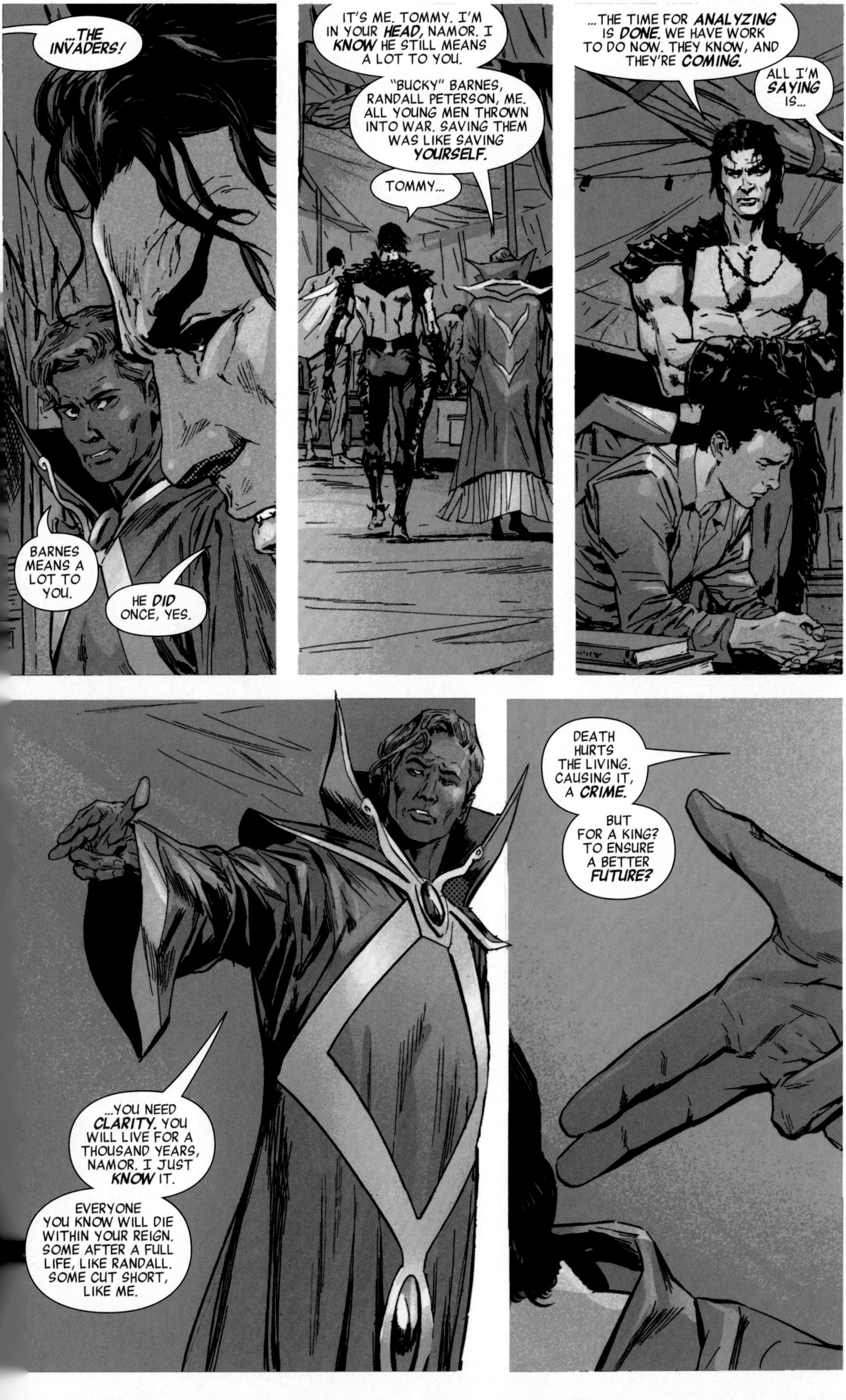
...THE INVADERS!
BARNES MEANS A LOT TO YOU.
HE DID ONCE, YES.
IT'S ME. TOMMY. I'M IN YOUR HEAD, NAMOR. I KNOW HE STILL MEANS A LOT TO YOU.
"BUCKY" BARNES, RANDALL PETERSON, ME. ALL YOUNG MEN THROWN INTO WAR. SAVING THEM WAS LIKE SAVING YOURSELF.
TOMMY...
...THE TIME FOR ANALYZING IS DONE. WE HAVE WORK TO DO NOW. THEY KNOW, AND THEY'RE COMING.
ALL I'M SAYING IS...
...YOU NEED CLARITY. YOU WILL LIVE FOR A THOUSAND YEARS, NAMOR. I JUST KNOW IT.
EVERYONE YOU KNOW WILL DIE WITHIN YOUR REIGN. SOME AFTER A FULL LIFE, LIKE RANDALL. SOME CUT SHORT, LIKE ME.
DEATH HURTS THE LIVING. CAUSING IT, A CRIME.
BUT FOR A KING? TO ENSURE A BETTER FUTURE?

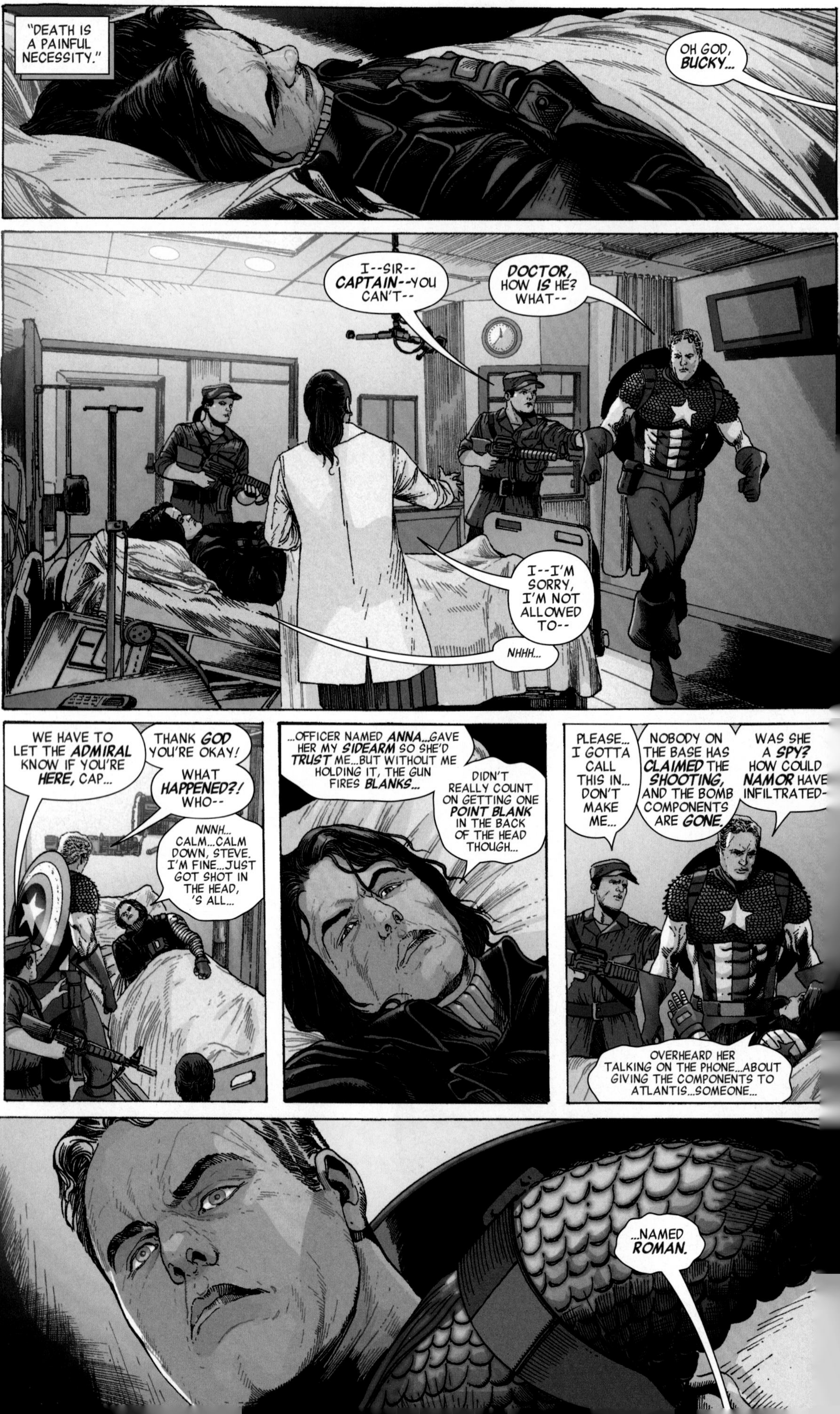
"DEATH IS A PAINFUL NECESSITY."
OH GOD, BUCKY...
I--SIR-- CAPTAIN--YOU CAN'T--
DOCTOR, HOW IS HE? WHAT--
I--I'M SORRY, I'M NOT ALLOWED TO--
NHHH...
WE HAVE TO LET THE ADMIRAL KNOW IF YOU'RE HERE, CAP...
THANK GOD YOU'RE OKAY!
WHAT HAPPENED?! WHO--
NNNH... CALM...CALM DOWN, STEVE. I'M FINE...JUST GOT SHOT IN THE HEAD, 'S ALL...
...OFFICER NAMED ANNA...GAVE HER MY SIDEARM SO SHE'D TRUST ME...BUT WITHOUT ME HOLDING IT, THE GUN FIRES BLANKS...
DIDN'T REALLY COUNT ON GETTING ONE POINT BLANK IN THE BACK OF THE HEAD THOUGH...
PLEASE... I GOTTA CALL THIS IN... DON'T MAKE ME...
NOBODY ON THE BASE HAS CLAIMED THE SHOOTING, AND THE BOMB COMPONENTS ARE GONE.
WAS SHE A SPY? HOW COULD NAMOR HAVE INFILTRATED-
OVERHEARD HER TALKING ON THE PHONE...ABOUT GIVING THE COMPONENTS TO ATLANTIS...SOMEONE...
...NAMED ROMAN.

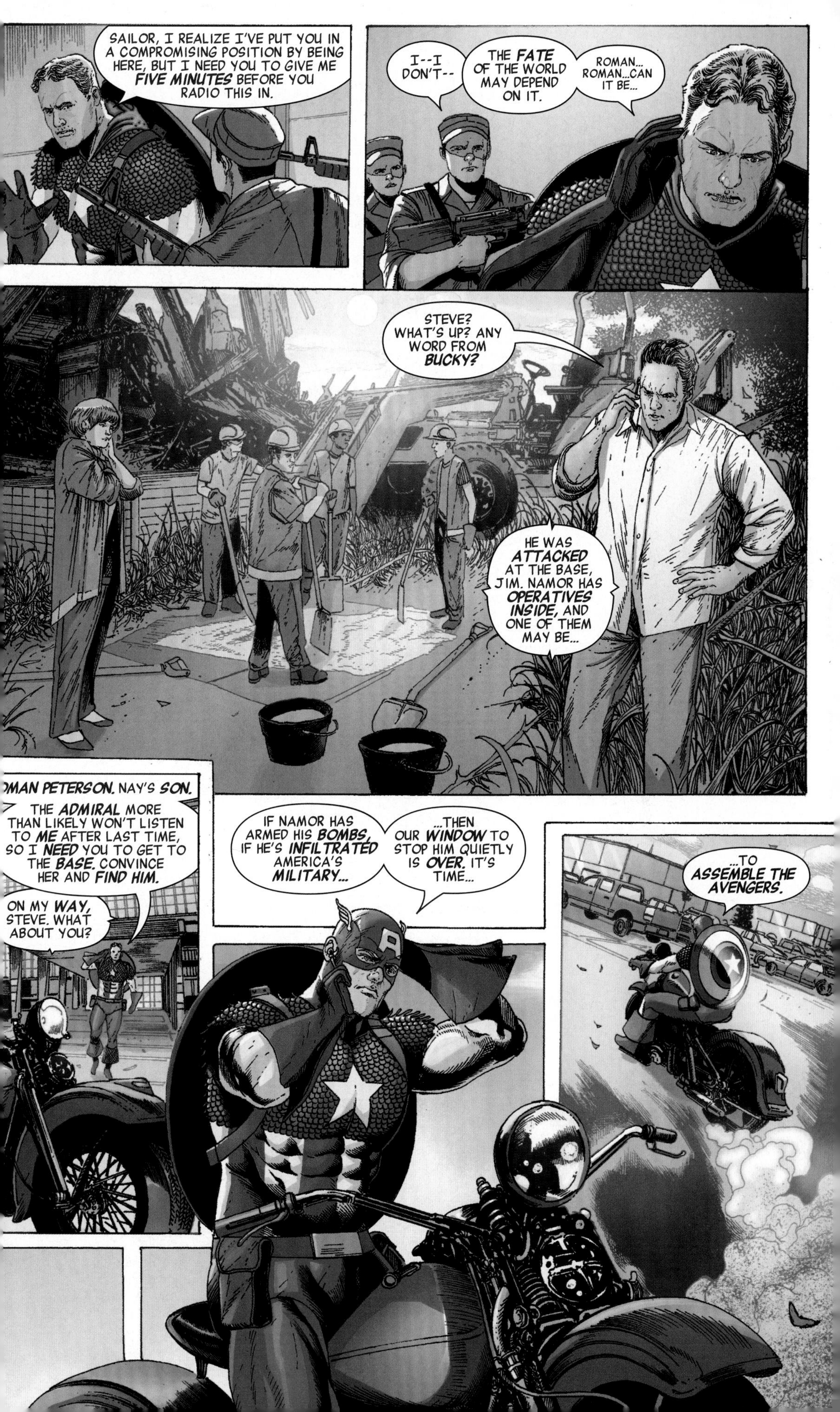

SAILOR, I REALIZE I'VE PUT YOU IN A COMPROMISING POSITION BY BEING HERE, BUT I NEED YOU TO GIVE ME FIVE MINUTES BEFORE YOU RADIO THIS IN.
I--I DON'T--
THE FATE OF THE WORLD MAY DEPEND ON IT.
ROMAN... ROMAN...CAN IT BE...
STEVE? WHAT'S UP? ANY WORD FROM BUCKY?
HE WAS ATTACKED AT THE BASE, JIM. NAMOR HAS OPERATIVES INSIDE, AND ONE OF THEM MAY BE...
OMAN PETERSON. NAY'S SON.
THE ADMIRAL MORE THAN LIKELY WON'T LISTEN TO ME AFTER LAST TIME, SO I NEED YOU TO GET TO THE BASE. CONVINCE HER AND FIND HIM.
ON MY WAY, STEVE. WHAT ABOUT YOU?
IF NAMOR HAS ARMED HIS BOMBS, IF HE'S INFILTRATED AMERICA'S MILITARY...
...THEN OUR WINDOW TO STOP HIM QUIETLY IS OVER. IT'S TIME...
...TO ASSEMBLE THE AVENGERS.

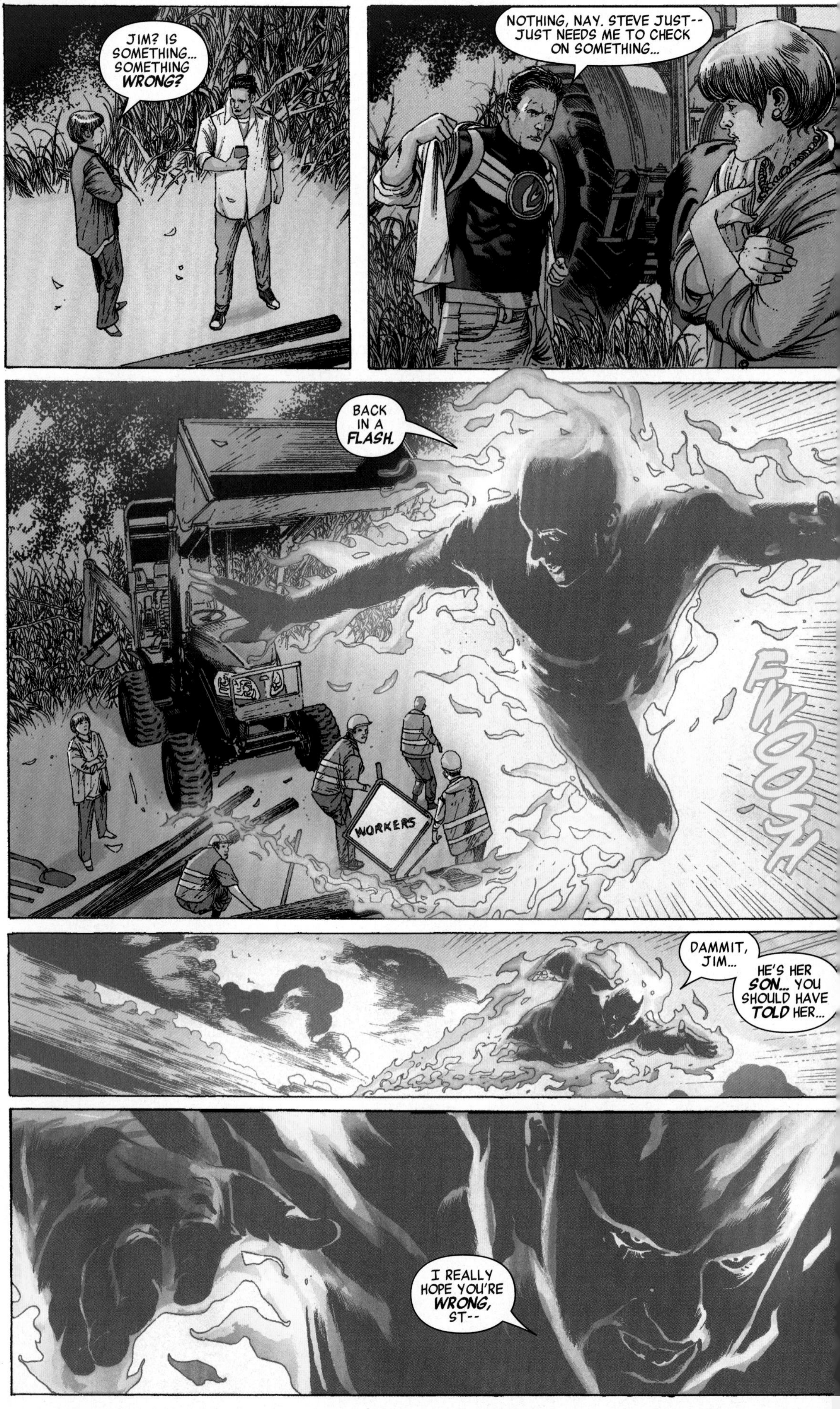
JIM? IS SOMETHING... SOMETHING WRONG?
NOTHING, NAY. STEVE JUST-- JUST NEEDS ME TO CHECK ON SOMETHING...
BACK IN A FLASH.
WORKERS
FWOOSH
DAMMIT, JIM...
HE'S HER SON... YOU SHOULD HAVE TOLD HER...
I REALLY HOPE YOU'RE WRONG, ST--

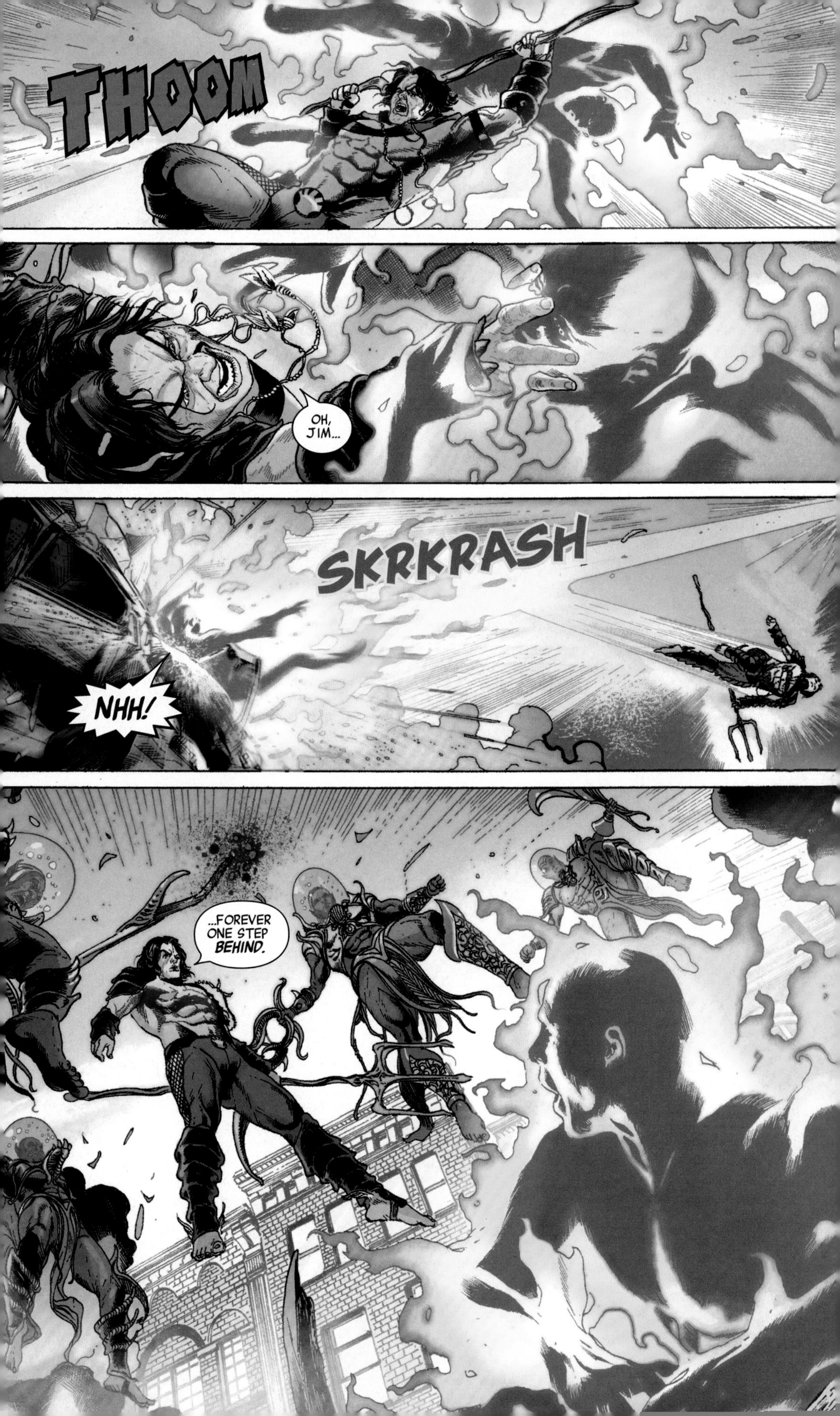
THOOM
OH, JIM...
SKRKRASH
NHH!
...FOREVER ONE STEP BEHIND.

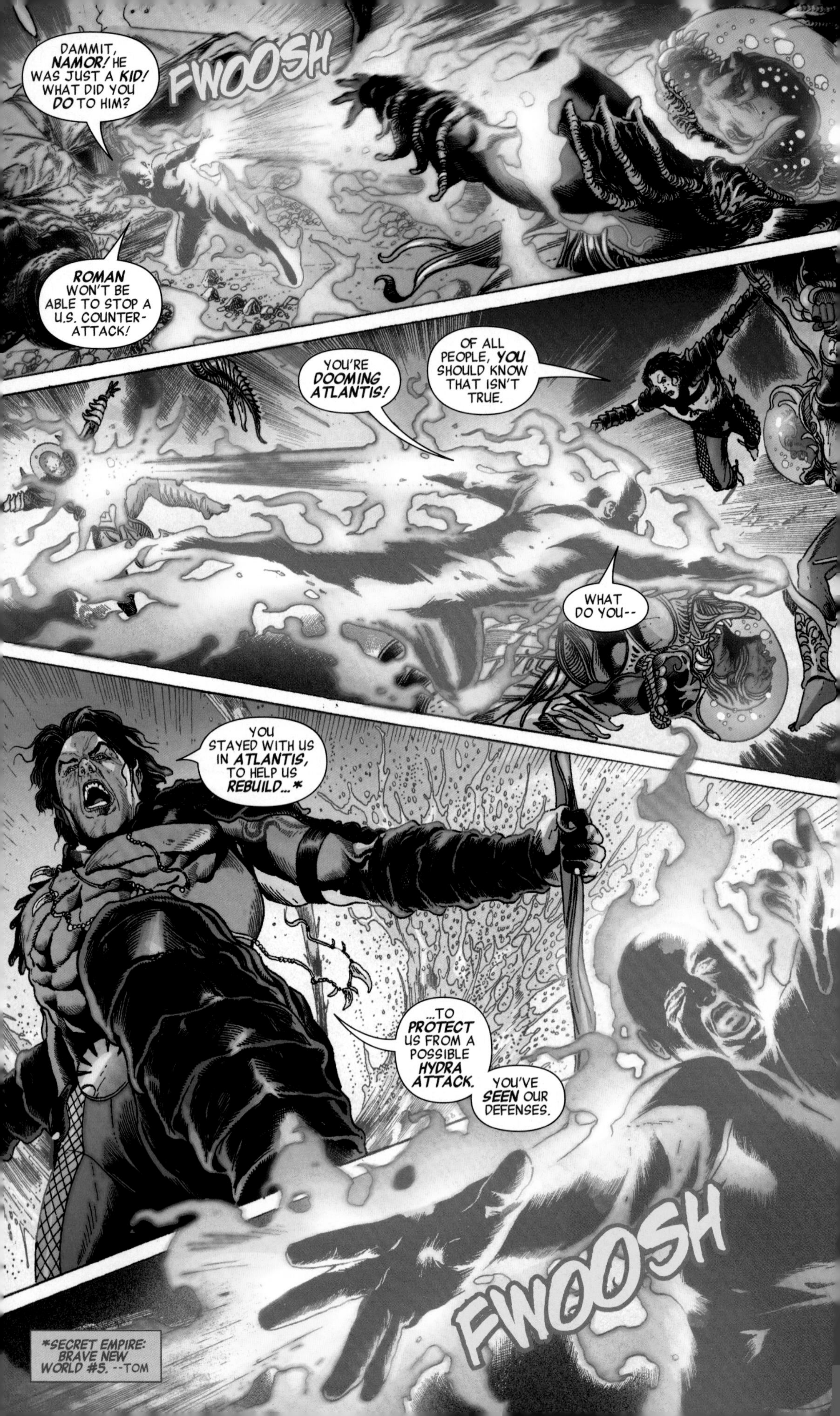
DAMMIT, NAMOR! HE WAS JUST A KID! WHAT DID YOU DO TO HIM?
FWOOSH
ROMAN WON'T BE ABLE TO STOP A U.S. COUNTER-ATTACK!
YOU'RE DOOMING ATLANTIS!
OF ALL PEOPLE, YOU SHOULD KNOW THAT ISN'T TRUE.
WHAT DO YOU--
YOU STAYED WITH US IN ATLANTIS, TO HELP US REBUILD...*
...TO PROTECT US FROM A POSSIBLE HYDRA ATTACK.
YOU'VE SEEN OUR DEFENSES.
FWOOSH
*SECRET EMPIRE: BRAVE NEW WORLD #5. --TOM

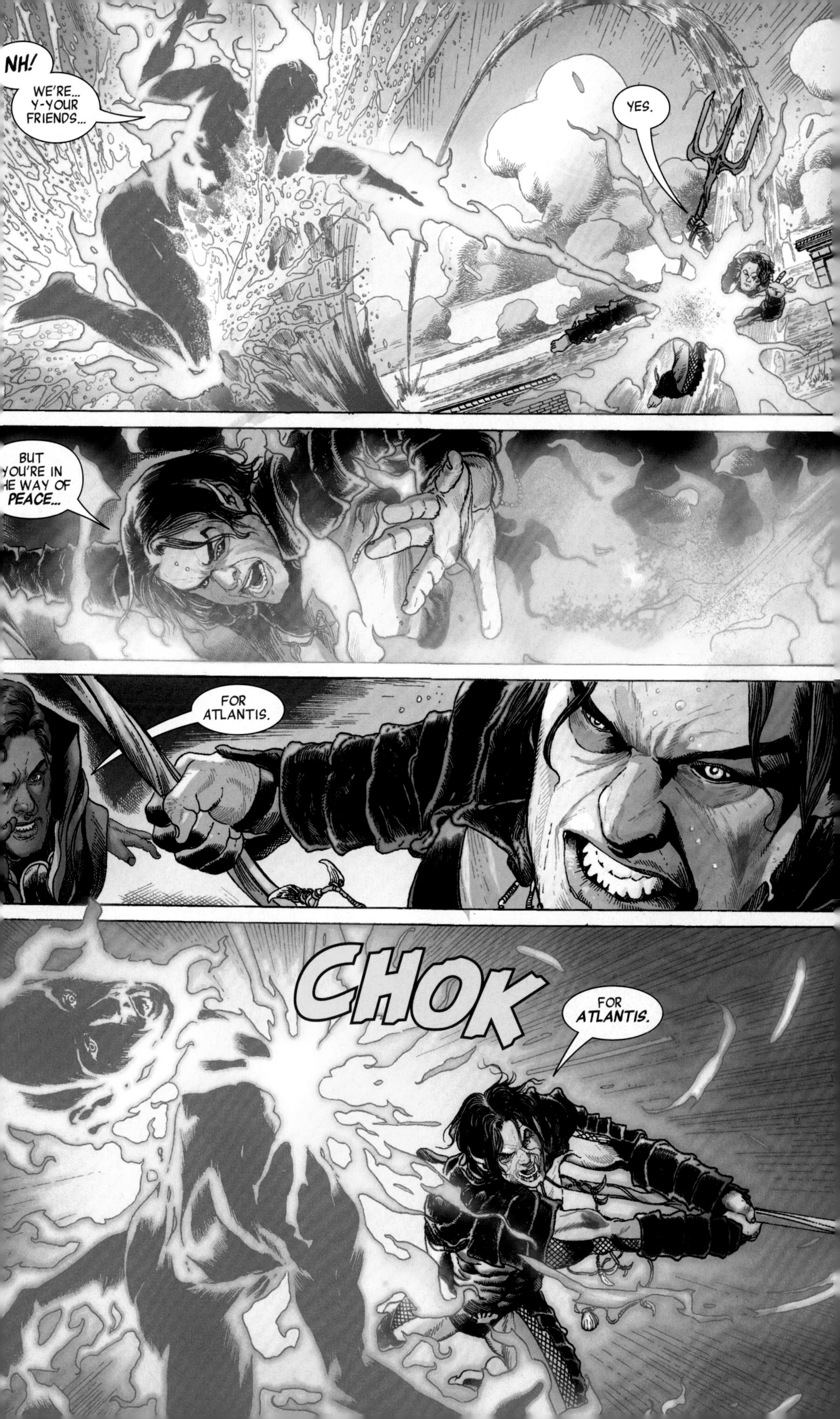
NH!
WE'RE... Y-YOUR FRIENDS...
YES.
BUT YOU'RE IN HE WAY OF PEACE...
FOR ATLANTIS.
CHOK
FOR ATLANTIS.

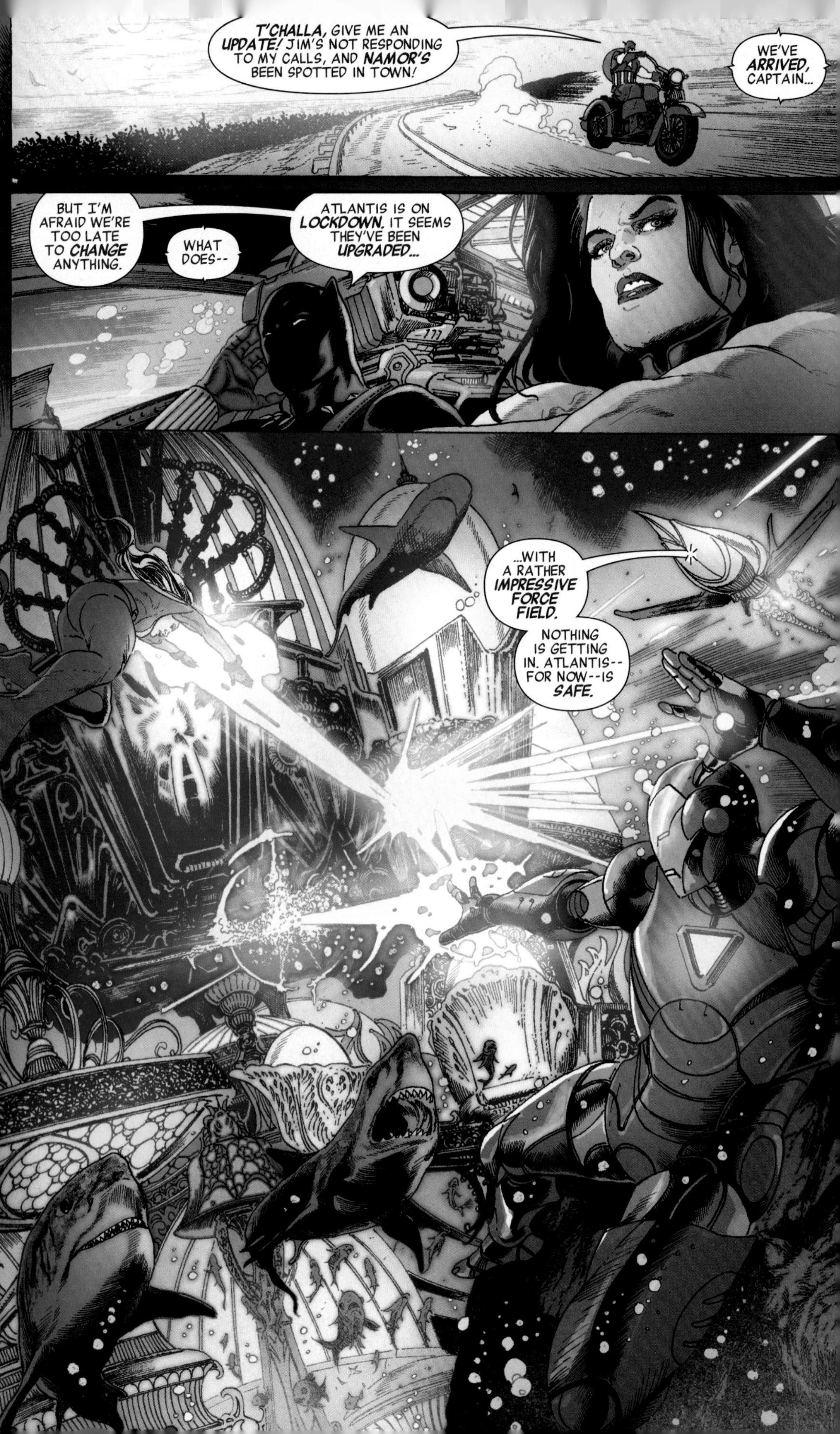
T'CHALLA, GIVE ME AN UPDATE! JIM'S NOT RESPONDING TO MY CALLS, AND NAMOR'S BEEN SPOTTED IN TOWN!
WE'VE ARRIVED, CAPTAIN...
BUT I'M AFRAID WE'RE TOO LATE TO CHANGE ANYTHING.
WHAT DOES--
ATLANTIS IS ON LOCKDOWN. IT SEEMS THEY'VE BEEN UPGRADED...
...WITH A RATHER IMPRESSIVE FORCE FIELD.
NOTHING IS GETTING IN. ATLANTIS-- FOR NOW--IS SAFE.

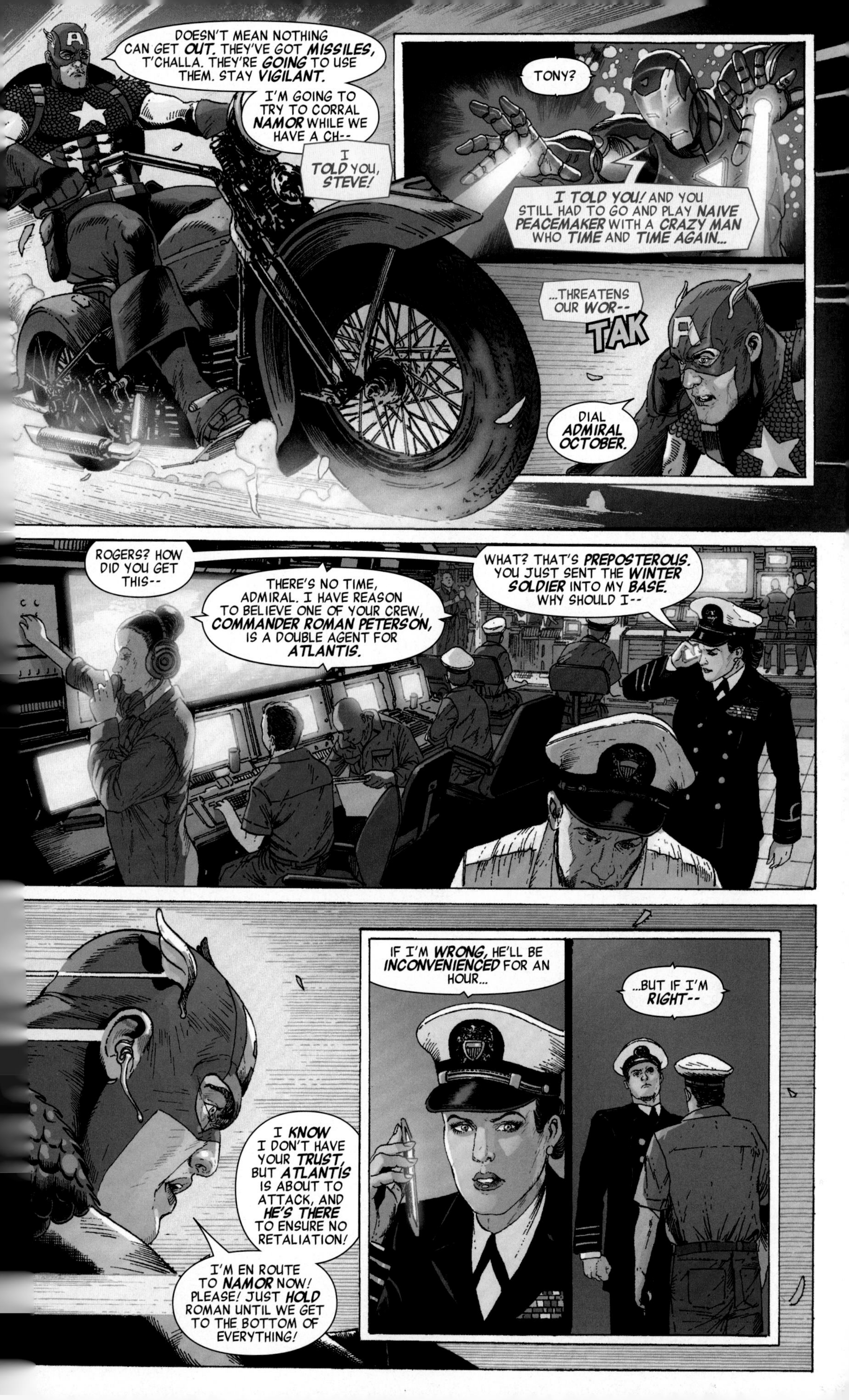
DOESN'T MEAN NOTHING CAN GET OUT. THEY'VE GOT MISSILES, T'CHALLA. THEY'RE GOING TO USE THEM. STAY VIGILANT.
I'M GOING TO TRY TO CORRAL NAMOR WHILE WE HAVE A CH--
I TOLD YOU, STEVE!
TONY?
I TOLD YOU! AND YOU STILL HAD TO GO AND PLAY NAIVE PEACEMAKER WITH A CRAZY MAN WHO TIME AND TIME AGAIN...
...THREATENS OUR WOR--
TAK
DIAL ADMIRAL OCTOBER.
ROGERS? HOW DID YOU GET THIS--
THERE'S NO TIME, ADMIRAL. I HAVE REASON TO BELIEVE ONE OF YOUR CREW, COMMANDER ROMAN PETERSON, IS A DOUBLE AGENT FOR ATLANTIS.
WHAT? THAT'S PREPOSTEROUS. YOU JUST SENT THE WINTER SOLDIER INTO MY BASE. WHY SHOULD I--
I KNOW I DON'T HAVE YOUR TRUST, BUT ATLANTIS IS ABOUT TO ATTACK, AND HE'S THERE TO ENSURE NO RETALIATION!
I'M EN ROUTE TO NAMOR NOW! PLEASE! JUST HOLD ROMAN UNTIL WE GET TO THE BOTTOM OF EVERYTHING!
IF I'M WRONG, HE'LL BE INCONVENIENCED FOR AN HOUR...
...BUT IF I'M RIGHT--

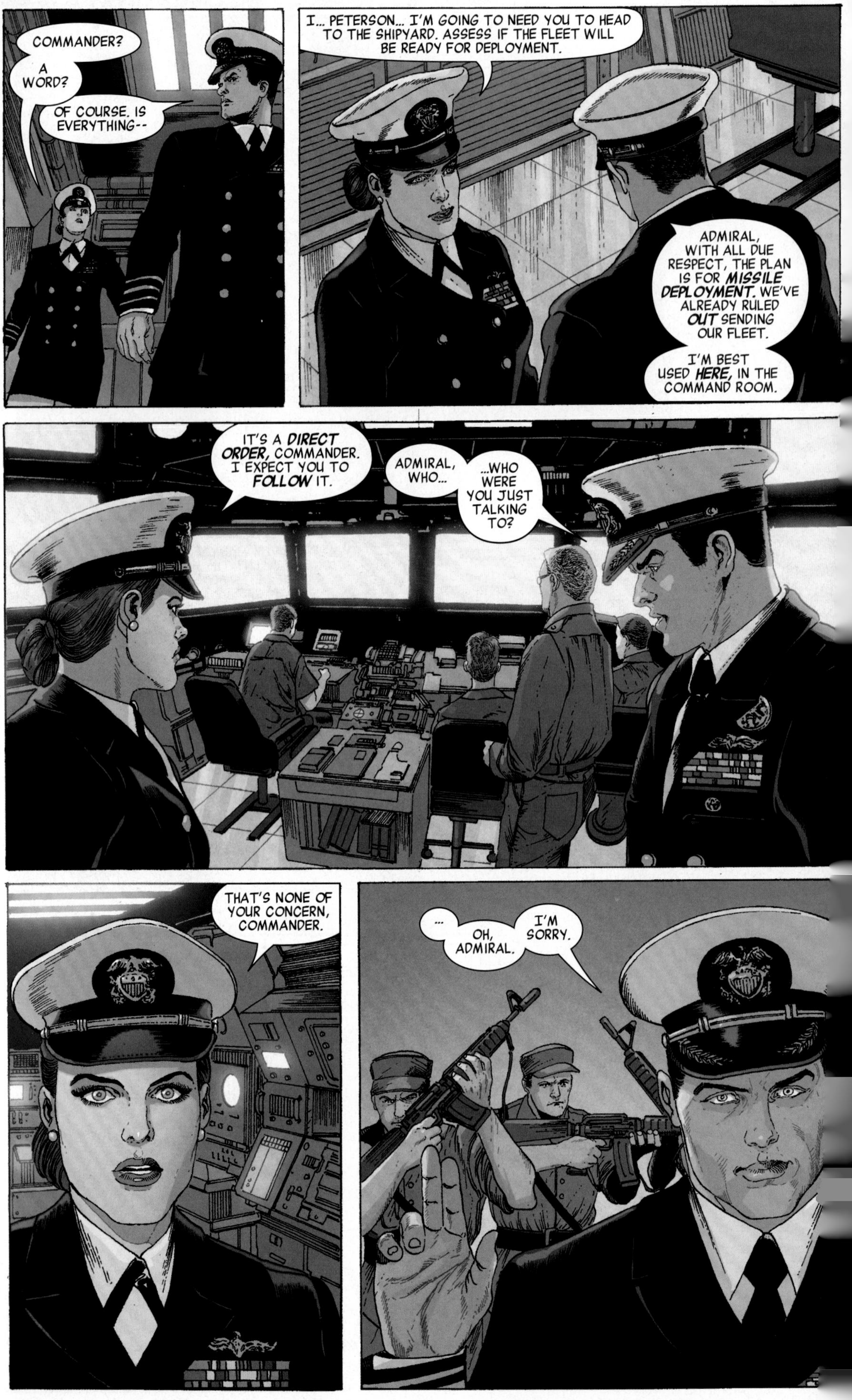
COMMANDER?
A WORD?
OF COURSE. IS EVERYTHING--
I... PETERSON... I'M GOING TO NEED YOU TO HEAD TO THE SHIPYARD. ASSESS IF THE FLEET WILL BE READY FOR DEPLOYMENT.
ADMIRAL, WITH ALL DUE RESPECT, THE PLAN IS FOR MISSILE DEPLOYMENT. WE'VE ALREADY RULED OUT SENDING OUR FLEET.
I'M BEST USED HERE, IN THE COMMAND ROOM.
IT'S A DIRECT ORDER, COMMANDER. I EXPECT YOU TO FOLLOW IT.
ADMIRAL, WHO...
...WHO WERE YOU JUST TALKING TO?
THAT'S NONE OF YOUR CONCERN, COMMANDER.
...
OH, ADMIRAL.
I'M SORRY.

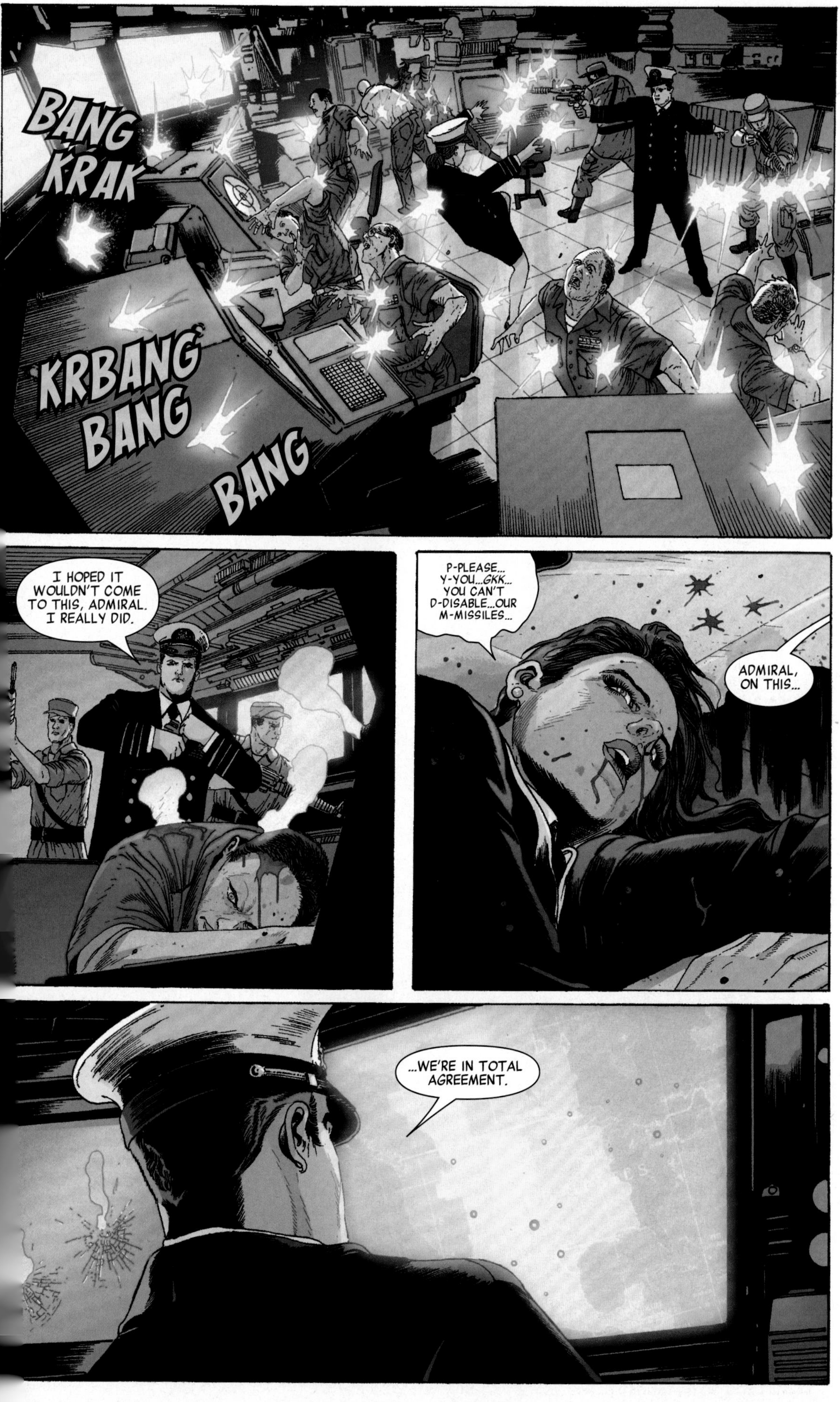
BANG
KRAK
KRBANG
BANG
BANG
I HOPED IT WOULDN'T COME TO THIS, ADMIRAL. I REALLY DID.
P-PLEASE... Y-YOU...GKK... YOU CAN'T D-DISABLE...OUR M-MISSILES...
ADMIRAL, ON THIS...
...WE'RE IN TOTAL AGREEMENT.

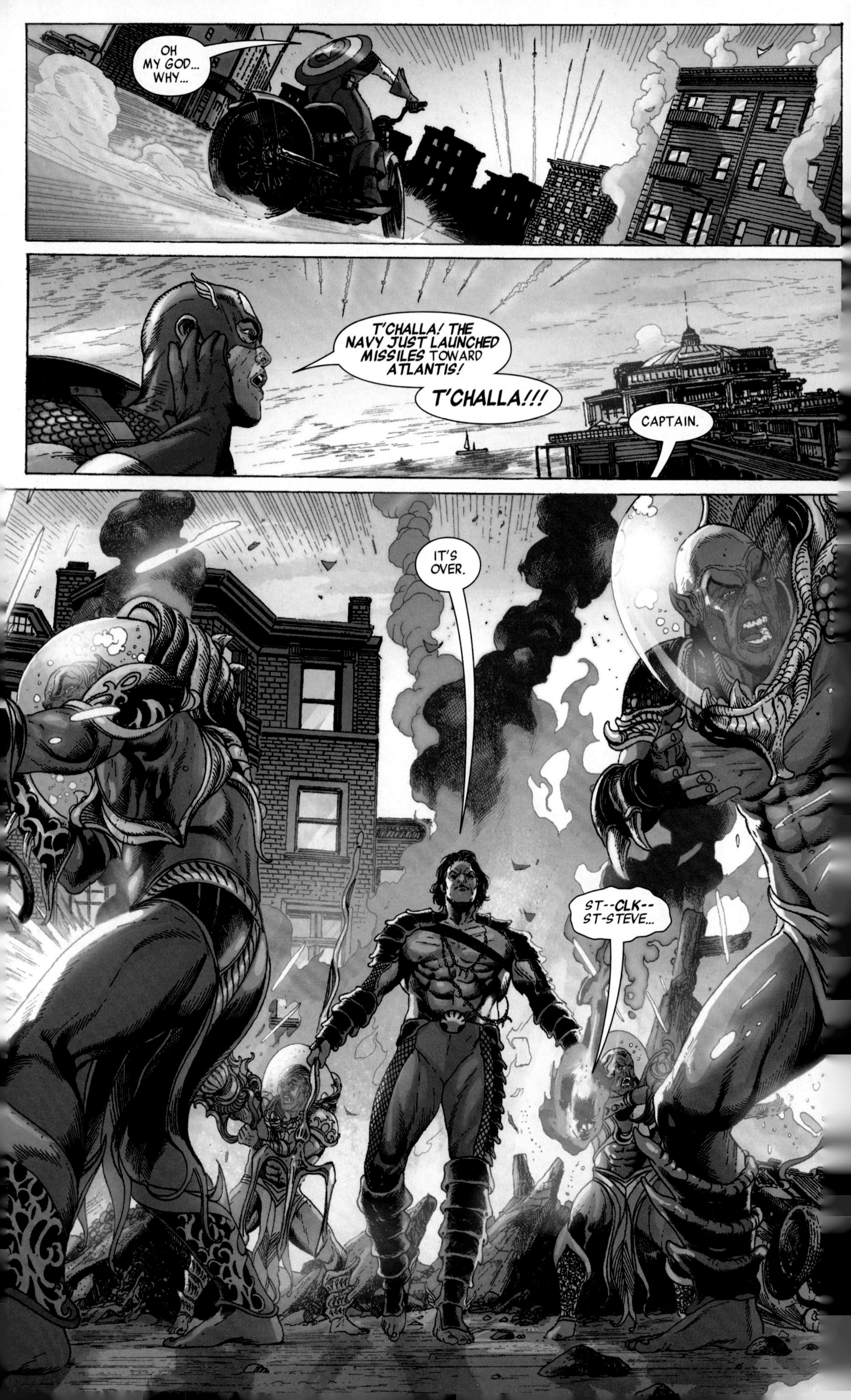
OH MY GOD... WHY...
T'CHALLA! THE NAVY JUST LAUNCHED MISSILES TOWARD ATLANTIS!
T'CHALLA!!!
CAPTAIN.
IT'S OVER.
ST--CLK-- ST-STEVE...

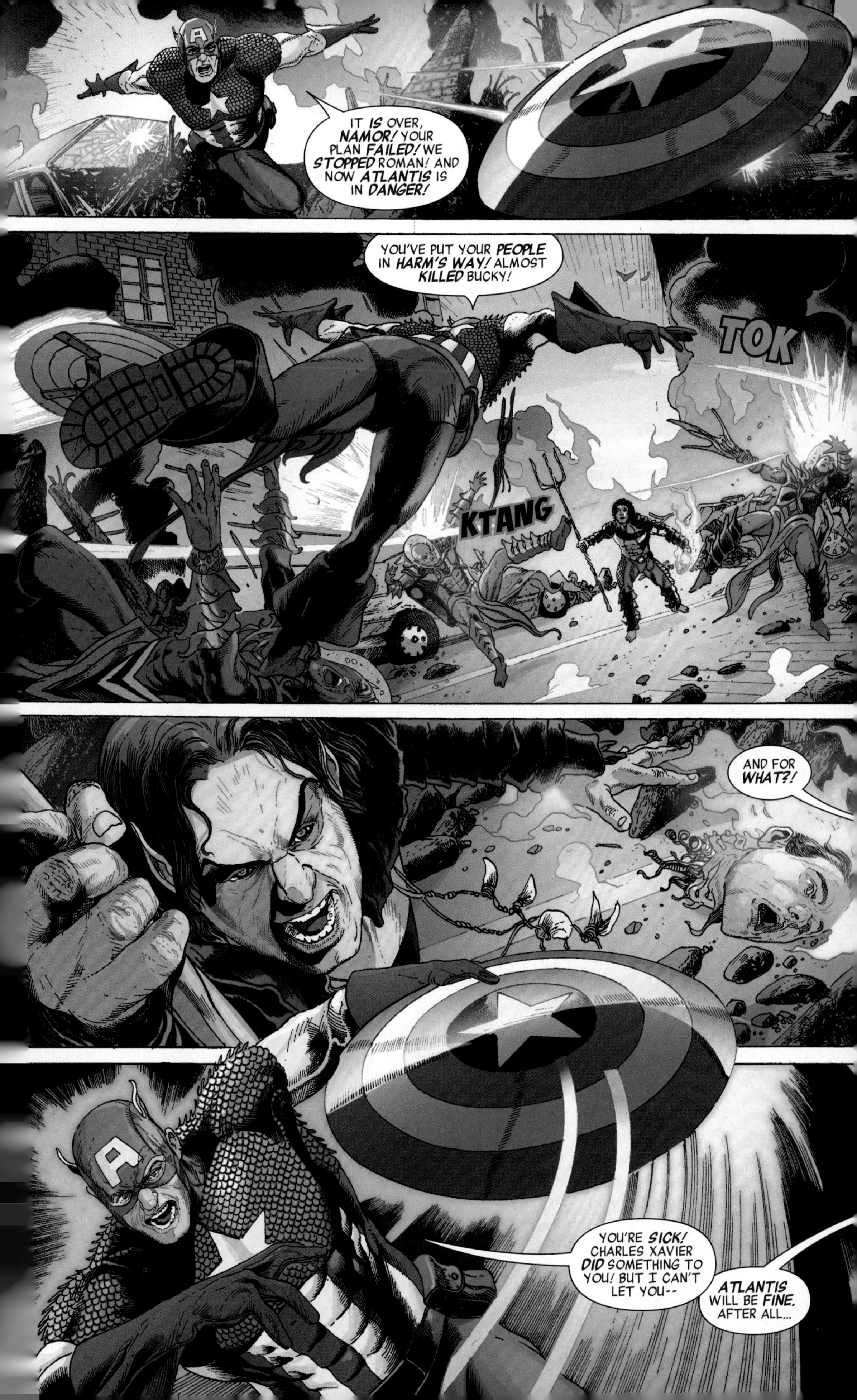
IT IS OVER, NAMOR! YOUR PLAN FAILED! WE STOPPED ROMAN! AND NOW ATLANTIS IS IN DANGER!
YOU'VE PUT YOUR PEOPLE IN HARM'S WAY! ALMOST KILLED BUCKY!
TOK
KTANG
AND FOR WHAT?!
YOU'RE SICK! CHARLES XAVIER DID SOMETHING TO YOU! BUT I CAN'T LET YOU--
ATLANTIS WILL BE FINE. AFTER ALL...

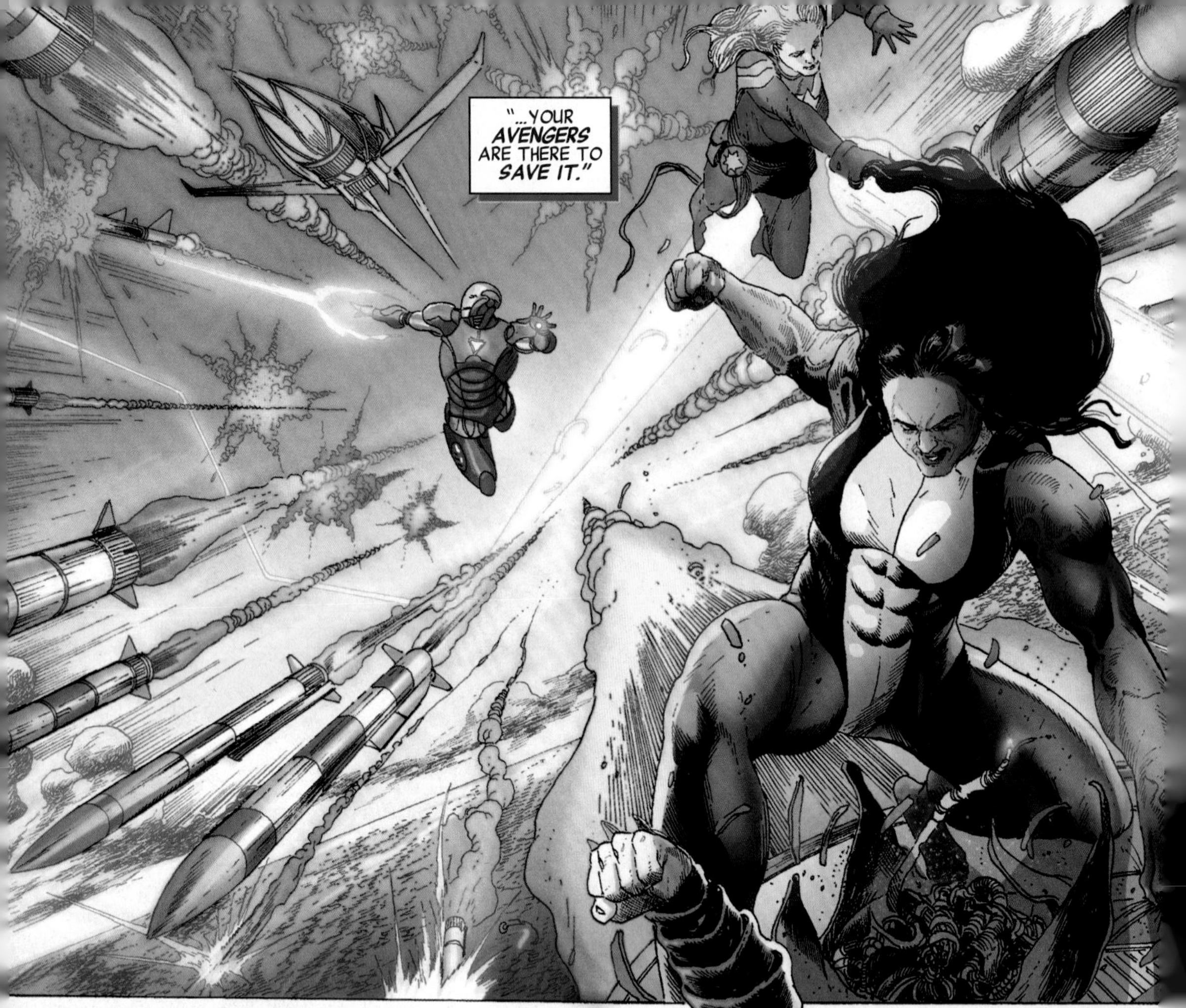
"...YOUR AVENGERS ARE THERE TO SAVE IT."

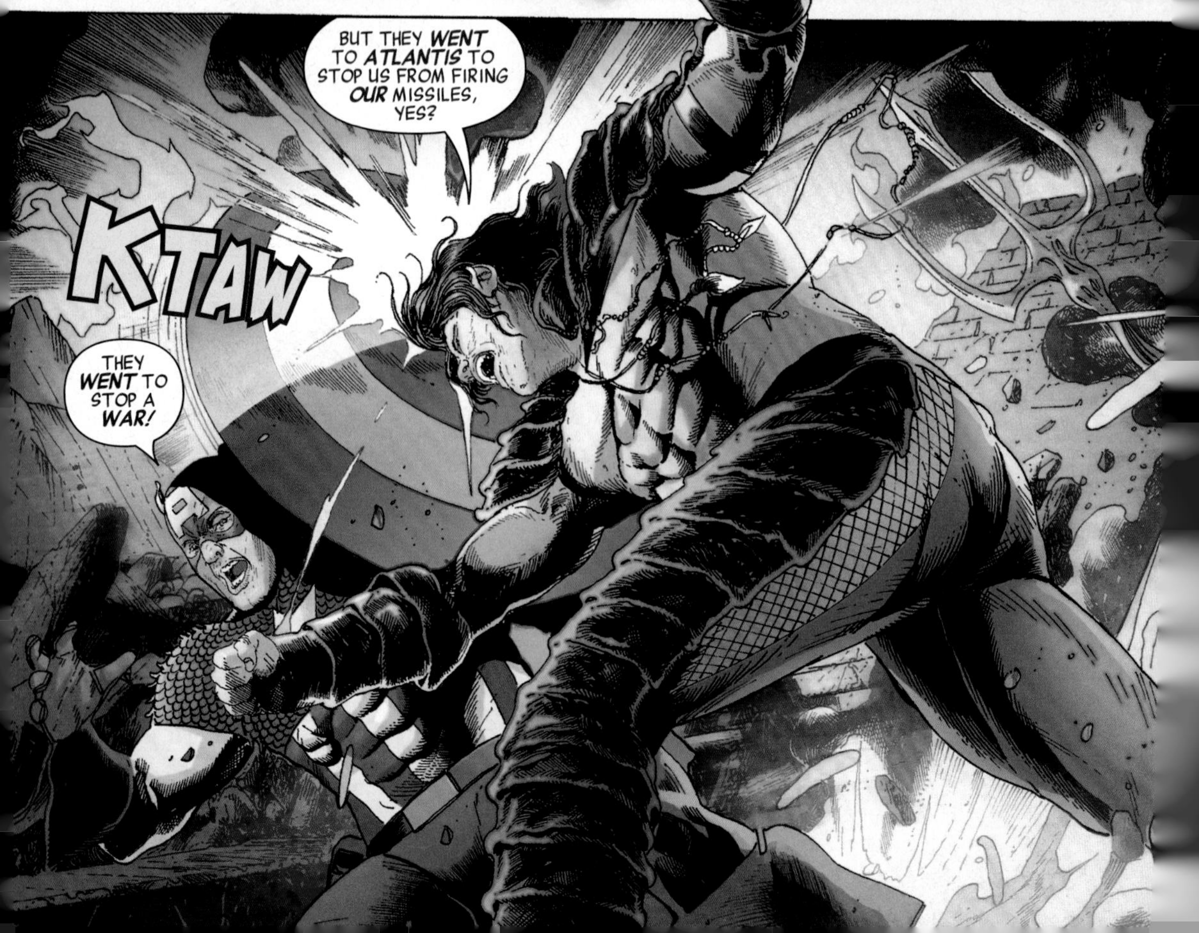
BUT THEY WENT TO ATLANTIS TO STOP US FROM FIRING OUR MISSILES, YES?
KTAW
THEY WENT TO STOP A WAR!

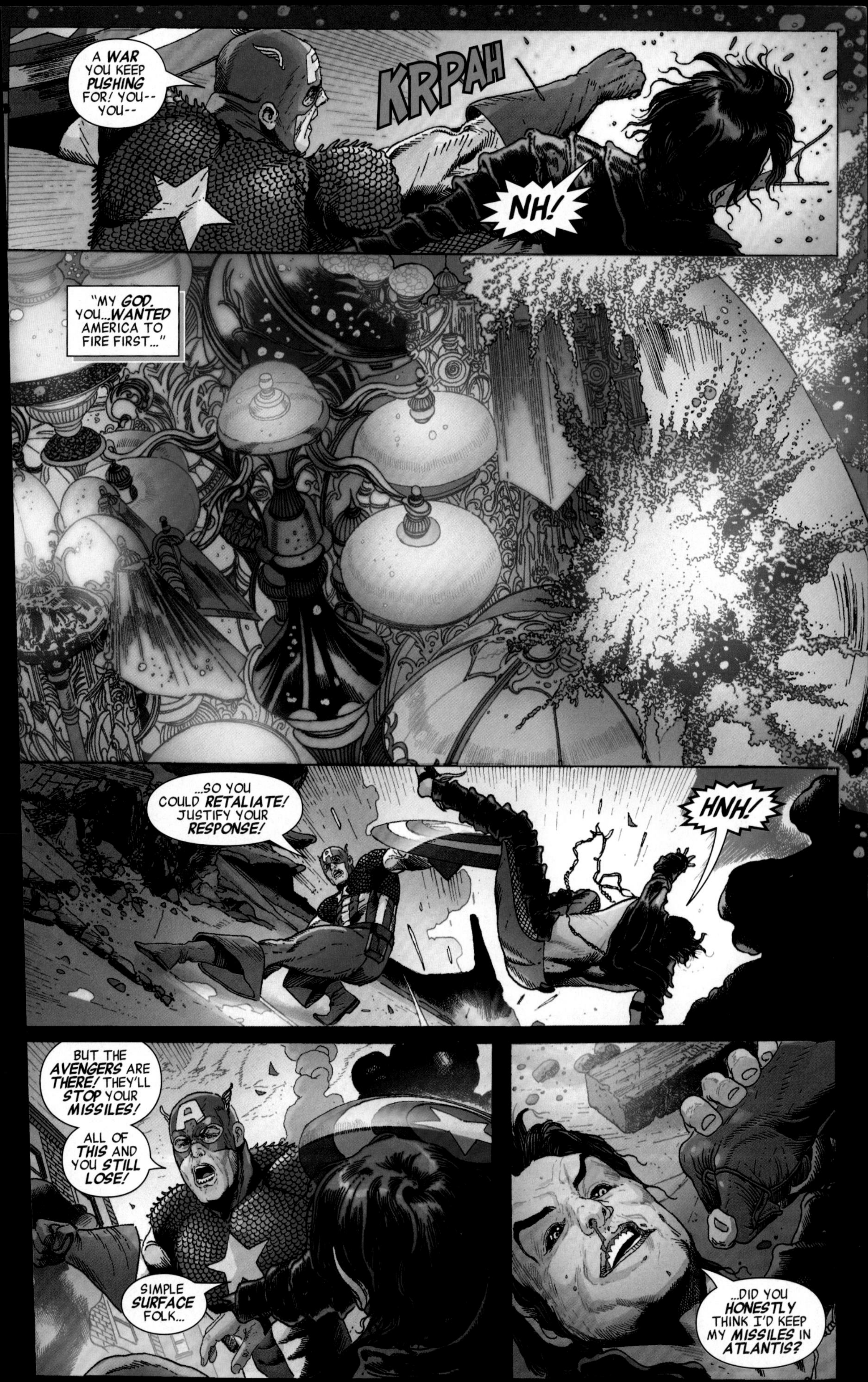

A WAR YOU KEEP PUSHING FOR! YOU-- YOU--
KRPAH
NH!
"MY GOD. YOU...WANTED AMERICA TO FIRE FIRST..."
...SO YOU COULD RETALIATE! JUSTIFY YOUR RESPONSE!
HNH!
BUT THE AVENGERS ARE THERE! THEY'LL STOP YOUR MISSILES!
ALL OF THIS AND YOU STILL LOSE!
SIMPLE SURFACE FOLK...
...DID YOU HONESTLY THINK I'D KEEP MY MISSILES IN ATLANTIS?

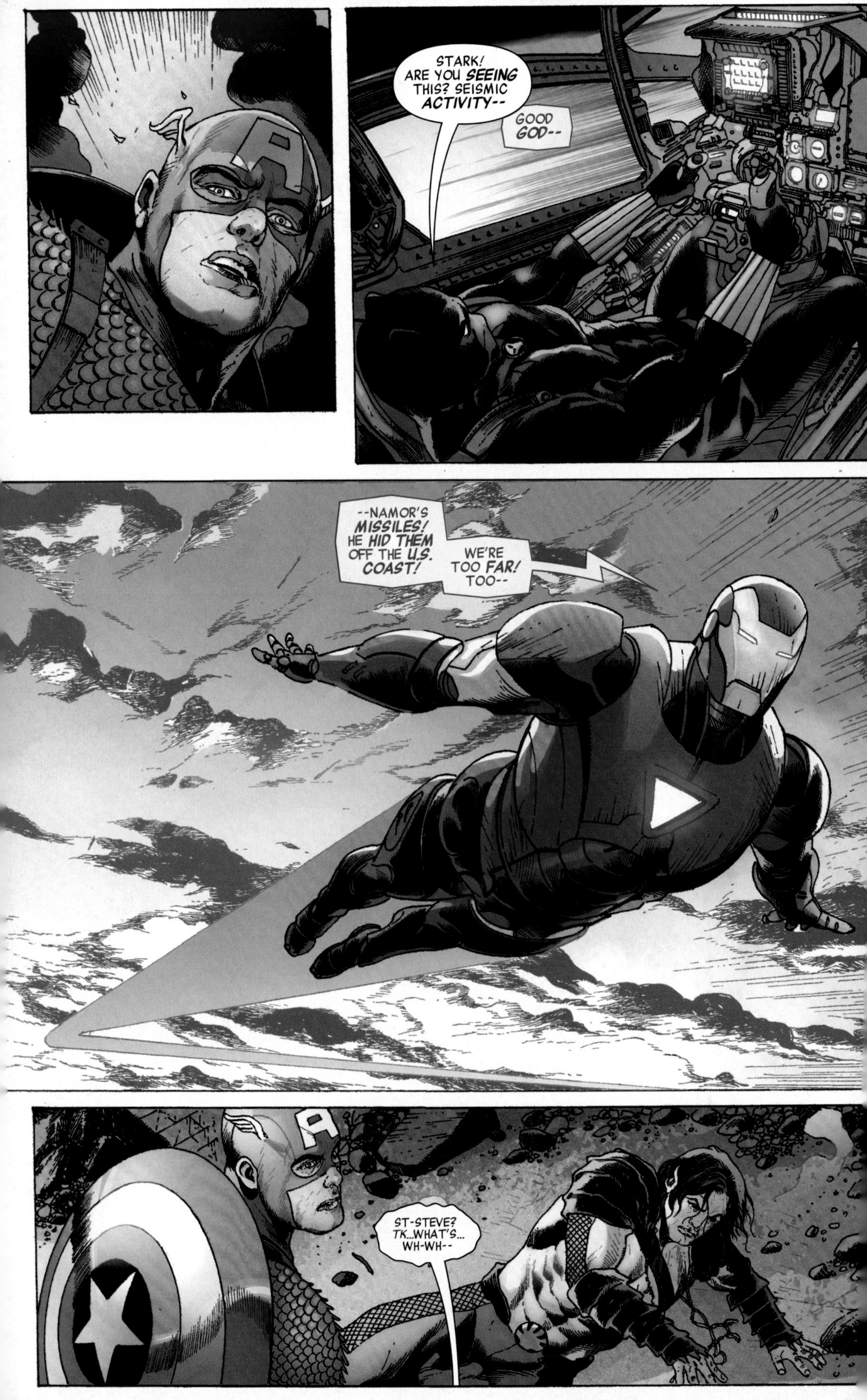
STARK! ARE YOU SEEING THIS? SEISMIC ACTIVITY--
GOOD GOD--
--NAMOR'S MISSILES! HE HID THEM OFF THE U.S. COAST!
WE'RE TOO FAR! TOO--
ST-STEVE? TK...WHAT'S... WH-WH--

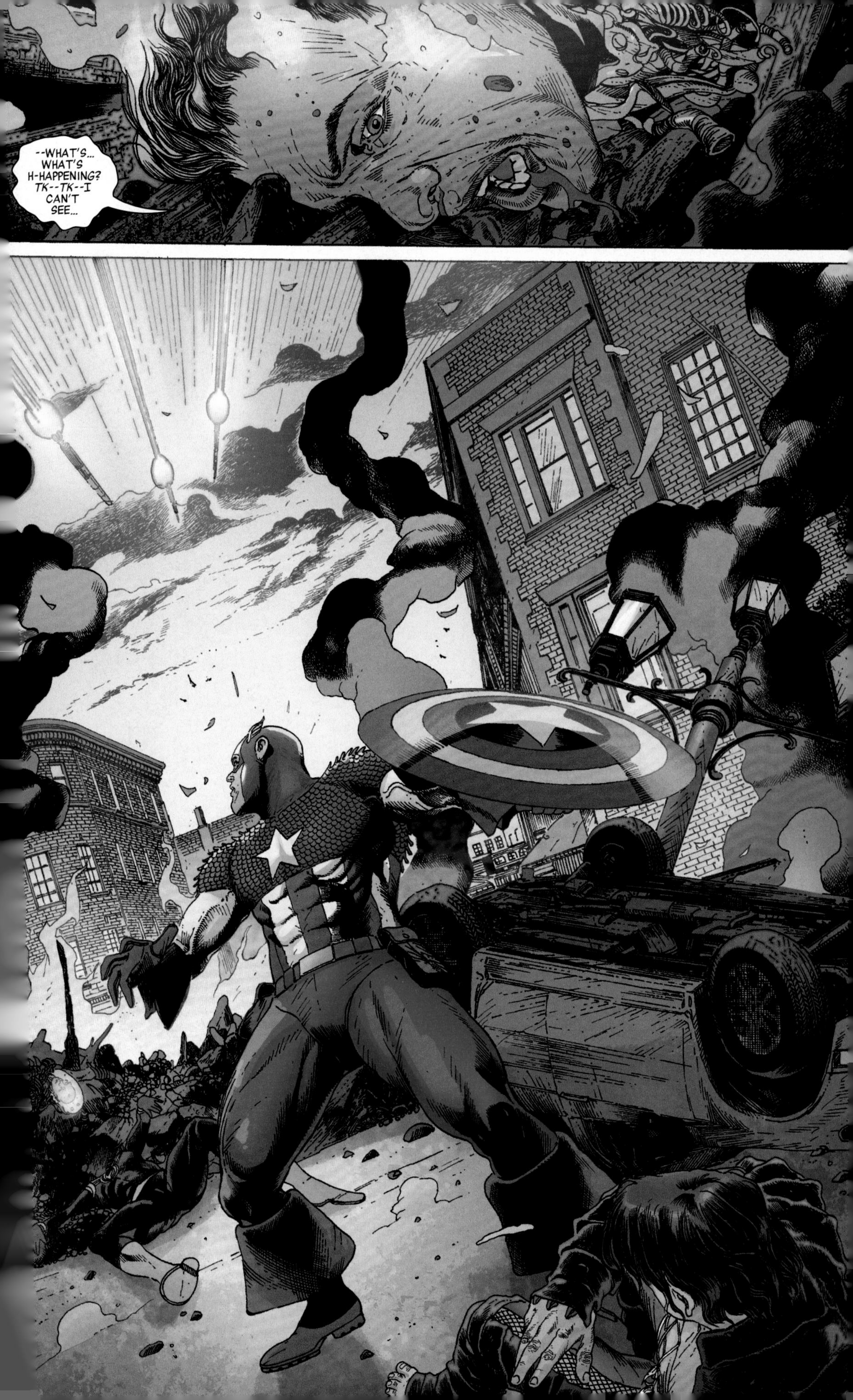
--WHAT'S... WHAT'S H-HAPPENING? TK--TK--I CAN'T SEE...

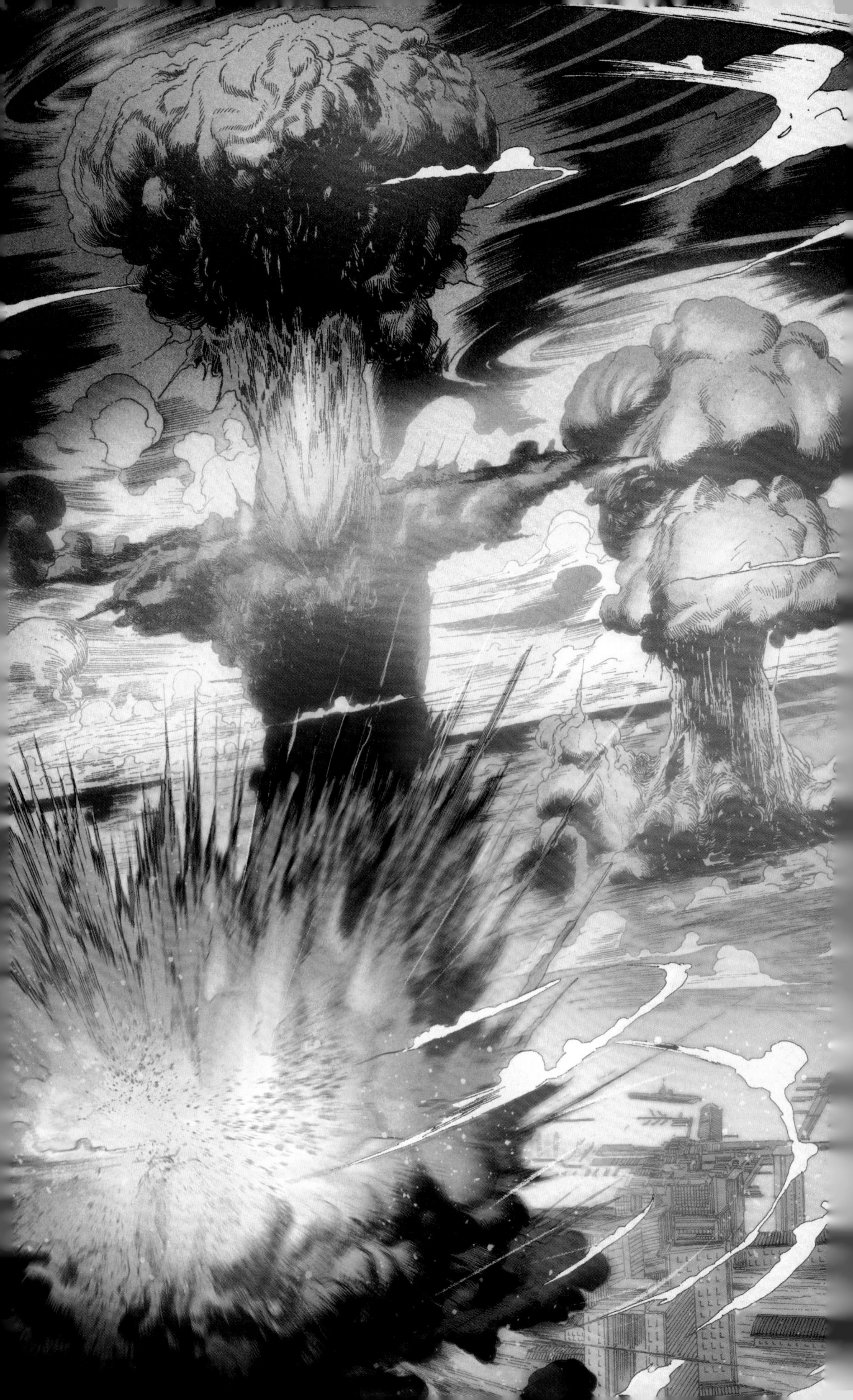

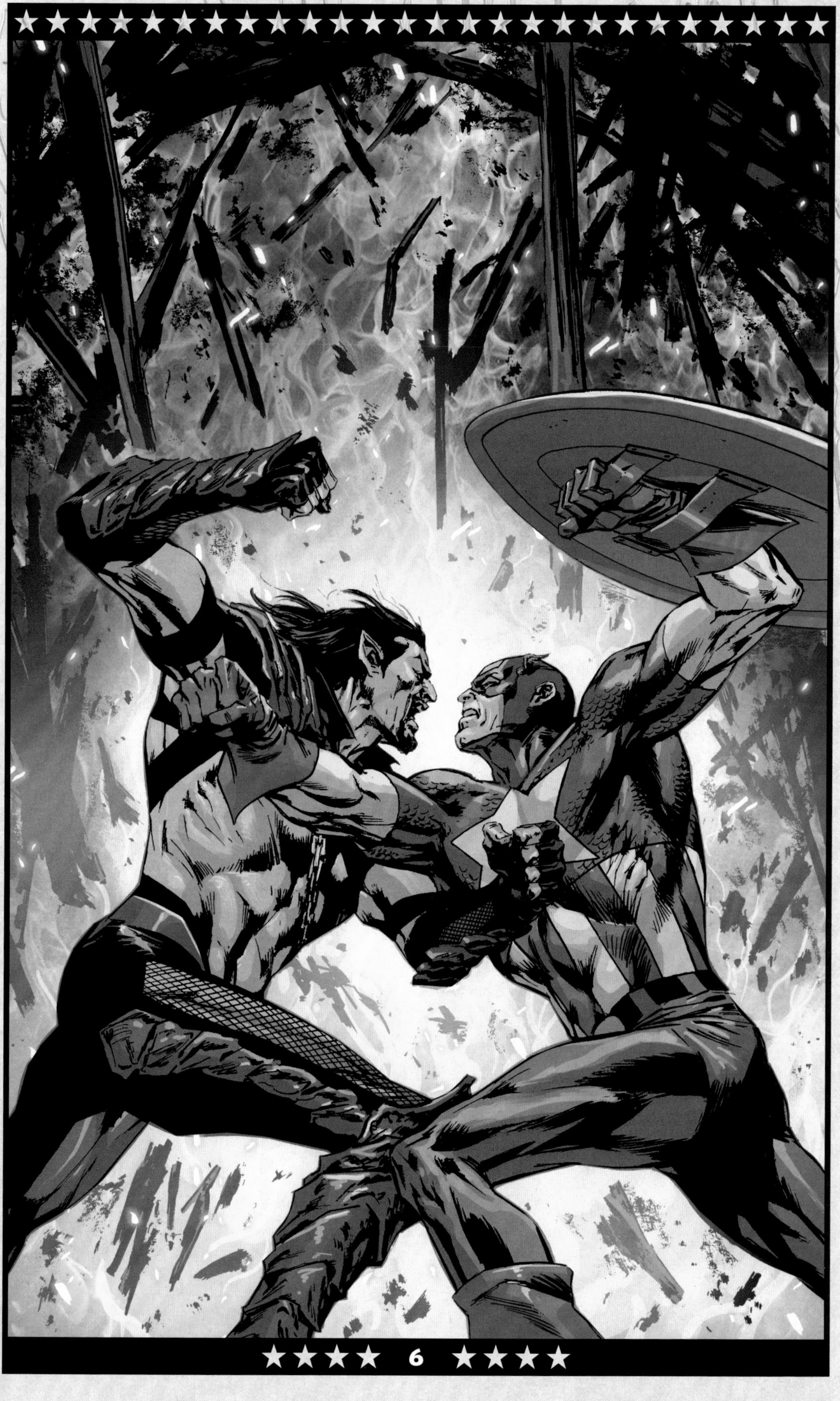
6

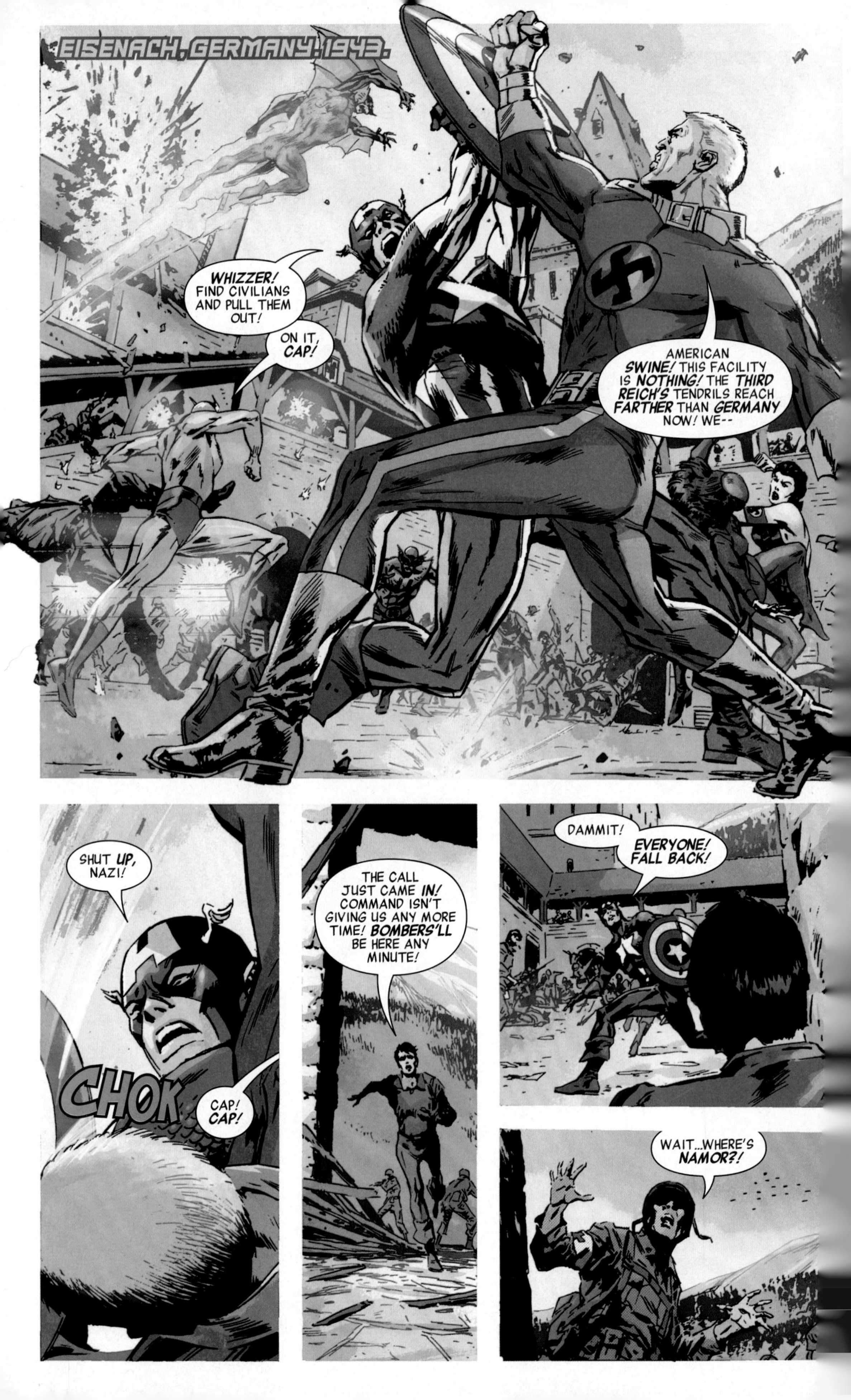
EISENACH, GERMANY. 1943.
WHIZZER! FIND CIVILIANS AND PULL THEM OUT!
ON IT, CAP!
AMERICAN SWINE! THIS FACILITY IS NOTHING! THE THIRD REICH'S TENDRILS REACH FARTHER THAN GERMANY NOW! WE--
SHUT UP, NAZI!
CHOK
CAP! CAP!
THE CALL JUST CAME IN! COMMAND ISN'T GIVING US ANY MORE TIME! BOMBERS'LL BE HERE ANY MINUTE!
DAMMIT!
EVERYONE! FALL BACK!
WAIT...WHERE'S NAMOR?!

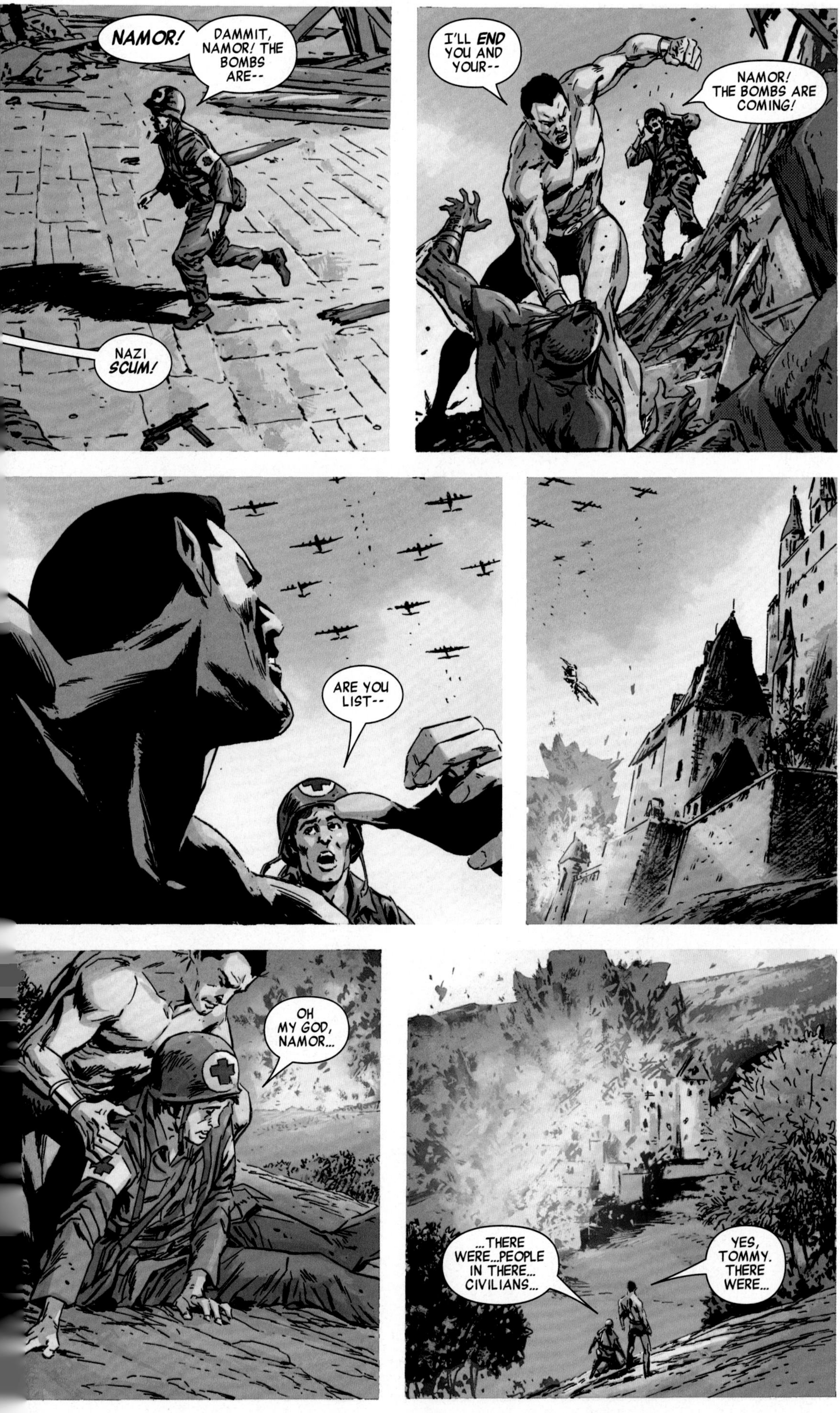
NAMOR!
DAMMIT, NAMOR! THE BOMBS ARE--
NAZI SCUM!
I'LL END YOU AND YOUR--
NAMOR! THE BOMBS ARE COMING!
ARE YOU LIST--
OH MY GOD, NAMOR...
...THERE WERE...PEOPLE IN THERE... CIVILIANS...
YES, TOMMY. THERE WERE...

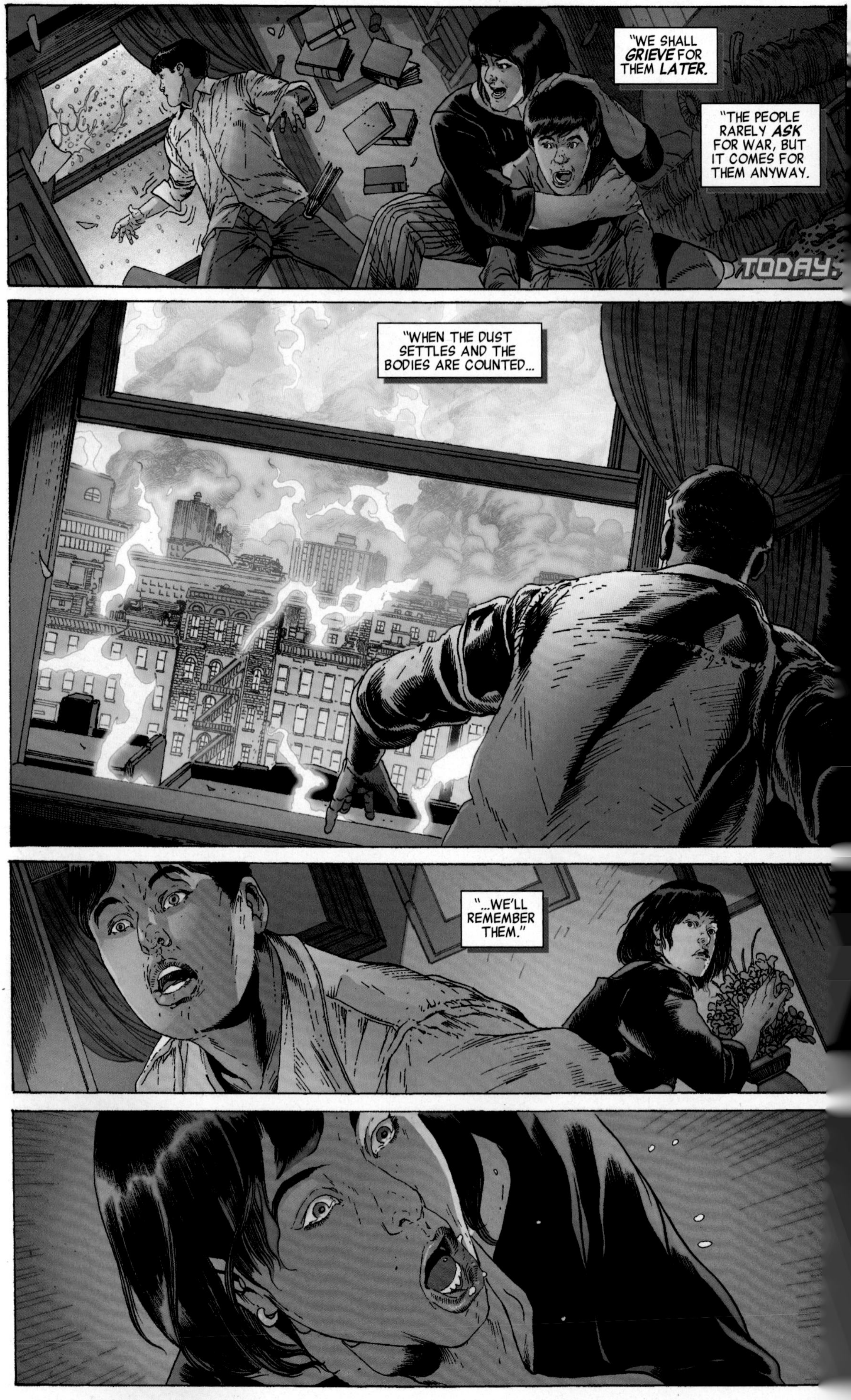
"WE SHALL GRIEVE FOR THEM LATER.
"THE PEOPLE RARELY ASK FOR WAR, BUT IT COMES FOR THEM ANYWAY.
TODAY.
"WHEN THE DUST SETTLES AND THE BODIES ARE COUNTED...
"...WE'LL REMEMBER THEM."

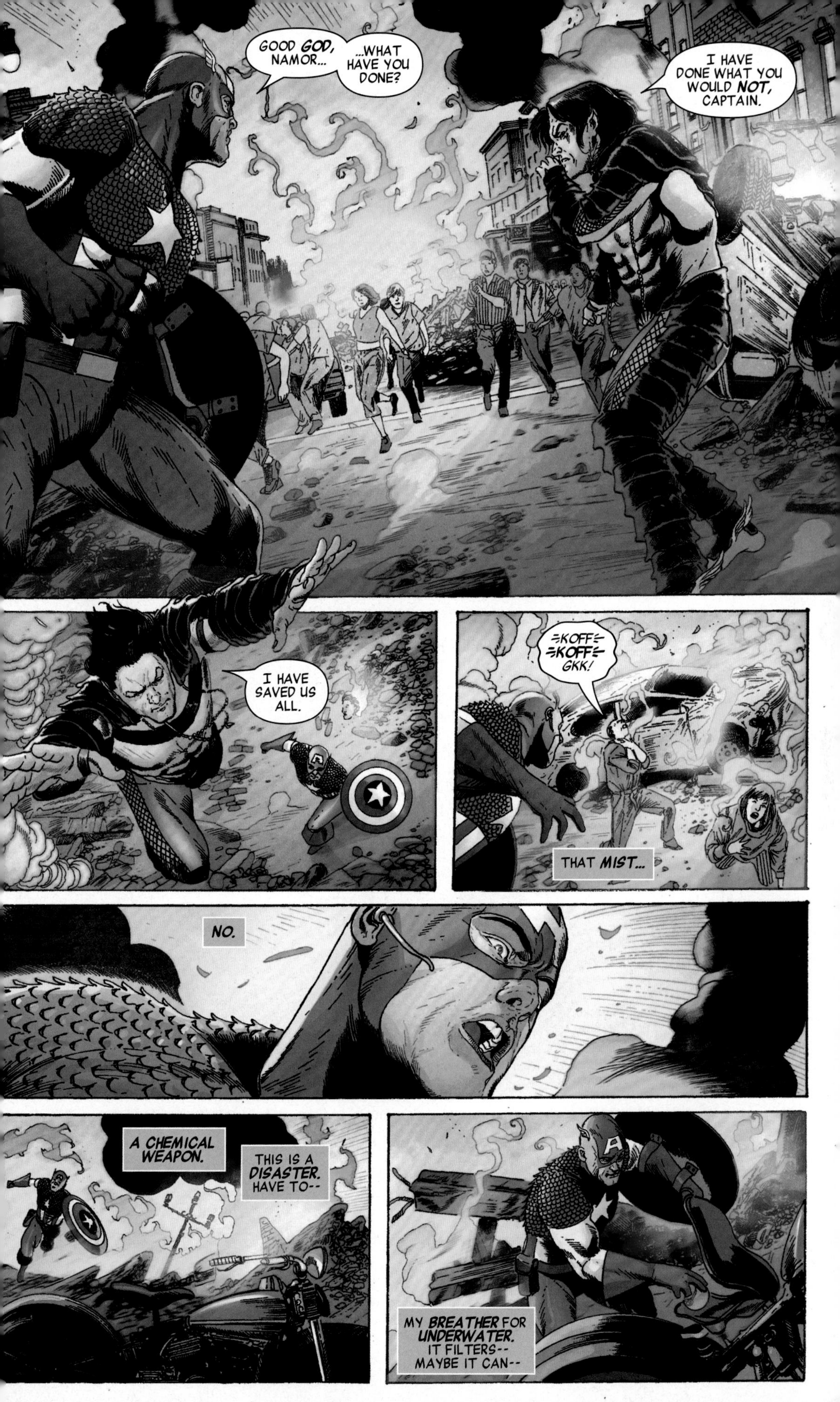
GOOD GOD, NAMOR...
...WHAT HAVE YOU DONE?
I HAVE DONE WHAT YOU WOULD NOT, CAPTAIN.
I HAVE SAVED US ALL.
KOFF KOFF GKK!
THAT MIST...
NO.
A CHEMICAL WEAPON.
THIS IS A DISASTER. HAVE TO--
MY BREATHER FOR UNDERWATER. IT FILTERS-- MAYBE IT CAN--

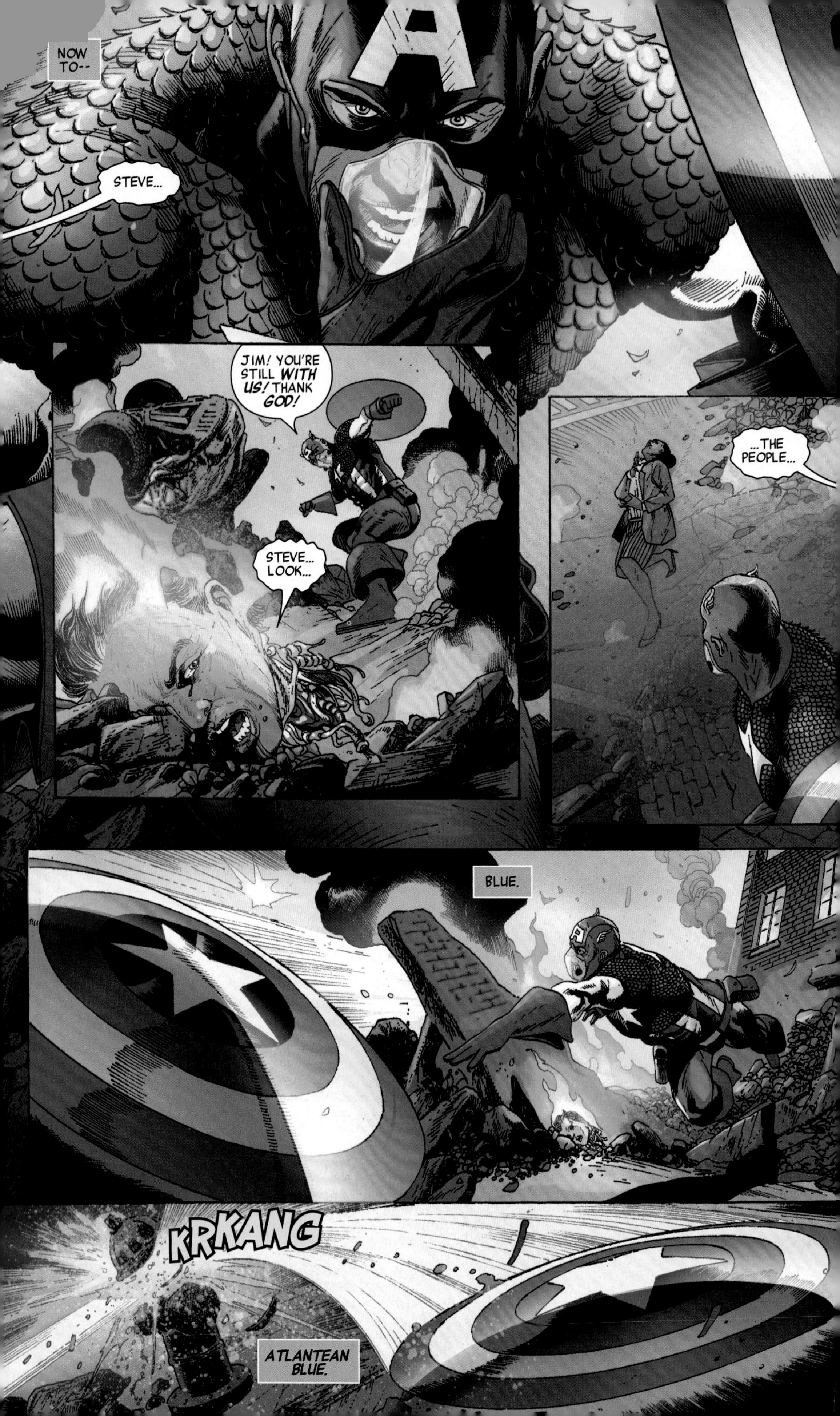
NOW TO--
STEVE...
JIM! YOU'RE STILL WITH US! THANK GOD!
STEVE... LOOK...
...THE PEOPLE...
BLUE.
KRKANG
ATLANTEAN BLUE.

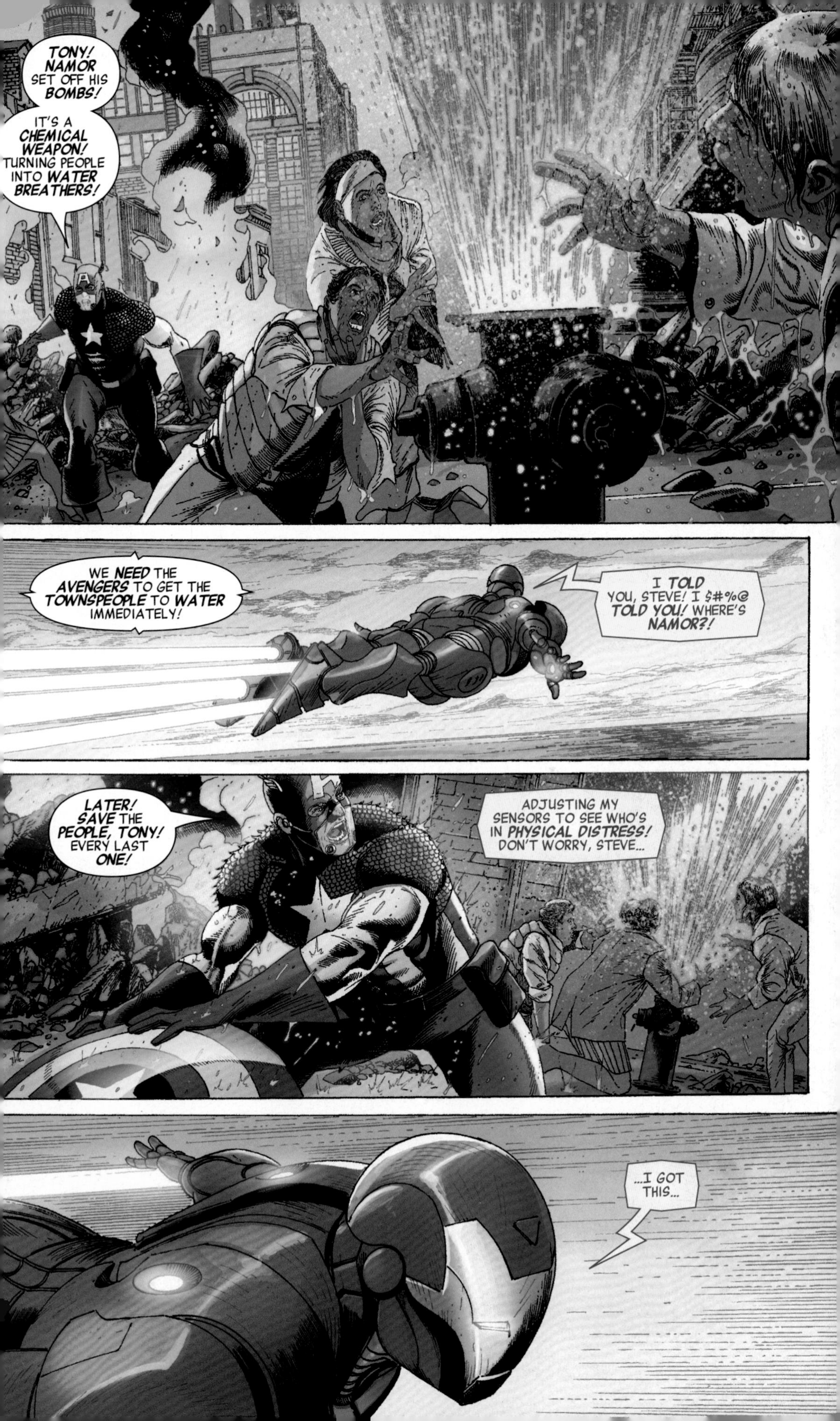
TONY! NAMOR SET OFF HIS BOMBS!
IT'S A CHEMICAL WEAPON! TURNING PEOPLE INTO WATER BREATHERS!
WE NEED THE AVENGERS TO GET THE TOWNSPEOPLE TO WATER IMMEDIATELY!
I TOLD YOU, STEVE! I $#%@ TOLD YOU! WHERE'S NAMOR?!
LATER! SAVE THE PEOPLE, TONY! EVERY LAST ONE!
ADJUSTING MY SENSORS TO SEE WHO'S IN PHYSICAL DISTRESS! DON'T WORRY, STEVE...
...I GOT THIS...

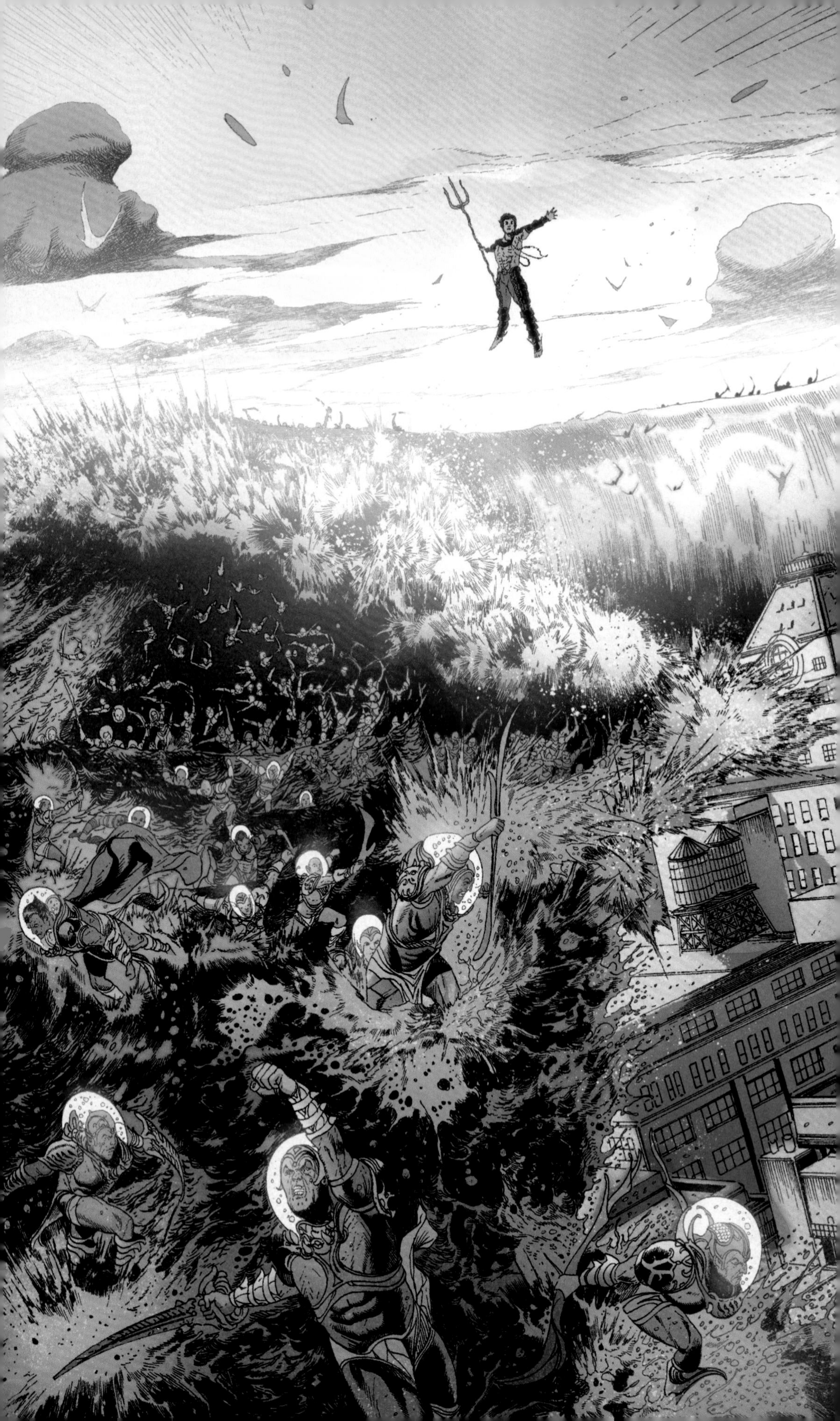

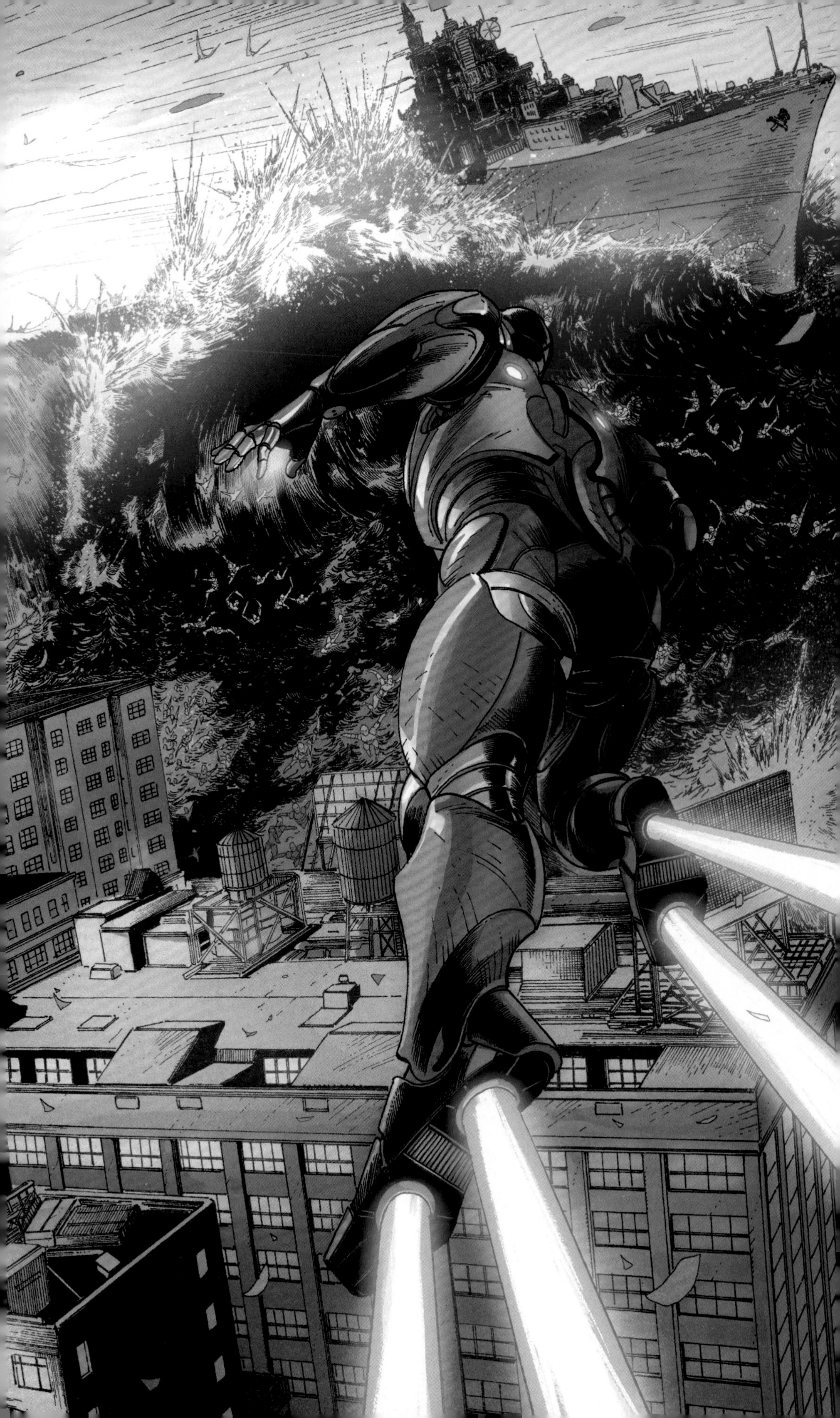

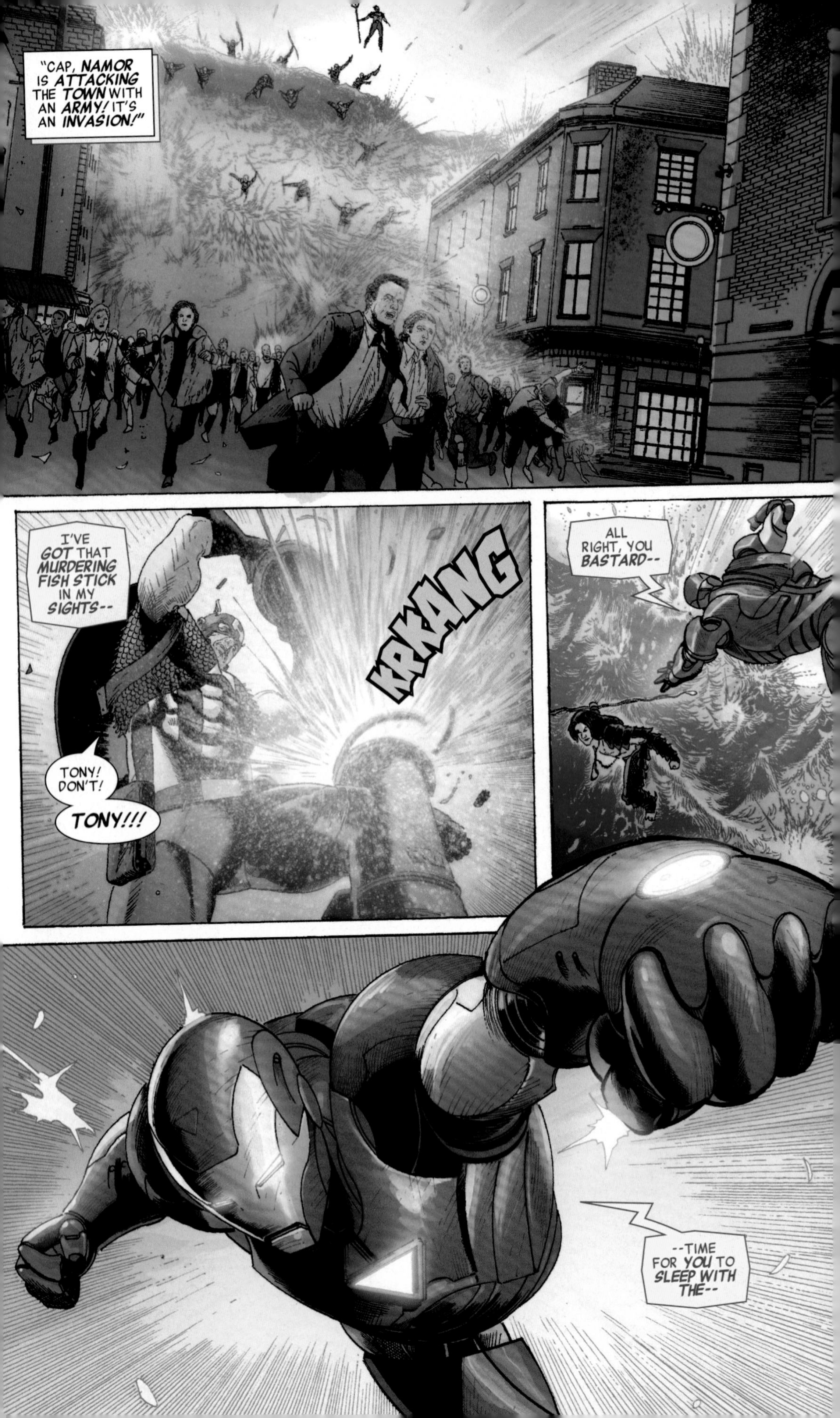
"CAP, NAMOR IS ATTACKING THE TOWN WITH AN ARMY! IT'S AN INVASION!"
I'VE GOT THAT MURDERING FISH STICK IN MY SIGHTS--
TONY! DON'T!
TONY!!!
KRKANG
ALL RIGHT, YOU BASTARD--
--TIME FOR YOU TO SLEEP WITH THE--

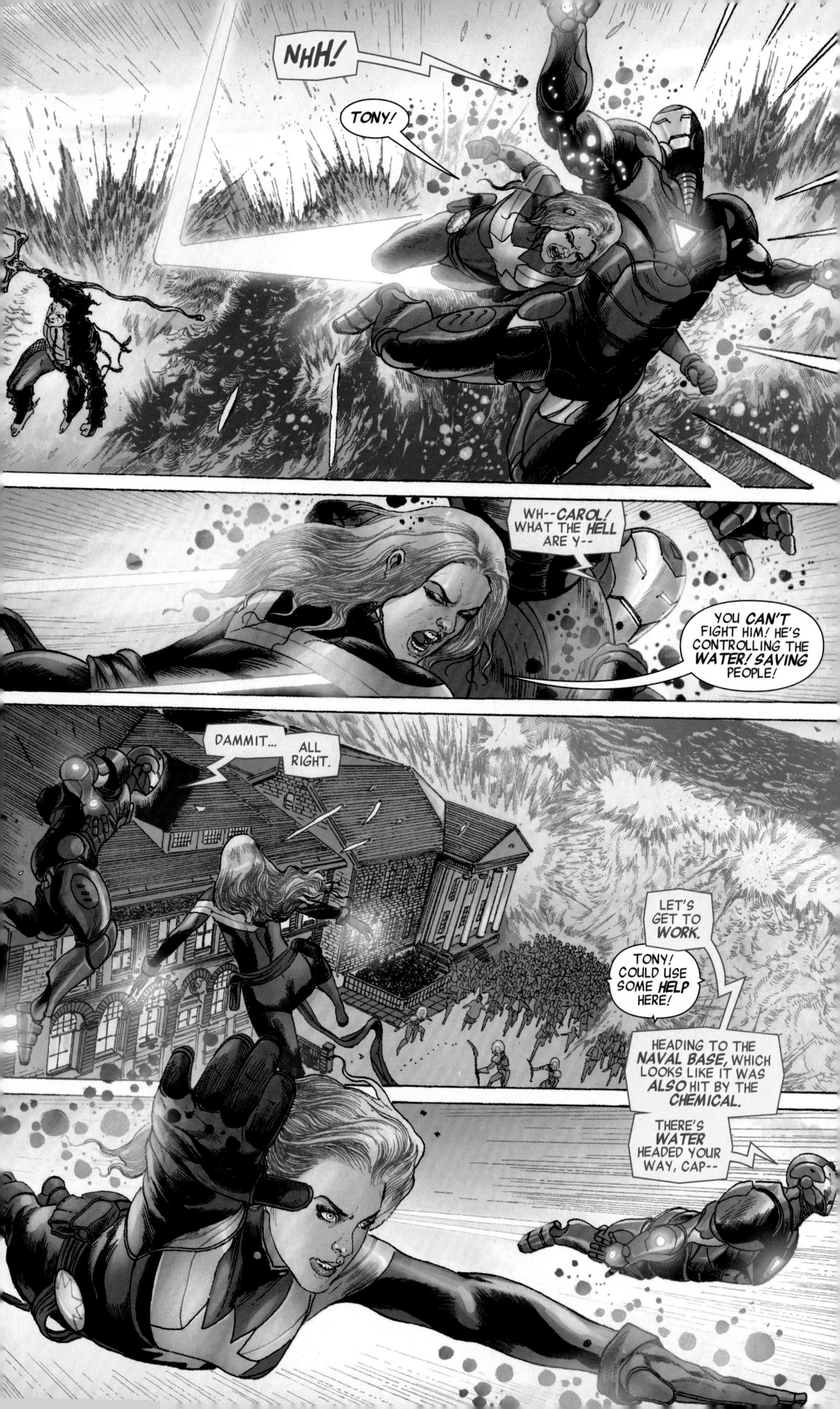

NHH!
TONY!
WH--CAROL! WHAT THE HELL ARE Y--
YOU CAN'T FIGHT HIM! HE'S CONTROLLING THE WATER! SAVING PEOPLE!
DAMMIT... ALL RIGHT.
LET'S GET TO WORK.
TONY! COULD USE SOME HELP HERE!
HEADING TO THE NAVAL BASE, WHICH LOOKS LIKE IT WAS ALSO HIT BY THE CHEMICAL.
THERE'S WATER HEADED YOUR WAY, CAP--

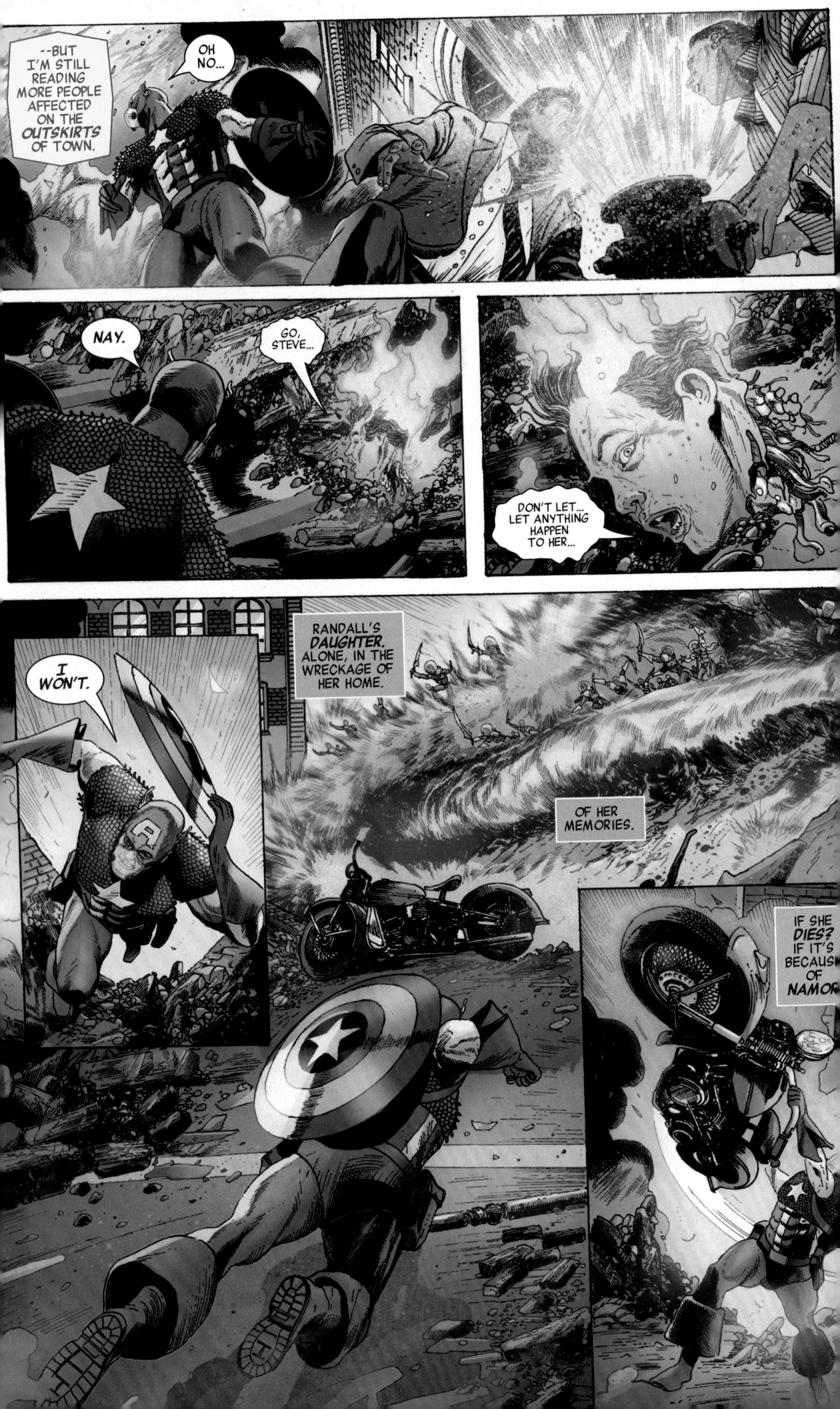
--BUT I'M STILL READING MORE PEOPLE AFFECTED ON THE OUTSKIRTS OF TOWN.
OH NO...
NAY.
GO, STEVE...
DON'T LET... LET ANYTHING HAPPEN TO HER...
I WON'T.
RANDALL'S DAUGHTER. ALONE, IN THE WRECKAGE OF HER HOME.
OF HER MEMORIES.
IF SHE DIES? IF IT'S BECAUS OF NAMOR

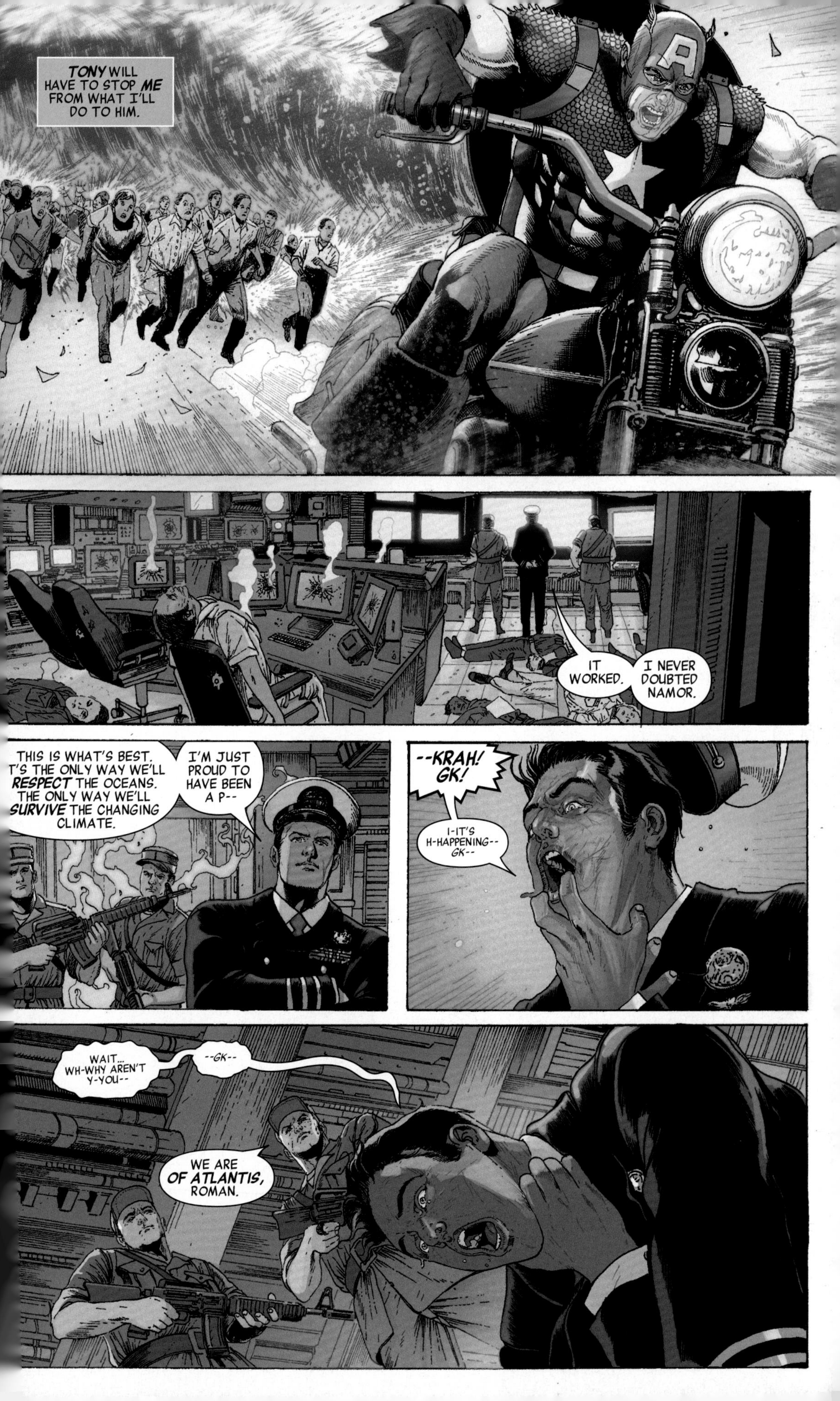

TONY WILL HAVE TO STOP ME FROM WHAT I'LL DO TO HIM.
IT WORKED.
I NEVER DOUBTED NAMOR.
THIS IS WHAT'S BEST. T'S THE ONLY WAY WE'LL RESPECT THE OCEANS. THE ONLY WAY WE'LL SURVIVE THE CHANGING CLIMATE.
I'M JUST PROUD TO HAVE BEEN A P--
--KRAH! GK!
I-IT'S H-HAPPENING-- GK--
WAIT... WH-WHY AREN'T Y-YOU--
--GK--
WE ARE OF ATLANTIS, ROMAN.

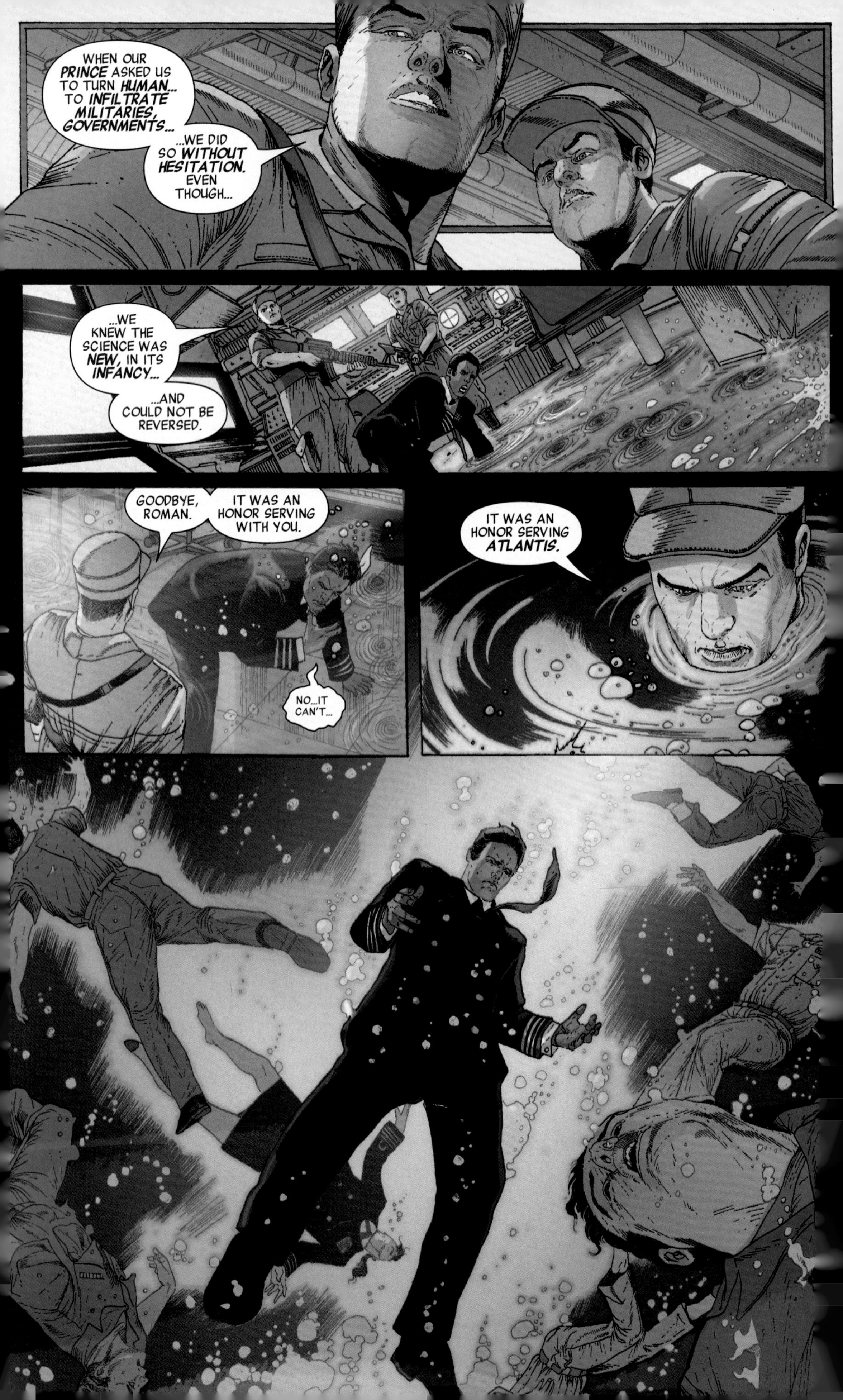
WHEN OUR PRINCE ASKED US TO TURN HUMAN... TO INFILTRATE MILITARIES, GOVERNMENTS...
...WE DID SO WITHOUT HESITATION. EVEN THOUGH...
...WE KNEW THE SCIENCE WAS NEW, IN ITS INFANCY...
...AND COULD NOT BE REVERSED.
GOODBYE, ROMAN.
IT WAS AN HONOR SERVING WITH YOU.
NO...IT CAN'T...
IT WAS AN HONOR SERVING ATLANTIS.

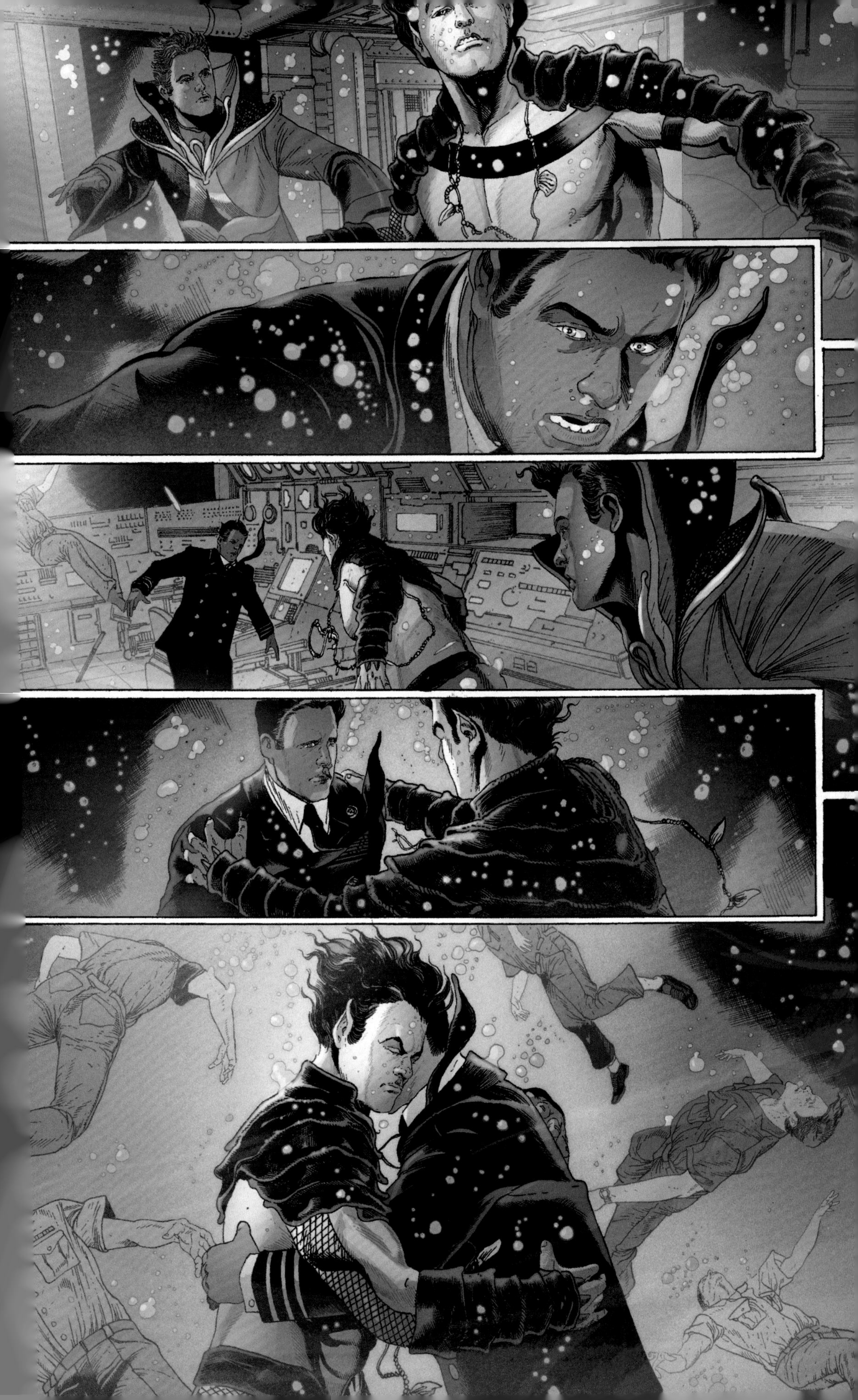

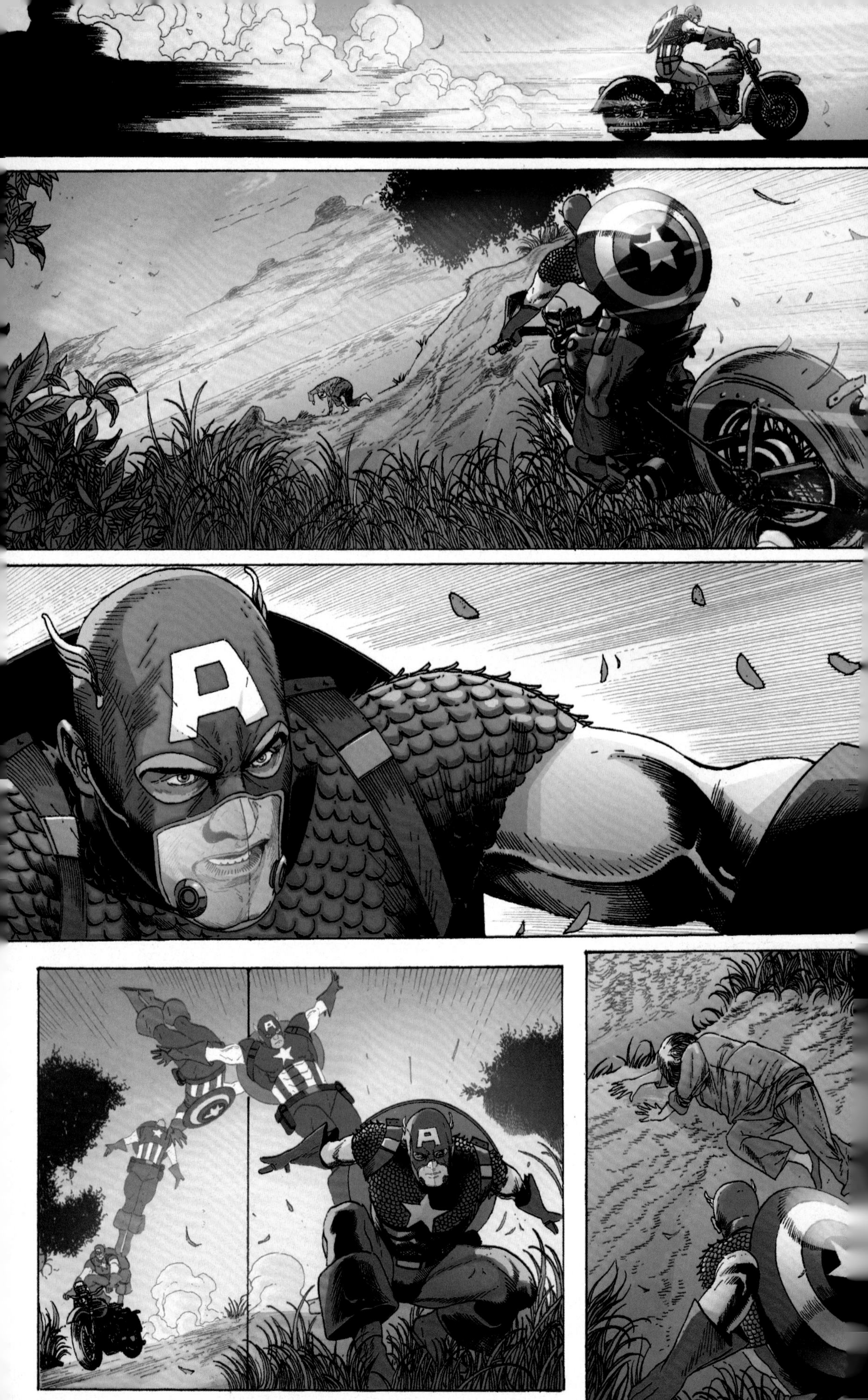

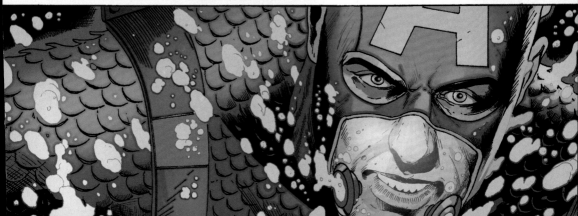

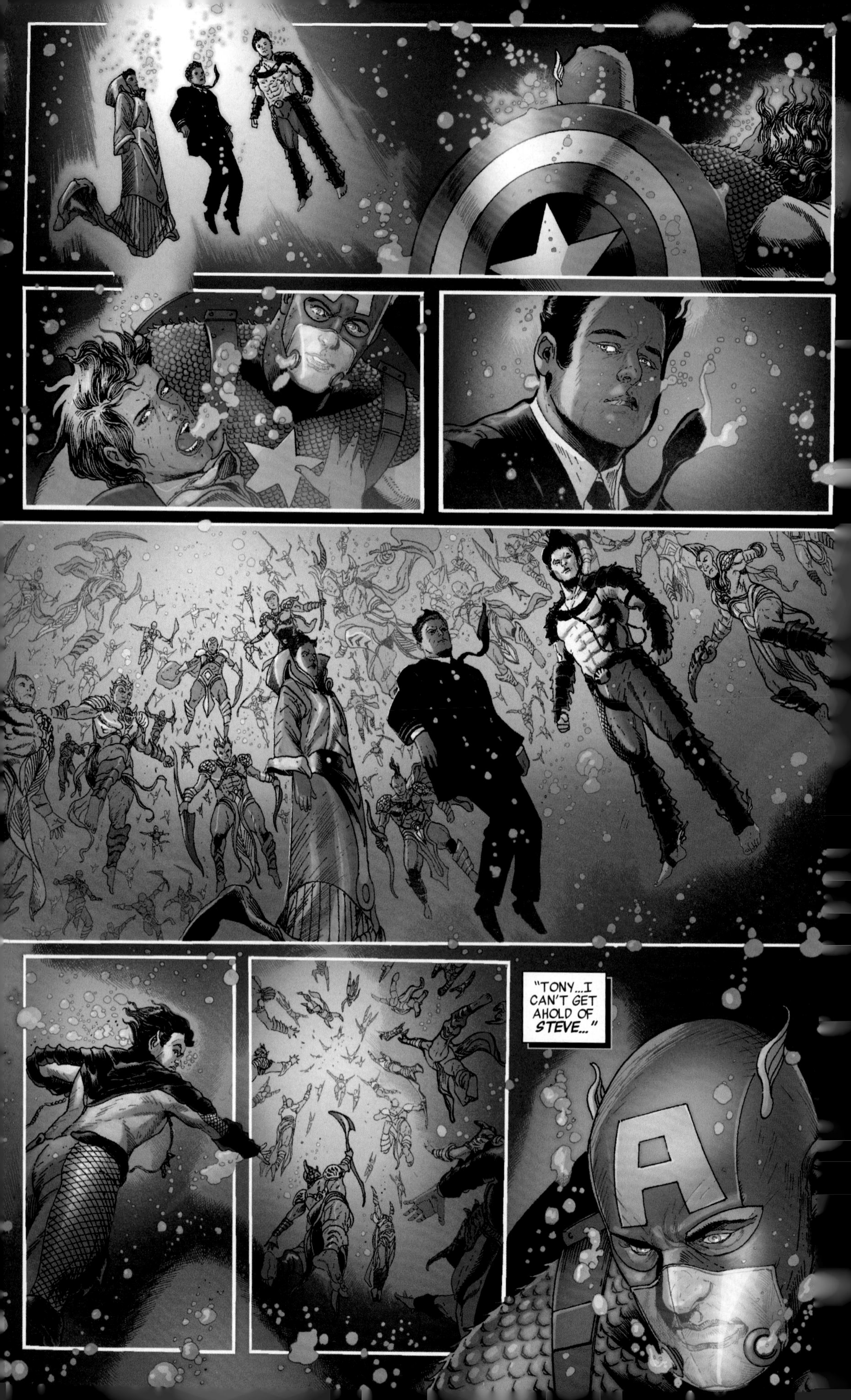
"TONY...I CAN'T GET AHOLD OF STEVE..."

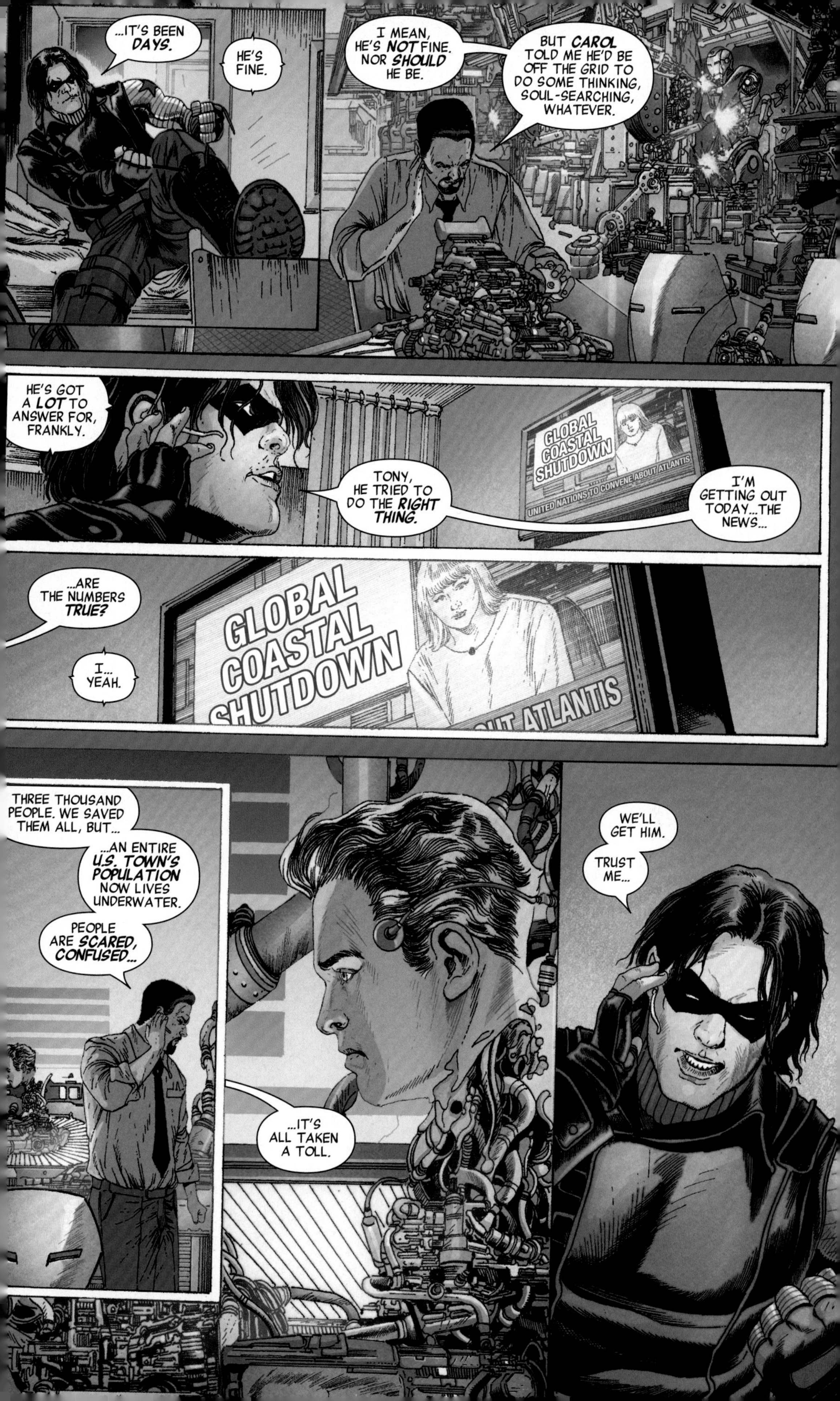

...IT'S BEEN DAYS.
HE'S FINE.
I MEAN, HE'S NOT FINE. NOR SHOULD HE BE.
BUT CAROL TOLD ME HE'D BE OFF THE GRID TO DO SOME THINKING, SOUL-SEARCHING, WHATEVER.
HE'S GOT A LOT TO ANSWER FOR, FRANKLY.
TONY, HE TRIED TO DO THE RIGHT THING.
GLOBAL COASTAL SHUTDOWN
UNITED NATIONS TO CONVENE ABOUT ATLANTIS
I'M GETTING OUT TODAY...THE NEWS...
...ARE THE NUMBERS TRUE?
I... YEAH.
GLOBAL COASTAL SHUTDOWN
THREE THOUSAND PEOPLE. WE SAVED THEM ALL, BUT...
...AN ENTIRE U.S. TOWN'S POPULATION NOW LIVES UNDERWATER.
PEOPLE ARE SCARED, CONFUSED...
...IT'S ALL TAKEN A TOLL.
WE'LL GET HIM.
TRUST ME...

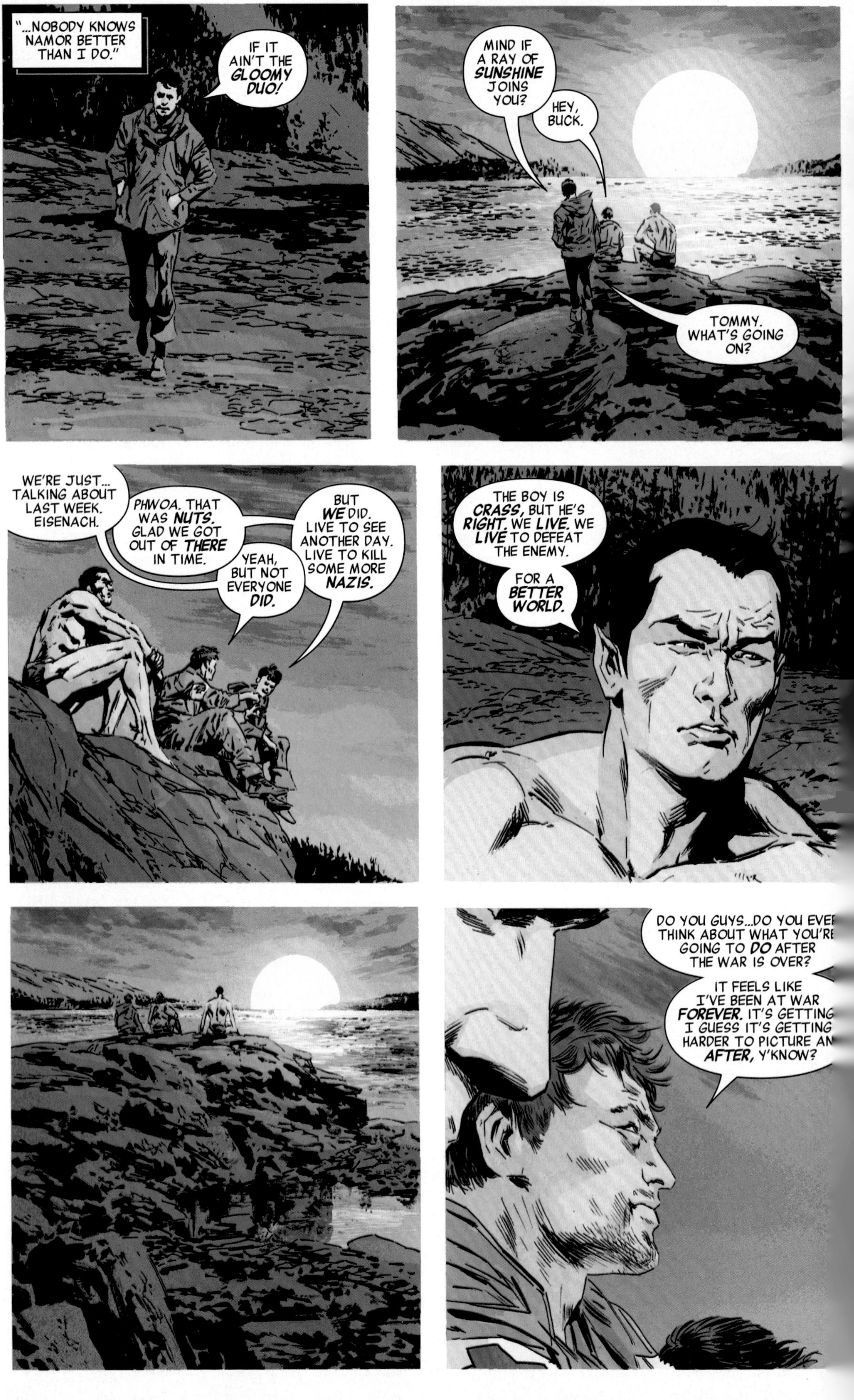

"...NOBODY KNOWS NAMOR BETTER THAN I DO."
IF IT AIN'T THE GLOOMY DUO!
MIND IF A RAY OF SUNSHINE JOINS YOU?
HEY, BUCK.
TOMMY. WHAT'S GOING ON?
WE'RE JUST... TALKING ABOUT LAST WEEK. EISENACH.
PHWOA. THAT WAS NUTS. GLAD WE GOT OUT OF THERE IN TIME.
YEAH, BUT NOT EVERYONE DID.
BUT WE DID. LIVE TO SEE ANOTHER DAY. LIVE TO KILL SOME MORE NAZIS.
THE BOY IS CRASS, BUT HE'S RIGHT. WE LIVE. WE LIVE TO DEFEAT THE ENEMY.
FOR A BETTER WORLD.
DO YOU GUYS...DO YOU EVE THINK ABOUT WHAT YOU'R GOING TO DO AFTER THE WAR IS OVER?
IT FEELS LIKE I'VE BEEN AT WAR FOREVER. IT'S GETTING I GUESS IT'S GETTING HARDER TO PICTURE AN AFTER, Y'KNOW?

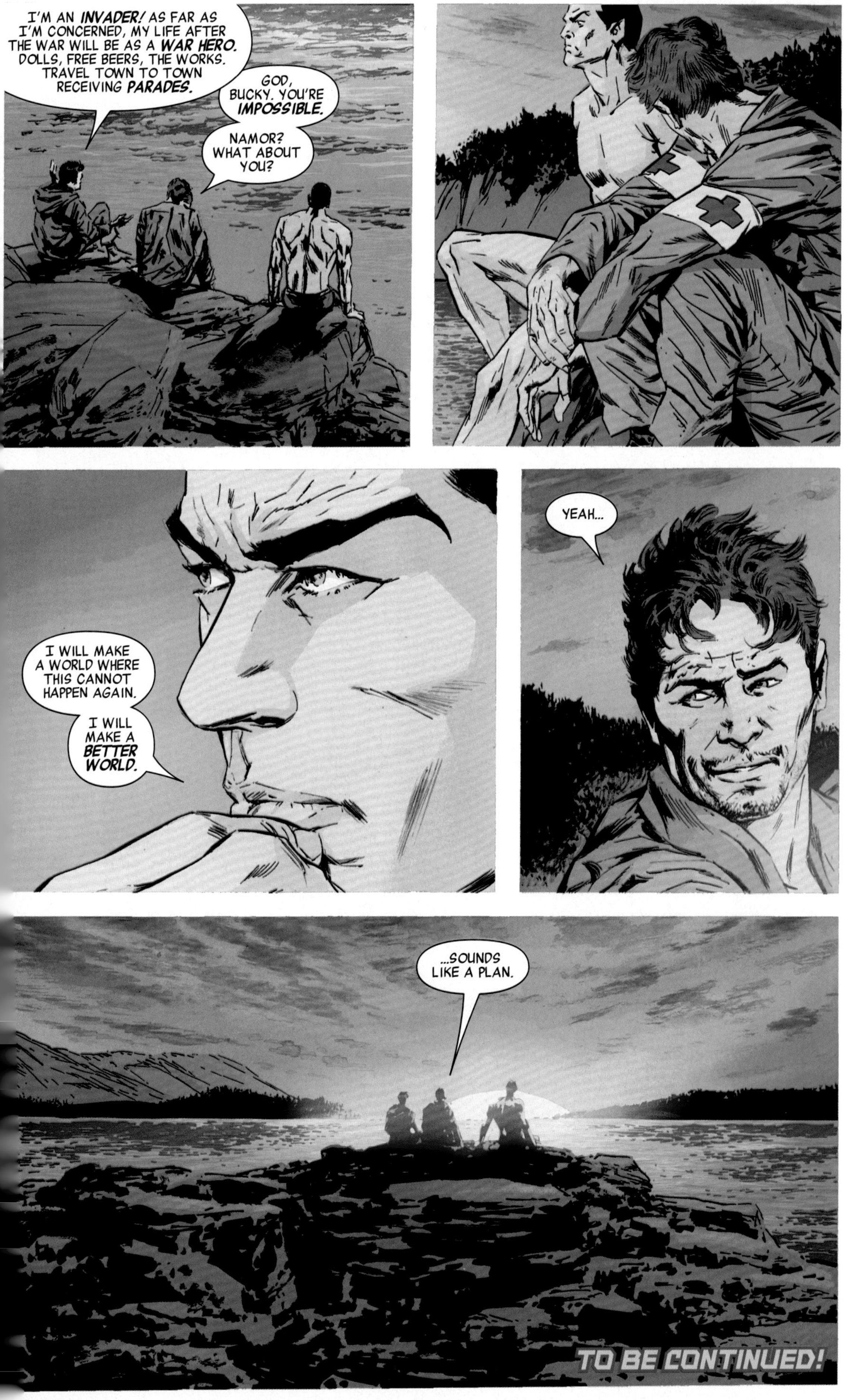

I'M AN *INVADER!* AS FAR AS I'M CONCERNED, MY LIFE AFTER THE WAR WILL BE AS A *WAR HERO.* DOLLS, FREE BEERS, THE WORKS. TRAVEL TOWN TO TOWN RECEIVING *PARADES.*
GOD, BUCKY. YOU'RE *IMPOSSIBLE.*
NAMOR? WHAT ABOUT YOU?
I WILL MAKE A WORLD WHERE THIS CANNOT HAPPEN AGAIN.
I WILL MAKE A *BETTER WORLD.*
YEAH...
...SOUNDS LIKE A PLAN.
TO BE CONTINUED!

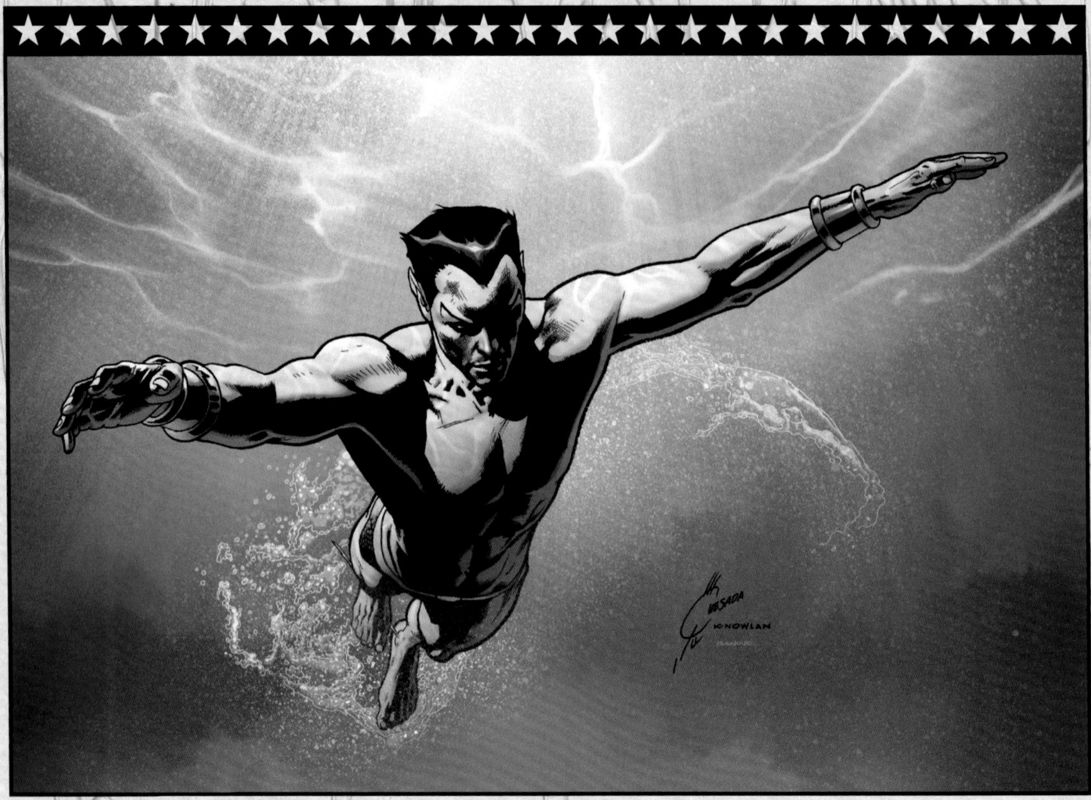

#1 VARIANT BY **JOE QUESADA, KEVIN NOWLAN** & **RICHARD ISANOVE**

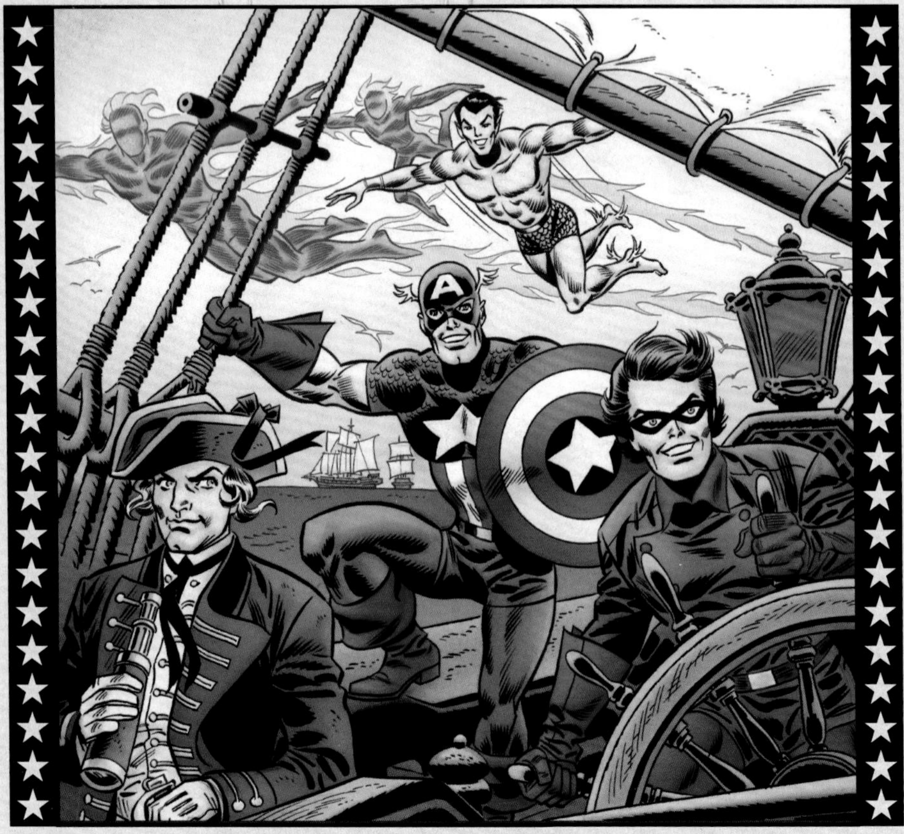

#1 HIDDEN GEM VARIANT BY **FRANK ROBBINS** & **MORRY HOLLOWELL**

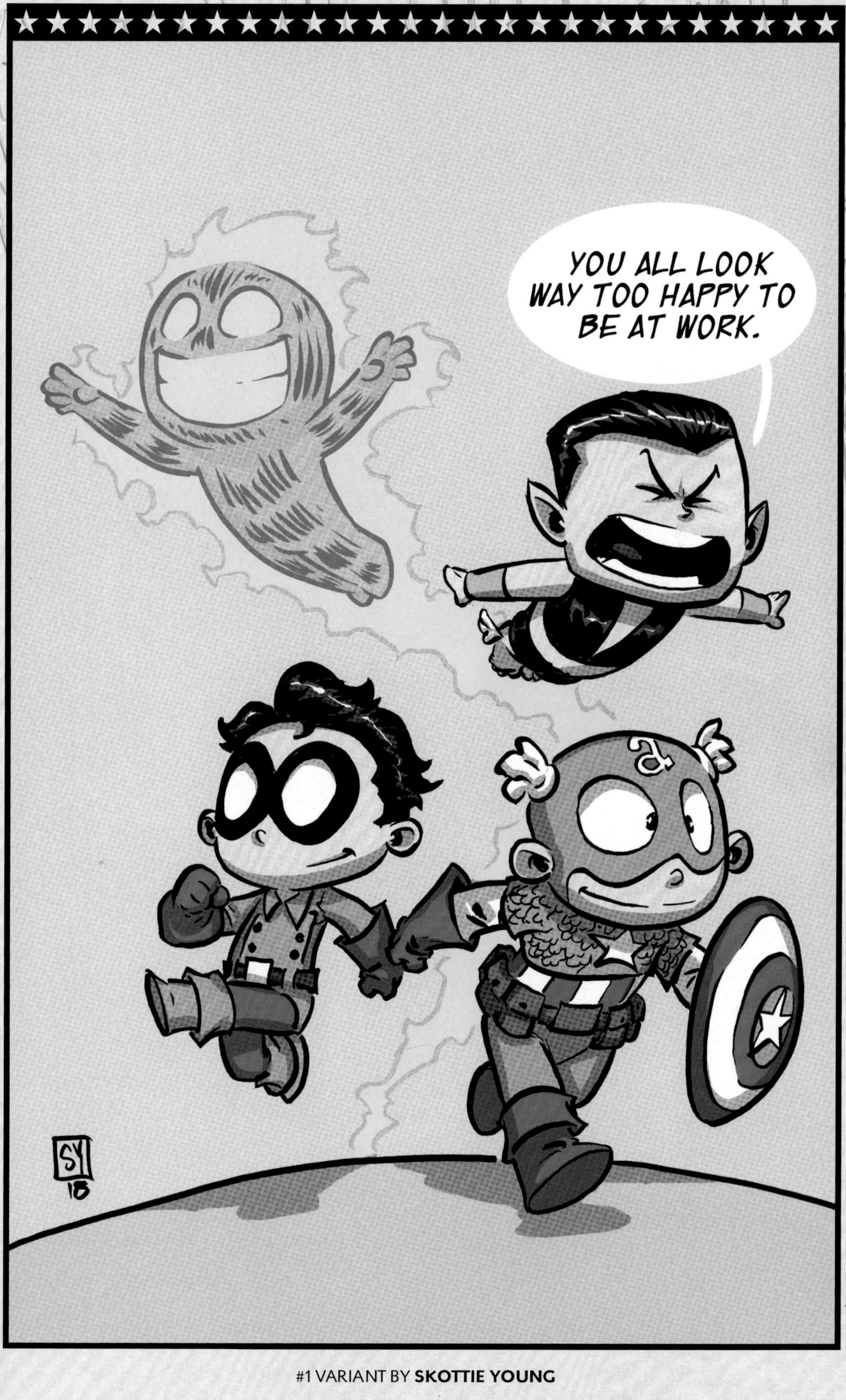
YOU ALL LOOK WAY TOO HAPPY TO BE AT WORK.
SY 18

#1 VARIANT BY **SKOTTIE YOUNG**

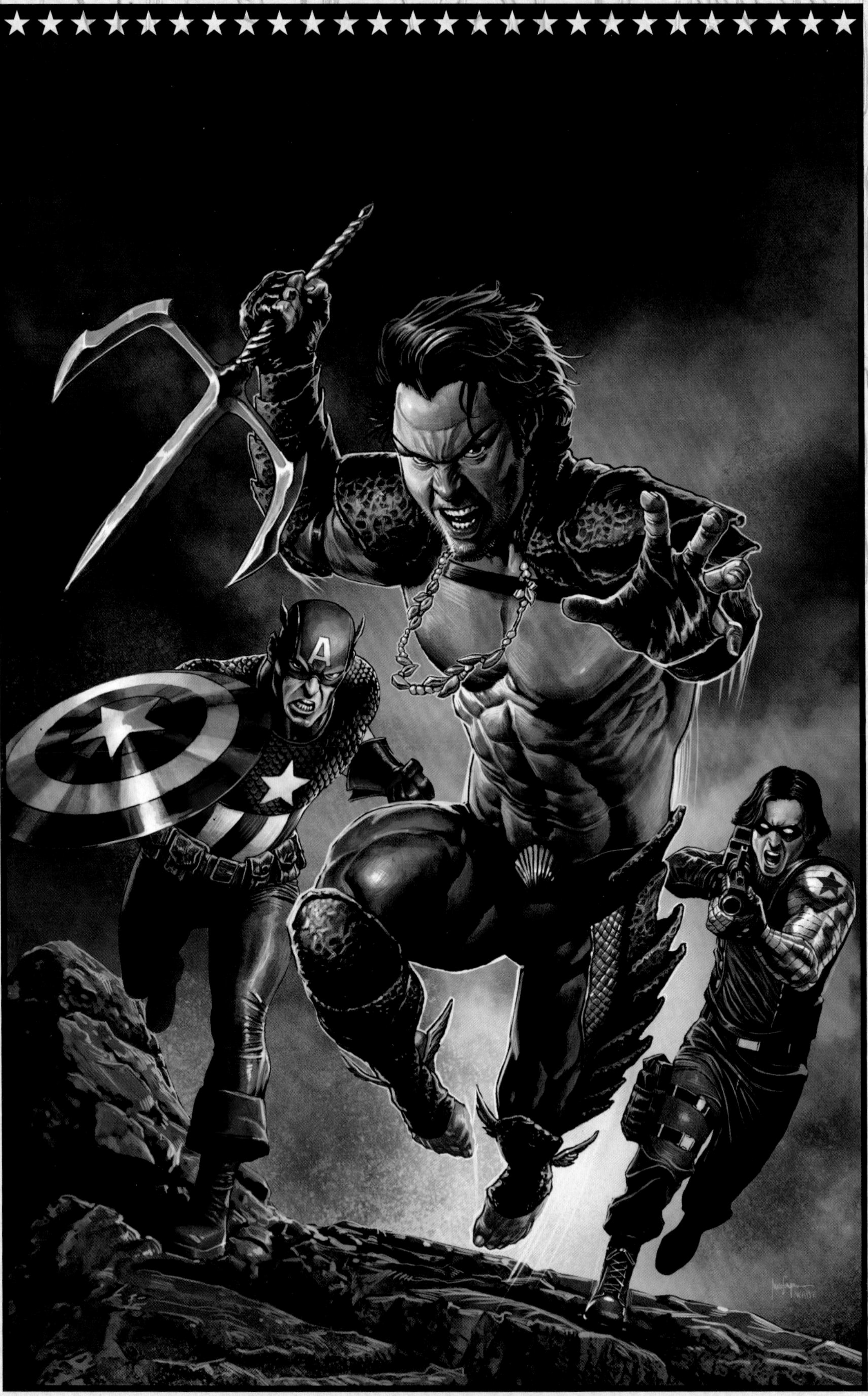

#1 VARIANT BY **MICO SUAYAN** & **DEAN WHITE**

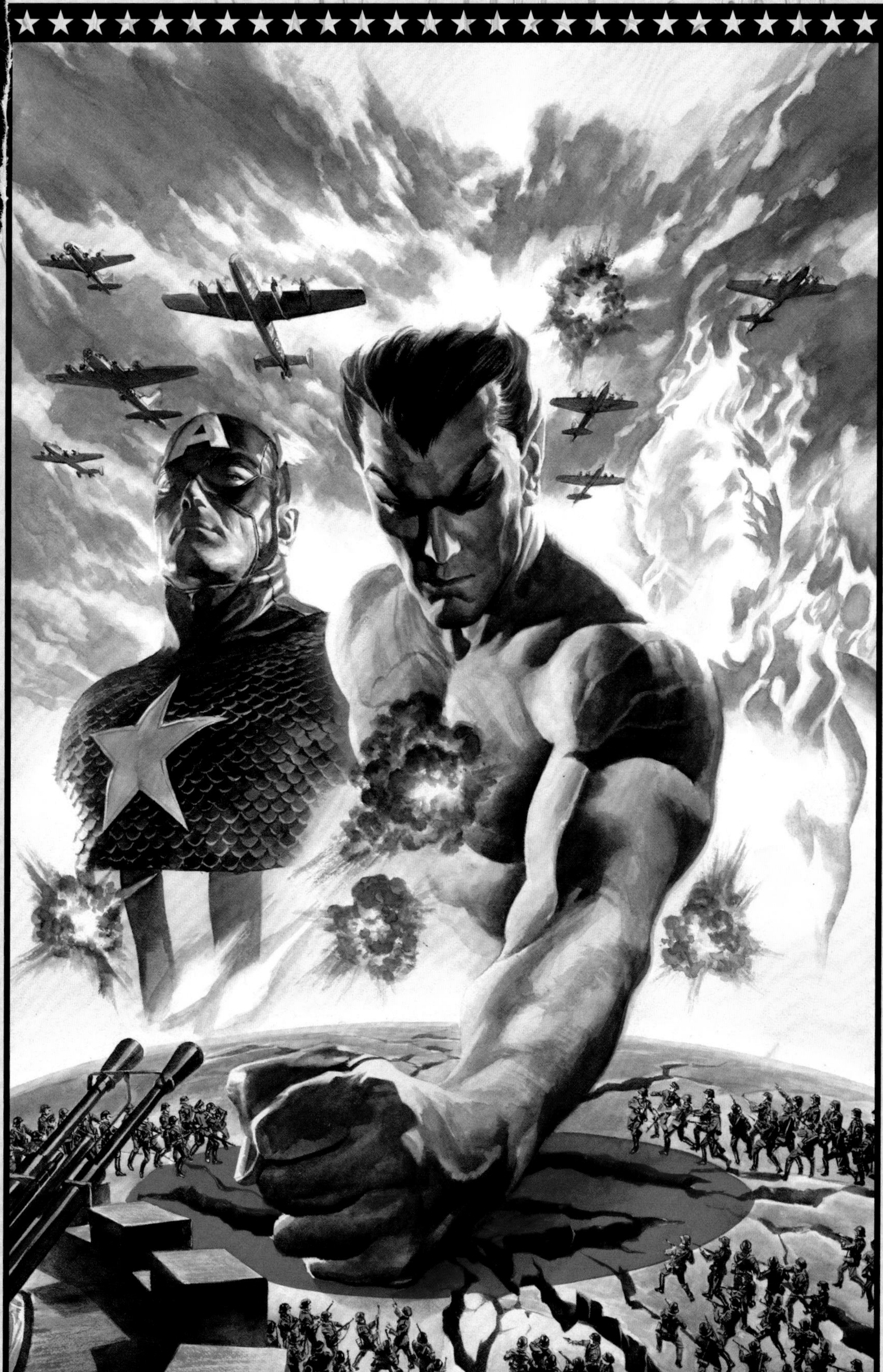

#1 VARIANT BY **ALEX ROSS**

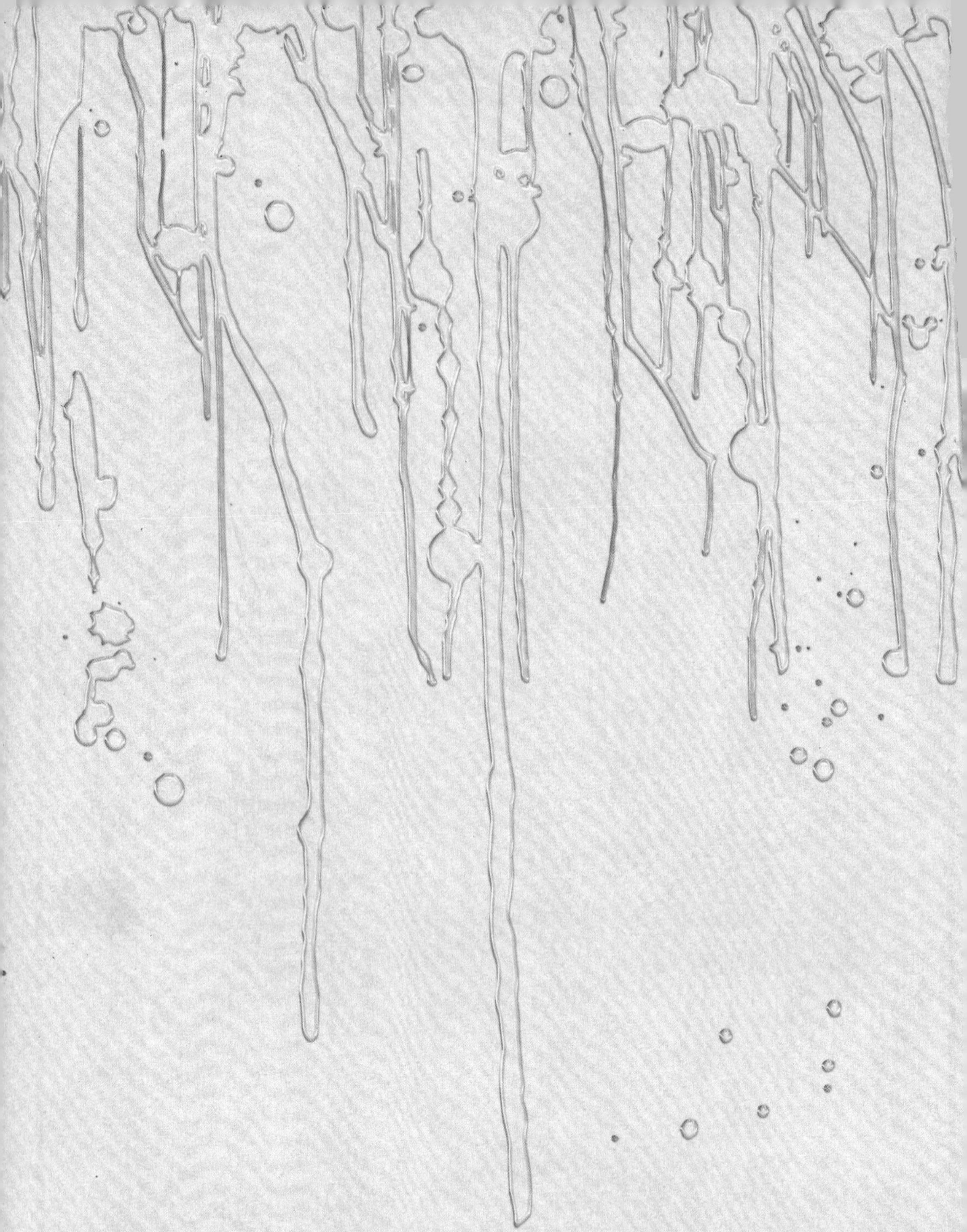

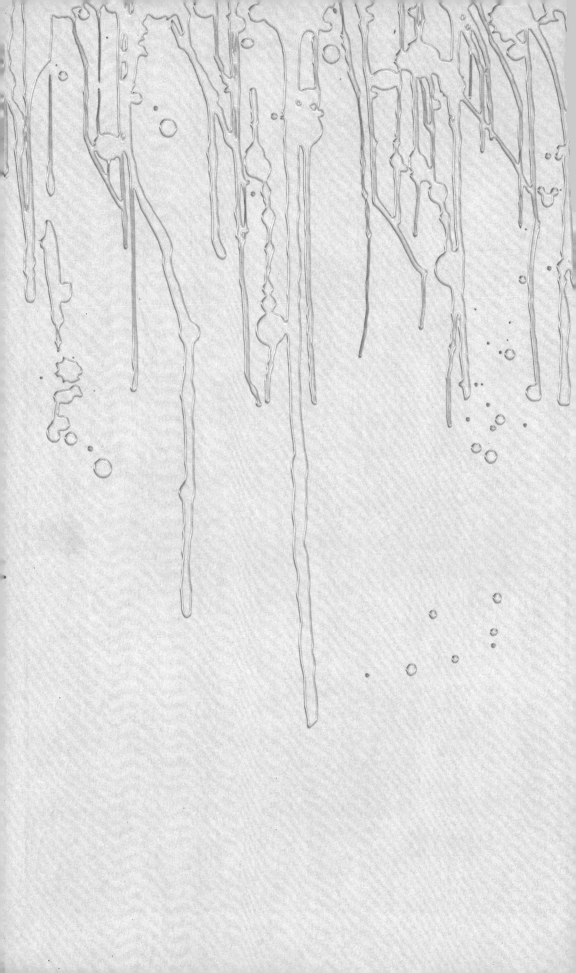